MARXIST THOUGHT ON IMPERIALISM

MARXIST THOUGHT ON IMPERIALISM

Survey and Critique

Charles A. Barone

M. E. Sharpe, Inc.
Armonk, New York

To my father, who taught me to be critical,
and to my mother, who had faith in me

Library of Congress Cataloging in Publication Data

Barone, Charles A.
    Marxist thought on imperialism.

    Bibliography: p.
    1. Imperialism. I. Title.
JC359.B36   1985   325'.32   84-23556
ISBN 0-87332-291-6
ISBN 0-87332-345-9 (pbk.)

Printed in the United States of America

Table of Contents

Acknowledgments

This book is an outgrowth of my dissertation, completed at the American University in Washington, D.C., and I wish first to thank the members of my committee, particularly John Weeks and James Weaver, for their invaluable assistance. I would also like to acknowledge the bold and pioneering efforts of the faculty members who in 1972 founded the university's Ph.D. program in radical political economy—the first of its kind in the United States. They were Chuck Wilber, Jim Weaver, Ron Müller, Howard Wachtel, Larry Stevens, and Rick Simons. It is to this program and the people behind it, including my fellow graduate students, that I owe my greatest debt of gratitude.

It has been a pleasure to work with the people at M. E. Sharpe, Inc., and I particularly want to thank Editorial Director Arnold C. Tovell and Social Sciences Editor Patricia A. Kolb for helping me transform my original manuscript into the present, much more readable book. My thanks also to the academic community at Dickinson College, where I now teach, for providing an environment conducive to productive scholarship of this kind. Finally, I am grateful to my wife, Susan, and my daughter, Sarah, for not allowing me to forget the importance of family life.

MARXIST THOUGHT ON IMPERIALISM

1
Marxist Foundations and the Theory of Imperialism

In the years since World War II there has been a resurgence of interest in theories of imperialism, both Marxist and non-Marxist. Not since the early decades of this century have there been so many studies and analyses of imperialism. This renewed interest has been fueled by dramatic changes in the world political economy, in particular the emergence of the United States after the war as the most powerful economic and political force among the capitalist countries of the West. As the United States exercised its economic and political hegemony over the international capitalist system, a reordering of political and economic relationships took place and new lines of demarcation were drawn. Under the leadership and tutelage of the United States, the international capitalist economy experienced tremendous rates of growth in foreign trade, investment, and public resource transfers. This created a highly integrated world economy characterized by complex interdependence. A growing proportion of this increased economic activity has been accounted for by the growth of multinational corporations, which have had a significant impact on the operation and dynamic of the international political economy.

A second factor has been the growing threat of the Soviet Union and socialist movements in general to the capitalist world and the balance of economic and political power. This balance has been further endangered by the large number of successful anticolonialist national liberation movements and the resulting creation of over a hundred new nations since the war. The continuing dependency of such nations on the rich capitalist countries, and the failure of economic development to take place in the Third World at the expected rate, has led to increasing international concern and to charges of neocolonialism and neo-imperialism. Military intervention by major capitalist powers attempting to maintain the status quo in such widely scattered countries as Vietnam, the Congo, and the Dominican Republic further exacerbated this situation. Currently the struggle between rich and poor countries takes the form of heated political debate over a new international order.

Preeminent among those analyzing these postwar events as imperialist phenomena are theorists associated with the left, i.e., those who analyze imperialism from within the Marxist intellectual tradition. Among the better-known contemporary Marxists who have written about imperialism are Paul Baran, Harry Magdoff, Andre Gunder Frank, Arghiri Emmanuel, and Samir Amin. Not since the seminal contributions of Rudolf Hilferding, Rosa Luxemburg, Vladimir Lenin, and Nikolai Bukharin during the first quarter of this century have Marxists given so much attention to this question. The result has been a tremendous growth in the literature on imperialism and a proliferation of Marxist theories that purport to explain the causes and effects of capitalist foreign economic expansion.

There have been few attempts to pull together the major strands of this literature, examine them, critique them, and place them in the history of Marxist intellectual thought on imperialism. The many available readers on imperialism do not fulfill this task.[1] Tom Kemp's excellent study, *Theories of Imperialism*, published in 1967, surveys major Marxist and non-Marxist theories of imperialism, but concentrates almost exclusively on prewar writers. Kemp's primary purpose was to vindicate Lenin in terms of contemporary relevance. Another work that partially meets the objective outlined above is Michael Barratt Brown's book *Economics of Imperialism* (1974). Brown develops the classical, Marxist, Keynesian, and neoclassical theories of imperialism and attempts to interpret the history of capitalist imperialism through each theory, in order to assess the positive aspects, as well as failings, of each. Such an ambitious undertaking can at best provide extensive knowledge of the many different theories of imperialism, and Brown's work certainly does an excellent job of this, but it does not give an intensive analysis. Indeed, by focusing on empirical verification it tends to obscure theoretical issues.[2]

This book is an attempt to provide a historical survey and analytical critique of contemporary Marxist theories of imperialism. It is not all-inclusive. Only works that represent major strands of Marxist thought on capitalist imperialism—and within each strand, only the most important theoretical works—are singled out for discussion. This means that many significant works had to be excluded from this study. Analyses of precapitalist forms of imperialism or of Soviet imperialism were excluded entirely, not because they were considered unimportant but because they require separate treatment.

The present study will give special attention to analyses of the causes of capitalist foreign economic expansion and the impact of that expansion on other countries. Although the actual character and operation of the imperialist system will not be ignored, this is dealt with in summary fashion and only to the extent that it exposes and clarifies these two more central theoretical concerns.

Our second task, providing an analytical critique of the theoretical literature, entails assessment of the theoretical differences, commonalities, and shortcomings of the various theories surveyed, and will include but not be limited to discussion of contemporary debates and critiques. It excludes empirical assessment, beyond a broad conformity with evidence "close at hand," and also assessment from non-Marxist theoretical perspectives. In short, this study is an analytical survey of the varieties of Marxist thought on imperialism, conducted from within the Marxist intellectual tradition and at the theoretical rather than the empirical level.

The rest of this chapter is devoted to a preliminary discussion of Marxist theory on imperialism. It begins with a brief outline of Marx's methodological approach and analysis of capitalism. This is followed by a discussion on Marx's ideas concerning imperialism. The final section of this chapter presents an overview of subsequent Marxist thought on imperialism.

The Marxist foundation

The intellectual ancestry of contemporary Marxist thought on the causes and impact of capitalist foreign economic expansion is to be found in the methodology and analysis developed by Karl Marx in the mid-nineteenth century. This body of thought was later expanded and modified, particularly on the problem of imperialism, by Marx's intellectual and political followers in the late nineteenth and early twentieth centuries, who will be the subject of the next chapter.

Marx's general method of analysis is unique in the history of thought. His approach to history and to the process of historical (social) change has been called historical and dialectical materialism. This method underlies Marx's analysis of capitalism, its historical origin as a socioeconomic system and its place in the history of humankind.

Marx's approach focuses on the material forces of society, that is, the concrete social existence of individuals as opposed to the realm of ideas, those "phantoms" formed in the brain. For Marx economic activities play a predominant role in shaping, or conditioning, the individual as well as society.

Marx conceptually divides society into a substructure and a superstructure. The substructure of society consists of its mode of production, that is, the relations that people enter into in the process of production and reproduction of the means of subsistence, and the material conditions of production. Marx refers to the latter as the material forces of production, which include labor, the organization of production, natural objects, and the instruments of production. The latter two forces of production Marx calls the means of production. Human beings take raw materials from the natural environment and with the use of tools (instruments of production) reshape or transform these natural objects into useful objects.

The relations that people enter into in the act of production Marx calls the social relations of production, which are definable in terms of control over the material forces of production. Marx observes that, except in tribal society, there have always been nonlaboring classes, able to live off the labor of others. This ability of one group to reap the fruits of others' labor is based, Marx thought, on control over the forces of production.

Control over the forces of production gives a class control over the social surplus, the portion of output that is produced by producers but appropriated by nonproducers. The mode of appropriation of the products of human labor, i.e., the mode of exploitation, takes different forms, depending on the level of development of the material powers of production and on the particular property relationships. One of the fundamental problems Marx sought to explain was how labor was exploited under capitalist, or bourgeois, relations of production.

It is upon the material substructure of society that the rest of society—its legal, political, religious, esthetic, and ideological elements, or superstructure—is built. These superstructural elements can take on the appearance of being independent social creations; once created they may follow a path of development divorced from the material circumstances in which they were born and may even influence the material substructure of society. Thus the various aspects of society interact. However, for Marx, the material base is the dominant, conditioning force and within broad confines restricts the superstructural elements as independent forces.[3]

Marx saw history as a series of different modes of production, each representing "epochs marking progress in the economic development of society." Each succeeding mode represents a higher level of economic development, and the process of social change from one mode to another is based on the internal dynamics of contradictions existing within each mode of production; the seeds of self-destrucion are also the seeds for a succeeding economic formation.

In each socioeconomic formation there exist conflicting forces. The basic conflict is between the material forces of society, which are dynamic, and the relations of production, which are not. The source of the antagonism between the social relations of production and the development of the material forces is divergent class interests. Social relations of production resist change, and the elevation of the formation to a more developed system of economic reproduction, because certain classes have vested interests in maintaining the status quo, i.e., they have a privileged position which they must protect along with the wealth derived from that position.

Class conflict is the motor force for change, a force that is created by the internal dynamics of society. The resolution of this conflict leads either to a new set of social relations of production, that is, new class relations, or to the stagnation of society and the common ruin of the contending classes. Marx thought that the bourgeois relations of production would be the last antagonistic social form of production. Thereafter, production would come under the collective, rational control of society and the interests of individuals would coincide with the community of interests.

For Marx the system-defining elements of any mode of production are the particular relations of production and the way surplus labor or product is extracted from the direct producers. One of the main tasks Marx set for himself was disclosing capitalist exploitation, which is obscured by complex exchange relationships among individuals and among classes.

Capitalist production is first of all characterized by the production of commodities, that is, production for exchange rather than for use by the producers. Production takes place within a social structure wherein the laborer is separated from the means of production, and the means of production are the private property of a minority class of capitalists. Most people, who are propertyless and without means of production, must for their survival sell their labor power to those who own the means of production. In capitalism labor power is thus reduced to a commodity bought and sold for a price, wages. Controlling the means of production gives the capitalist the prerogative of buying labor power, and thus of managing both the laborer and the product of labor. The sphere of production, and the class relations on which it is based, are the key to Marx's analysis of the laws of motion of capitalism.

The prerequisite for such a system is that labor power be "free" to be bought and sold. Historically this meant the abolition of serfdom, which tied producers to the land and to feudal lords. It also meant separating the producers from their means of production and means of subsistence, so that they would be compelled to sell their labor power to live.

These conditions were established in the period of what Marx refers to as the "primitive" or "original" accumulation of capital. For Marx capital is a social relation expressing the power of one class over another, rather than a physical or technical relationship. Capital commands means of production and labor. The original accumulation of capital represents the creation of a proletariat, "conjuring whole populations out of the ground," as well as the concentration of financial capital of sufficient size to command labor and the means of production. According to Marx, this corresponds roughly to the mercantilist era of early capitalism.

Marx viewed capitalism as a social system that conceals the real productive activities of society behind commodities (land, labor, and capital, as well as products). What is obscured is the class nature of capitalism, the origin of profit in surplus labor, and the exploitation of workers. Because capitalism produces commodities and the "factors of production" are themselves treated as commodities at the level of market exchange, i.e., in the sphere of circulation, all exchange appears not only as the relation of things but as the exchange of equivalents.

These two spheres, production and circulation, are treated as different moments in an organic whole; their unity becomes apparent through Marx's labor theory of value, which attempts to explain the causal links and interrelationships between these two moments. Indeed Marx's value theory is crucial to his entire economic analysis of the origins of capitalism, as well as its inner nature and its inherent contradictions.[4] It was upon this analysis that Marx derived his famous "laws of motion" of capitalism.

The "immanent law of capitalism," capital accumulation, was based on the production of surplus value. Capital is self-expanding, traveling through several circuits as follows:

$$\text{M} - - - - - - \text{C}^{L(v)}_{MP(c)} - - - - -\text{P}- - - - -\text{C}' - - - - -\text{M}'$$

Circulation	*Production*	*Circulation*
Money-	Productive-	Commodity-
capital	capital	capital
period	period	period

$$\text{C} = c + v$$
$$\text{C}' = c + v + s$$

$$\text{M}' - \text{M} = \text{surplus value} = \text{C}' - \text{C}$$

The capitalist begins with a sum of money or financial capital (M) with which he buys productive commodities (C), (labor power [L], and means of production [MP]). During the productive-capital period, products are produced that contain more value than the value of the capital advanced (M = C); the difference C' – C is equal to surplus value, which in turn is equal to the difference between the value of labor power and the value created by labor. During the commodity-capital period, the capitalist returns to the sphere of circulation to realize the total value, and thus his surplus value, by selling the commodity for money (M') in the market. His capital has now expanded from M to M', the difference equaling the surplus value created by labor and appropriated by the capitalist.

The circuit of capital does not stop here. The capitalist must invest a portion of the newly created surplus value in advanced technologies and labor power or else be driven out of business by competitors. This driving force behind the capitalist exerts itself as an external, objective force (in addition to any subjective motives of the capitalist) over which the capitalist has little control. Only by constantly extending his capital and by "revolutionizing" the means of production can the capitalist preserve his capital in the competitive struggle for profits. This process, by which capital reproduces not only itself but itself plus surplus value, is referred to as the expanded reproduction of capital.

The dynamics of capitalist commodity production, i.e., the "laws of motion of capitalism," are predicated on one independent variable—the process and rate of capital accumulation. This process gives rise to several "general laws" and tendencies, according to Marx, of which six seem to be the most important: first, an increase in what Marx calls the rate of composition of capital; second, the progressive concentration and centralization of capital as expanded accumulation continues; third, an increase in what Marx called the reserve industrial army; fourth, the uneven development of capital across different branches of production, regions, and countries; fifth, the tendency for the rate of profit to fall; and finally, the tendency toward economic crises that periodically interrupt the accumulation process.

In summary, Marx's laws of motion of capitalism are derived utilizing a historical materialist approach and are based on an analysis centered in the sphere of production and the labor theory of value. The central dynamic of capitalism is identified as the expanded reproduction of capital, which is based on the exploitation of wage labor and production of surplus value. Capitalism's inherent need to expand brings more and more constant as well as variable capital under its sway, as it expands into every branch of production and every region and every corner of the globe, confronting an ever greater portion of the population as an objective and subjective power over the labor process. This process results in the concentration and centralization of capital, a rising industrial reserve army, uneven development, and economic crises. These contradictions form a partial basis for the demise of capitalism and the rise of socialism.

Marx on imperialism

Marx did not develop a theory of imperialism; in fact he never used the term. Although he planned to write a book about capitalism and world markets, he did not live to do so. However, it is clear from what Marx did write that he thought that capitalism was inherently expansionary and that as it expanded, it would transform the noncapitalist world "in its own image," so that capitalist relations of production would be reproduced everywhere.

While Marx did not treat capitalist expansion or its impact in a comprehensive manner, he did make many references to both in his writings. It is clear from the very first volume of *Capital* that Marx thought the "foreign sector" played an important role in the period of primitive or original capital accumulation. The growth of foreign markets during this period both accelerated the destruction of domestic noncapitalist sectors and branches of production, and accelerated the amassing of the money capital necessary for undertaking capitalist forms of production, through plunder, tribute, and trade carried out under monopoly conditions. It should be noted, however, that the extension of the market is not a sufficient condition for the rise of capitalism, nor is the emergence of merchant capital. What was in the beginning its *basis* becomes, with capitalism's further development, the *product* of capitalist economic development. In other words, what was one of the conditions of the early internal development of capitalism becomes in a later, "mature" period the overflow of capitalism beyond its national frontiers.

Marx explicitly treats the need for world markets as a reaction to the tendency of the rate of profit to fall. Foreign trade can raise the rate of profit by cheapening elements of constant capital (e.g., cheap raw materials) and by cheapening the necessities of life, thus lowering the value of variable capital. These results are obtained both by the import of cheap commodities from abroad and by economies of scale made possible by the expansion of markets.[5]

Furthermore, the advanced country is able to sell goods in foreign markets above their value in the home country, but below their value in the competing country, thus earning a surplus profit. However, this is a characteristic of merchant capital, not productive capital. Capital can also be invested in a backward country that has a lower organic composition of capital, for the purpose of realizing a higher rate of profit. It can obtain a higher rate of profit in foreign lands by using forced labor, "coolies and slaves," from whom absolute surplus value can be extracted more easily than from labor in the more developed country, where labor has become more organized and resistant.[6]

In another context, Marx speaks of the "furious combat" for market shares, which leads to rapid technological changes. This causes production to increase "by leaps and bounds that finds no hindrance except in the supply of raw materials and in the disposal of the produce."[7] Marx goes on to show how this process creates both the raw materials and the markets necessary for capitalist expansion. A new division of labor, suitable to the major industrial centers, is imposed upon the rest of the world.[8]

Marx also envisioned the impact that monopoly would have on foreign expansion, something that later Marxists were to emphasize. It will be useful to quote Marx on this, for it is a point often overlooked by some of his followers:

> In practical life we find not only competition, monopoly, and the antagonism between them, but also the synthesis of the two, which is not a formula, but a movement. Monopoly produces competition, competition produces monopoly. Monopolists compete among themselves; competitors become monopolists . . . and the more the mass of the proletarians grows as against the monopolists of one nation, the more desperate competition becomes between monopolists of different nations. The synthesis is such that monopoly can only maintain itself by continually entering into the struggle of competition.[9]

As will be seen in the next chapter, Marx's statement here anticipates some of the early Marxist theories of imperialism, especially Lenin's. These aspects of capitalist expansion only noted by Marx—the international division of labor, the expansion of markets, the export of capital, and international monopoly competition—became the very aspects of imperialism that later Marxists emphasized.

From the above discussion one might get a mixed picture of the anticipated impact of capitalist expansion on the noncapitalist world. On the one hand it would "create a world in its own image"; on the other hand it would impose an international division of labor "suited to the requirements of the chief centers of modern industry." Marx argued that such a change in the international division of labor would be a positive development. For example, it resulted in "radical changes in agriculture" which in the United States led to capitalist development.[10]

Shlomo Avineri has pointed out that Marx's view of capitalist expansion as a progressive force was not restricted to those regions populated by Europeans, but was also applicable to the colonies. In Marx's words, England would fulfill "a double mission in India; one destructive, the other regenerating—the annihilation of old Asiatic society, and the laying of the material foundations of Western Society in Asia."[11] The expanded reproduction of capital would thus transform all precapitalist modes of commodity production to capitalist commodity production in the colonies, just as it had in its home countries:

> I know that the English millocracy intend to endow India with railways with the exclusive view of extracting at diminished expenses, the cotton and other raw materials for their manufactures. . . . You cannot maintain a net of railways over an immense country without introducing all those industrial processes necessary to meet the immediate and current wants of railway locomotion, and out of which there must grow the application of machinery to those branches of industry not immediately connected with railways. The railway system will therefore become, in India truly the forerunner of modern industry.[12]

But, Marx added:

> The Indians will not reap the fruits of the new elements of society scattered among them by the British bourgeoisie, till in Great Britain itself the now ruling classes shall have been supplanted by the industrial proletariat, or till the Hindoos themselves shall have grown strong enough to throw off the English yoke altogether.[13]

Thus, while the British bourgeoisie would be the beneficiaries of the "regeneration" of India, still the material foundations would be laid there for modern industry. Though he was aware of the "barbaric" treatment of the Indians and the havoc that ensued from British colonial policies, Marx nonetheless thought that this would speed their development to a higher stage, for he viewed Asiatic societies as inherently stagnant, regressive, and incapable of transcending their own limitations.[14]

We know one hundred years later that economic regeneration in the former colonies has not taken place, that successful anticolonial liberation movements have not been able to take advantage of the material base established by colonialism. Marx's thinking on colonialism, although perceptive, was fragmentary and incomplete. It would remain for his followers to develop a more coherent theory of imperialism and to more thoroughly analyze capitalist expansion and its impact on the world.

Marxists on imperialism

Marx's theory of imperialism has been developed by a number of twentieth-century Marxists, who have pursued in diverse ways the lines of analysis established by Marx. The early Marxists Hilferding, Bukharin, and Lenin focused especially on the causes of capitalist foreign expansion and interimperialist rivalries. Luxemburg, who was the only one of the early Marxists to analyze in any detail the impact of foreign expansion on other countries, came to essentially the same conclusions as the others. In agreement with Marx, all thought that capitalist encroachment on other countries would create the conditions for their successful capitalist development.

This view predominated until the postwar period, when Marxists had to confront the problem of explaining why the Third World had not achieved successful capitalist development in the wake of national liberation. They responded with theories of neocolonialism and dependency, asserting that the Third World had become capitalist but that its industrialization was blocked by the forces of imperialism, which continued to operate in negative ways even in the absence of formal colonial rule. The causes of foreign expansion and interimperialist rivalries no longer commanded much attention. The predominant feature of imperialism had become the exploitation of underdeveloped countries by advanced capitalist countries, to the detriment of the underdeveloped.

In comparing subsequent Marxist theories of imperialism with Marx's methodological approach and his analysis of capitalism, we find on a certain level broad conformity with Marx. The primacy of material forces, the critical view of capitalism as a transitory and contradictory system, and the belief in the eventual replacement of capitalism by socialism all play predominant roles in Marxist thought on imperialism. However, at another level, many of these works have the descriptive flavor of Marx's writings, but little of the substance of Marx's method and analysis.

The trend in these studies has been to focus on empirical or descriptive analyses of imperialism, and to restrict analysis to the sphere of exchange, or circulation. But Marx treated the capitalist system, or mode of production, as an organic whole embracing three interacting phases or "moments": production, circulation, and distribution. The production moment predominates and within certain limits determines the other two moments, referred to as the spheres of exchange.[15] This is not the place to discuss the relatedness of these three moments or the predominance of one over the other.[16] The point is that those who followed in Marx's footsteps tended to eschew analysis of the sphere of production, concentrating instead on exchange relations.

This trend in Marxist thought is not restricted to those concerned with imperialism, but is a more general trend and indeed one of the most important and controversial issues among contemporary Marxists.[17] Such basic divergence from Marx's method, or what is called revisionism, characterizes several of the Marxists discussed in this study.[18] For example, Baran and Sweezy (see chapter 3), the primary architects of what has come to be known as the "monopoly capital" school of Marxist thought, significantly revised Marx,[19] and their influence is evident in the work of others, including Andre Gunder Frank and Samir Amin (see chapters 4 and 6). The rationale for their break with Marx has little to do with a criticism of Marx's methodological approach, but rather with the assertion that monopoly conditions make Marx's analysis obsolete inasmuch as it rests on the neoclassical assumption of perfect competition. In fact, however, Baran and Sweezy not only relax this assumption, they abandon Marx's analytic approach without offering any explanation for doing so.

In another case, revision has been justified on the basis of difficulties with the transformation of labor values into prices of production—a crucial theoretical link between the sphere of production and the sphere of exchange. One proposed solution to the transformation problem makes redundant the labor theory of value as well as analysis of the sphere of production. Proponents of this solution make up yet another school of thought, referred to as "neo-Ricardian,"[20] which has influenced the theory of imperialism through the work of Arghiri Emmanuel and to a lesser extent that of Samir Amin (see chapters 5 and 6).

Of what importance is the sphere of production in Marx's analysis? Marx devoted considerable attention to demonstrating how the classical economists had reached erroneous conclusions because their analysis was restricted to the sphere of exchange. It was through an analysis of the sphere of production that Marx sought to "pierce the veil of appearances," to see beyond the exchange of commodities, in which all commodity owners (including capitalists and workers) appear to confront each other as equals and to exchange equivalents. A look at any neoclassical microeconomics textbook will confirm that this view is alive and well today. Marx probed *behind* such appearances, to establish the domination of capital over labor, the exploitation of wage labor as the source of surplus value, the rhythms of the capital accumulation process, and the laws of motion of capitalism. Certainly, then, to ignore an analysis of the sphere of production is to ignore Marx.

Why have so many Marxists abandoned the methodology of Marx's major works on capitalism? Is it because they were analyzing a very changed form of capitalism? Perhaps. But then why has there been so little recognition, let alone acknowledgment, of their methodological divergence from Marx?

There are several possible answers. Perhaps these Marxists were in essential agreement with Marx's basic theory, and sought to provide a more empirically based analysis and extension of the laws of motion of capitalism that Marx had already established. Certainly they enriched our understanding of the nature of capitalism and imperialism. However, in their work there was such a lack of fit between empirical analysis and theory that eventually they abandoned the theoretical base.

A second explanation might be that in the international political economy, exchange relations are not only the most visible, they tend to encompass the entire landscape, so that the power of exchange relations to obscure productive relations (commodity fetishism) is stronger internationally than it is nationally.[21]

A third explanation might be that twentieth-century Marxists have not always had access to all of Marx's works. Marx's *Grundrisse*, which contains a discussion of the three moments of production, has only recently been published. So it is not surprising that many Marxists have not had a full understanding of Marx's method of analysis. This problem is compounded by the fact that the study of Marxist political economy has not exactly been promoted in academic communities, particularly in the United States, so that the conventional formal training of many contemporary Marxists may itself have led them to misinterpret his method and analysis. [22]

Whatever the explanation for twentieth-century revisions of Marx, the more important issue here is their reflection in the theory of imperialism. For although our understanding of imperialism has certainly grown immeasurably, it has several deficiencies that can be attributed to a lack of attention to the sphere of production. This sphere is crucial to a complete understanding of imperialism, because, as Marx showed, it is only through an analysis of production relations that we can understand the origins and nature of class, capital, surplus product, exploitation, and the contradictory nature of the expanded reproduction of capital. [23]

These aspects of the capitalist (or any) mode of production are for the most part absent from twentieth-century Marxist theories of imperialism, or are treated only tangentially. Among contemporary Marxists this deficiency has received attention in recent years, particularly in the debate over dependency theory, and attempts have been made to remedy it—with some success, as discussed in fuller detail in the final chapter of this book. There remains, however, much to be done before we will have a unified and complete Marxist theory of imperialism.

2

Early Marxist Theories of Imperialism

Some of the most important early twentieth-century Marxists—among them Rudolf Hilferding, Rosa Luxemburg, Nikolai Bukharin, and Vladimir Lenin—were the first to take up the task of systematically analyzing the phenomenon of imperialism from a Marxist perspective. It held central importance for them in the analysis of this period of capitalist development, just before or at the outbreak of World War I. Little of significance was to be added to this body of thought during the interwar period, which saw a solidification—for some, a dogmatization—of Marxism.[1]

The capitalism of 1870–1914 was much changed from Marx's days: it was becoming increasingly a global, international system of production and exchange. The period was characterized by intense international rivalries and a tremendous increase in the number and size of territories brought under formal or informal control by the very few advanced capitalist nations. Such were the conditions that preceded, and according to these theorists ultimately caused, the first world war. Thus it is not surprising that understanding imperialism was for them a central concern. And although they have been criticized for restricting their analysis to capitalism, and to a late phase of capitalist development, they were clearly aware of precapitalist forms of domination and did not deny the existence of domination in earlier phases of capitalism. They did not pretend to develop general theories of imperialism, transcending all historical epochs; they did not think such theories would be useful.

Because they are widely misunderstood and misread on these points, it may be useful to quote from Lenin and Bukharin, to show that they were aware of other forms of domination but chose not to attempt to develop a general theory of imperialism. First, Lenin:

> Colonial policy and imperialism existed before this latest stage of capitalism, and even before capitalism. Rome, founded on slavery, pursued a colonial policy and achieved imperialism. But "general" arguments about imperialism, which ignore or put into the background the fundamental difference of social-economic systems, inevitably degenerate into absolutely empty banalities, or into grandiloquent comparisons like "Greater Rome and Greater Britain." Even the colonial policy of capitalism in its previous stages is essentially different from the colonial policy of [present-day capitalism].[2]

Bukharin criticized a then widespread theory that defined imperialism

> . . . as the policy of conquest in general. From this point of view one can speak with equal right of Alexander the Macedonian's and the Spanish conqueror's imperialism, of the imperialism of Carthage and Ivan III, of ancient Rome and modern America, of Napoleon and Hindenburg. Simple as this theory may be, it is absolutely untrue. It is untrue because it "explains" everything, i.e., it explains absolutely nothing.[3]

Bukharin goes on to specify conditions for a correct theory of imperialism:

> If a certain phase of development is to be theoretically understood, it must be understood with all its peculiarities, its distinguishing trends, its specific characteristics, which it shares with none. . . . The historian or economist who places under one denominator the structure of modern capitalism, i.e., modern production relations, and the numerous types of production relations that formerly led to wars of conquest, will understand nothing in the development of modern world economy. One must single out the specific elements which characterize our time, and analyze them.[4]

In this chapter attention will be given separately to Hilferding, Luxemburg, Bukharin, and Lenin. There is considerable overlap among these four and with later theorists who were to draw upon and modify earlier works. This survey will both compare and contrast theories and place them within the Marxist paradigm.

Rudolf Hilferding

Exposition

What Marx had hypothesized as one of the laws of motion of capitalism—the increasing concentration and centralization of capital—had been borne out by Rudolf Hilferding's time. Monopoly (which for Marx meant highly centralized, and not a specified number of sellers in the product market) was becoming the dominant productive form in the more advanced capitalist countries. Hilferding's analysis[5] centers upon the process of concentration and centralization, and the structural changes that accompany it.[6] The advantages put forth by Hilferding for concentration and centralization are as follows:

> Combination levels out the fluctuations of trade and therefore assures to the combined enterprises a more stable rate of profit. Secondly, combination has the effect of eliminating trading. Thirdly, it has the effect of rendering possible technical improvements, and consequently, the acquisition of superprofits over and above those obtained by the "pure" (i.e., non-combined) enterprises. Fourthly, it strengthens the position of the combined enterprises compared with that of "pure" enterprises in the competitive struggle in periods of serious depression.[7]

Hilferding points out two structural changes that accompany and extend the process of the concentration and centralization of capital. First, the corporate form of business organization not only limited the liability of individual capitalists, but also facilitated the development of stock ownership and securities markets wherein industrial corporations could be promoted and stocks bought and sold. One of the consequences of this was a higher division of labor between the management of production and the management of money capital, the "transformation of the shareholder from an industrial capitalist receiving profit into a money capitalist receiving interest."[8]

Second, and paralleling this, was the development of what Hilferding called "finance capital." With a greater outlay necessary for a productive undertaking, due to concentration, and with money capital seeing profitable investment outside its original branch of production, there is both a need for large sums of money and an abundant number of smaller money capitals looking for employment. Both forces create a new role, an intermediary role between money capital and industrial capital: the role of finance capital. In Hilferding's words:

> A steadily increasing proportion of capital in industry does not belong to the industrialists who employ it. They obtain the use of it only through the medium of banks, which in relation to them, represent the owners of capital. On the other hand, the bank is forced to keep an increasing share of its funds engaged in industry. Thus to an increasing degree the bank is being transformed into an industrial capitalist. The bank capital, i.e., capital in money form which is thus really transformed into industrial capital, I call "finance capital." . . . Finance capital is capital controlled by banks and employed by industrialists.[9]

Thus, with the concentration and centralization of capital there is created a specialized need for financial institutions to allocate money capital from one productive enterprise to another, from one owner of money capital to another.

Subject to the same laws of concentration and centralization, this financial capital increasingly becomes concentrated into large masses of money centralized in the hands of a few powerful groups. Out of such centralization

> . . . arises a kind of personal union, on the one hand between the different corporations themselves, on the other between the latter and the banks, a circumstance which must be of the greatest importance for the policy of these institutions since among them there has arisen a community of interests.[10]

This "community of interest" implies that competition is further restricted. Indeed, the formation of trusts, cartels, and other forms of combination seems to support this contention by Hilferding.

If the tendency toward the concentration of finance capital were to be carried to its logical end it "would lead to a situation in which the entire money capital would be at the disposal of one bank or group of banks. Such a 'central bank' would then exercise control over the whole of social production."[11] For Hilferding such control over social production was more than just a theoretical tendency; it was an actual possibility:

> If we now pose the question as to the real limits of cartelization, the answer must be that there are no absolute limits. On the contrary there is a constant tendency for cartelization to be extended. As we have seen, the independent industries become increasingly dependent upon the cartelized industries until they are finally annexed by them. The ultimate outcome of this process would be the formation of a general cartel. The whole of capitalist production would then be consciously regulated by a single body which would determine the volume of production in all branches of industry.[12]

Hilferding went on to argue that cartelization would overcome the anarchy of capitalist production and economic crises; in other words, that monopoly and the rise of finance capital create the possibility for capitalism to overcome its internal contradictions, except that between the bourgeoisie and the workers. This latter contradiction is resolved, according to Hilferding, by putting workers in control of "organized capitalism" which could be accomplished, he thought, by seizing control of the state through parliamentary means.[13]

Imperialist expansion is explained by the needs of monopoly capitalists for new areas of raw material exploitation, export markets for the output of monopoly capitalists, and profitable markets for capital investment. If a country does not expand it will lose out on profitable opportunities, lose its competitive edge over its rivals, and in extreme cases will become a satellite of other countries.[14]

In its "conquest of the world" finance capital needs the assistance of a strong state to look after its foreign interests and to help extend its interests:

> It needs a strong state which recognizes finance capital's interests abroad and uses political power to extort favorable treaties from smaller states, a state which can exert its influence all over the world in order to be able to turn the entire world into a sphere of investment. Finance capital finally needs a state which is strong enough to carry out a policy of expansion and to gather in new colonies.[15]

Looking at the experience of the late nineteenth and early twentieth centuries, Hilferding saw that Great Britain was losing its preeminence as the "workshop of the world." Germany, Japan, France, and the United States were rising fast as industrial powers and were beginning to challenge British economic hegemony. The period also saw a scramble for new territories and the solidification of control over old territories by the leading capitalist countries.

Competition among domestic rival firms becomes transformed in the international arena into competition between nation states, each trying to preserve and extend the reaches of its own financial capital, its own bourgeoisie. International competition gives rise to what Hilferding refers to as the ideology of imperialism—racism and nationalism. The struggle between capitalists of different nationalities appears, with the union of the state and finance capital, as the struggle between different nations and races, a "collective" struggle. Nationalism and racism are for Hilferding the natural outgrowth of the foreign expansion of finance capital.[16]

Despite the formation of international cartels, trusts, and other forms of the suspension of international competition, Hilferding thought that such combinations would bring only temporary respite to the competitive struggle. Peace would be always interrupted by warfare when members of these anticompetitive agreements achieved some advantage that they thought would enable them to resume the competitive struggle from a position of strength. Hilferding thought it illusory to believe in the possibility of a harmony of interests "in a world of capitalistic struggle when superiority of arms alone decides."[17] Thus one of the consequences of the international spread of finance capital is the rise of militarism.

One of the state policies used in this international struggle is protective tariffs. During the period of history that Hilferding was considering, tariffs were being used not to protect infant industries but, according to Hilferding, to enable already mature industries to achieve world monopoly positions. Tariffs allowed monopolists to charge a higher price in domestic markets in order to obtain surplus profits which could then be used to subsidize exports (dumping) in international markets:

> With the development of the subsidy system, protective tariffs completely change their function, even turn it into its opposite. From being a means of defense against foreign conquest of domestic markets they become a means of conquering foreign markets, from a weapon of protection for the weak they become a weapon of aggression for the strong.[18]

In addition, the state supported the needs of finance capital by guaranteeing loans to foreign countries for public works, railroads, and public utilities. The state also ensured other more direct requirements of finance capital in foreign countries, such as a proper environment for profitable capital accumulation. Primary to this effort was the "forcible expropriation which creates the necessary free wage proletariat."[19] This, according to Hilferding, called for a strong colonial policy.

Hilferding's analysis of the impact of capital expansion in the colonies is similar to Marx's. He thought expansion would have a regenerative effect by promoting the conditions for industrialization. Furthermore, colonialization would create strong movements for independence:

> In the newly opened countries themselves the capitalism imported into them intensifies contradictions and excites the constantly growing resistance against the intruders of the peoples who are awakening to national consciousness. This resistance can easily become transormed into dangerous measures directed against foreign capital. The old social relations become completely revolutionized. The age-long agrarian incrustation of "nations without a history" is blasted away, and they are drawn into the capitalist whirlpool. . . . This movement for national independence threatens European capital just in its most valuable and most promising field of exploitation, and European capital can maintain its domination only by continually increasing its means of exerting violence.[20]

Hilferding goes on to argue that this tendency towards national liberation pushes finance capital to demand stronger state policies to preserve and control its sphere of trade and investment.[21]

Hilferding thought that foreign expansion would eventually result in the equalization of profit rates as capital flowed from regions of overproduction to regions of underproduction and that it would equalize economic development between countries as well. On the one hand, this would increase the viability of capital accumulation; on the other hand, it would increasingly be undermined by the threat of war between rival national bourgeoisie.[22]

Summary and critique

Hilferding saw the growth of monopolies, the intense competition between rival national capitals, the increasing spread of capital into foreign areas and countries, and the increasing hostility of armed nation states as the logical development of capitalism, as the manifestation of Marx's laws of motion of capitalism. The key points that Hilferding makes are the importance of "finance capital" in the monopoly stage of capitalism and the role of banks in controlling this finance capital as opposed to the industrial enterprises that merely "employ it." Capitalist foreign expansion is the result of a worldwide competitive struggle for dominance. This requires a strong state that will pursue the interests of finance capital. Foreign expansion is not a peaceful affair. It embraces nationalism, racism, and militarism, outgrowths of the competitive struggle of capitals of different nations over foreign markets and spheres of investment. Still, Hilferding thought that capitalist development would be accelerated in those areas penetrated by foreign capital.

Hilferding's most important contribution was to extend Marx's earlier analysis of the concentration of capital in the monopoly stage of capitalism. In terms of the circuit of capital, the expanded reproduction process outgrows the narrow parameters of the productive enterprise and a new division of labor is imposed which separates the money-capital phase from the productive and realization phases of the circuit. Marx anticipated such a division; in Hilferding's time it was well on its way to being complete. Although Hilferding did not analyze financial capital in the same conceptual terms that Marx used, his essentially empirical analysis extends the understanding of finance capital and its important role in the national as well as international political economy.

Hilferding has been criticized for placing too much emphasis on banks, and it is questionable that banks are as independent from the industrial or productive base of capitalism as Hilferding makes out. Paul Sweezy notes that banks were important in the formative stages of monopoly, but once this process became stabilized these industrial monopolies had sizable financial resources that were internally generated and thus were no longer dependent upon banks.[23]

Be this as it may, the more fundamental criticism is the emphasis placed on banking institutions rather than on the bankers and industrial capitalists who, I would argue, both became financial capitalists in this period. In this view, it makes no difference whether banks or industries are dominant as long as the men behind them are joined together in a union of interests. Contemporary research has shown that these "financial interest groups" do in fact exist and that they span both financial institutions and productive enterprises.[24] The issue of control is still unsettled today. Hilferding must be credited with one of the first far-reaching studies of finance capital.[25]

Another debatable assumption of Hilferding's analysis is the supposed ability of capitalism to overcome all of its contradictions but one, class conflict. The key question here is whether or not the concentration and centralization of capital replaces the anarchy of competition with planning. Unlike Marx, who thought that monopoly heightened competition, Hilferding thought the opposite, at least at the national level. On the international level Hilferding thought that rates of profit, growth, and development would be equalized, due to foreign expansion, but that this tendency would be interrupted by war, since the lack of a common culture and nationalism would prevent the globalization of tendencies generated at the national level. Although one could not deny the operation of these factors in the international political economy, history has shown Hilferding wrong at the national level: economic crisis and uneven development persist.

From a theoretical point of view Hilferding is at odds with Marx, who derives the laws of motion and contradictions of capitalism from an analysis rooted in the sphere of production; they are inherent in the process of capitalist production. If they are not, as Hilferding implicitly assumes, then much of the Marxist case against capitalism evaporates, and we are left with simple class conflict over distribution. Right or wrong, this places Hilferding among the revisionists.

A final point is Hilferding's view that capitalist foreign expansion into the noncapitalist world would promote capitalist industrialization there. Like Marx, Hilferding provided very little in the way of concrete analysis and clearly underestimated the negative impact of capitalist foreign expansion.

Rosa Luxemburg

Exposition

Rosa Luxemburg's theory of imperialism is contained for the most part in *The Accumulation of Capital*, published in 1913, and in a reply to her critics entitled *The Accumulation of Capital—An Anti-Critique*, which was written in 1915 but not published until 1921.[26] There are some references in her other writings that are relevant to a discussion of imperialism;[27] however, these are not as important to her overall thesis.

Luxemburg's analysis of imperialism is quite diferent from those of Hilferding and the other early Marxists. She focuses on the problem of realizing surplus-value, or what is more generally referred to as underconsumption. In Volume II of *Capital* Marx shows by using reproduction schemes that capital accumulation can take place on an expanded basis. He assumes the existence of only two classes (workers and capitalists) and a closed economy. The purpose of these schemes was to demonstrate that if certain supply and demand conditions are met, accumulation can proceed unabated.

Luxemburg, however, saw a conflict between Volumes II and III of *Capital*. In Volume III, in his analysis of the contradictions of capitalism, Marx argued that frequently the supply and demand conditions for continuous expanded reproduction are not met, in turn producing economic crises. This led Luxemburg to the question of how capitalism can in real life, under the assumptions of Volume II, produce the right conditions between supply and demand to ensure capital accumulation? In her mind it was not enough to show, with reproduction schemes, the "technical" prerequisites for accumulation to exist:

> A further condition is required to ensure that accumulation can in fact proceed and production expand; the effective demand for commodities must also increase. Where is this continually increasing demand to come from, which in Marx's diagram forms the basis of reproduction on an ever rising scale.[28]

The problem for Luxemburg, then, was how, in a society composed of only workers and capitalists, can capital ensure sufficient markets for its needs. For social capital as a whole sufficient buyers must be found for the total social product. Luxemburg in her search for buyers can only account for that portion of the social production which is destined for the replacement of the means of production used up in the production process and that portion of the product that maintains the workers and capitalists.

According to Luxemburg, there must be a third portion which can account for the surplus value, otherwise expanded reproduction cannot take place. She discounts workers and the expanded consumption of the capitalists as consumers of the surplus value. Other strata of society, e.g., lawyers, military, etc., are treated as merely "parasites in the consumption of the two major classes." She then goes on to discuss the possibility of capitalists "as mutual customers for the remainder of the commodities." However, in this case "what else is accumulation but extension of capitalist production? Those goods that fulfill this purpose must not consist of luxurious articles for the private consumption of capitalists, but must be composed of various means of production (new constant capital) and provisions for the workers (variable capital)." Luxemburg goes on to discount this possibility.

> All right, but such a solution only pushes the problem from this moment to the next. After we have assumed that accumulation has started and that the increased production throws an even bigger amount of commodities on to the market the following year, the same question arises again: where do we then find the consumers for this growing amount of commodities? Will we answer: well, this growing amount of goods will again be exchanged among the capitalists to extend production again, and so forth year after year? Then we have the roundabout that revolves around itself in empty space. That is not capitalist accumulation, i.e., the amassing of money capital, but the contrary: producing commodities for the sake of it; from the standpoint of capital an utter absurdity.[29]

Having exhausted all possibilities, Luxemburg is forced to conclude that when capitalist production is the sole and exclusive mode of production expanded capital reproduction cannot take place, because there are no other classes that can buy "the surplus goods in order to change the surplus value into money, and thus accumulate capital." However, she notes that capitalism has never existed in isolation from other modes of production, even within the confines of national geographic boundaries. There have always been noncapitalist producers to whom the surplus product is sold and the money is supplied for capitalist accumulation.[30]

The solution to the problem, then, is that surplus value is realized in a third, noncapitalist market. Luxemburg warns that this is not just a theoretical exercise; it is connected "with the most outstanding fact of our time: imperialism."[31] Capitalism cannot, according to Luxemburg, exist as a closed system; it must (in order to realize surplus value) constantly seek out new noncapitalist markets and expand into noncapitalist areas. Thus imperialism is a capitalist necessity in order to keep the accumulation process going.

Rosa Luxemburg thought, in agreement with Marx and Hilferding, that this would transform noncapitalist societies:

> Through destruction of the primitive barter relations in these countries, European capital opens the doors to commodity exchange and production, transforms the population into customers of capitalist commodities and hastens its own accumulation by making mass raids on their natural resources and accumulated treasures.[32]

Not only is capitalism inherently expansionary; the process of expansion transforms noncapitalist societies into capitalist ones. However, this creates a contradiction. As expansion approaches "the point where humanity only consists of capitalists and proletarians, further accumulation will become impossible."[33] However, long beore that point is actually reached, as noncapitalist areas become rarer, the competition stiffens between national capitals, so that a

> chain of political and social catastrophes in the form of crises, will make impossible the continuation of accumulation and will make necessary the rebellion of the international working class against the domination of capital even before the latter smashes itself against its own self-created economic barriers.[34]

Luxemburg, more than any other early Marxist, analyzed the impact of imperialism on noncapitalist societies in some detail and with what turned out to be remarkable insight. We have already seen she thought that the assimilation of noncapitalist societies into the capitalist orbit transforms them in its own image. Luxemburg derives three historical stages in the assimilation of these noncapitalist societies.[35] The first stage is the struggle by capital against natural economy which presents barriers to the realization of surplus value. Capitalism "annihilates" the natural economy with political, military, and economic weapons. There are four intermediate objectives in this process of annihilation: "The appropriation of natural wealth, the coercion of the labor force into service, the introduction of a simple commodity economy (that is, one in which a large part of producers' output is traded), and the elimination of rural industry.''[36] The result is the establishment of a simple commodity-producing economy.

However, as soon as simple commodity production is established, capital must turn against it to compete with it for means of production, labor power, and markets. The aim of the second stage is to "take the means of production away from the small manufacturer" and to turn these small producers into an industrial proletariat. Agriculture is no sooner transformed from production for use, to production for exchange, than it is again transformed into capitalist farming. The peasants are either driven into debt peonage or are driven from the land. Of course, the small manufacturer cannot compete with industrial capital and is driven from business.[37]

Luxemburg was one of the few to anticipate this dualism as well as the human cost of rapid socioeconomic transformations:

> To capitalist economists and politicians, railroads, matches, sewerage systems and warehouses are progress and culture. Of themselves such works, grafted upon primitive conditions, are neither culture nor progress, for they are too dearly paid for with the sudden economic and cultural ruin of the peoples who must drink down the bitter cup of misery and horror of two social orders, of traditional agriculture landlordism, of super-modern, super-refined capitalist exploitation, at one and the same time.[38]

The final stage in the process of assimilation of precapitalist societies is the industrialization of these backward economies. This is achieved through loans from the metropolitan centers, which can take the form of state loans, share capital in independent enterprises, direct investment in overseas subsidiaries, or purchase of controlling shares in existing enterprises.[39] These loans create a demand for metropolitan capital goods in the satellite countries and extend the process of capital accumulation. Realized surplus value (profit, interest, dividends, and rent) that cannot be invested in the metropolitan country is exported as money capital, whereupon it is converted to productive capital produced by the metropolitan center but employed in the satellite.

Luxemburg thought that the source of the realization of surplus value produced in the satellite would be internal, i.e., that the sales of these firms would take place domestically. The necessary demand would come, she thought, from the rapid expansion of consumer demand that the newly created industries fostered and from the demands stimulated by the formation of social overhead capital. In addition, and consistent with Luxemburg's analysis of the reproduction of capital above, realization is facilitated by the noncapitalist hinterland within the satellite.[40]

The process of assimilation into the capitalist industrial orbit was not considered by Luxemburg an automatic process. A modern state must be created, first of all to ensure the exploitation of the internal peasant sectors, but more importantly perhaps, to wrest control of its own economy out of the hands of the metropolitan centers. Control was strengthened through financial dependency: "Though foreign loans are indispensable for the emancipation of the rising capitalist states, they are yet the surest ties by which the old capitalist states maintain their influence, exercise financial control and exert pressure."[41] On national liberation Luxemburg writes:

> Just as the substitution of commodity economy for a natural economy, and that of capitalist production for a simple commodity production, was achieved by wars, social crises and the destruction of entire social systems, so at present the achievement of capitalist autonomy in the hinterland and backward colonies is attained amidst wars and revolutions. Revolution is an essential for the process of capitalist emancipation. The backward communities must shed their obsolete political organizations, relics of natural and simple commodity economy, and create a modern state machinery adapted to the purposes of capitalist production.[42]

Projecting this trend into the future, Luxemburg argued that this stage brought with it certain contradictions. First, as more and more countries achieved capitalist autonomy this would limit the areas that were available for capitalist exploitation, and which for Luxemburg were essential to realizing surplus value and steady accumulation. Further, these new capitalist states become rival centers of accumulation, competing against the old capitalists for what remains of the noncapitalist world. Ultimately, when all territories have been brought under the capitalist form of commodity production, "the collapse of capitalism follows inevitably, as an objective historical necessity."[43]

For Luxemburg "collapse" meant the ruin of society, but before this would happen, she argued, the international proletariat would overthrow world capitalism and establish a world socialist order. If they did not, the proletariat would sink with capitalism.

Summary and critique

Luxemburg, beginning with Marx's reproduction schemes, developed a theory of imperialism that explains the necessity of foreign expansion as a need for external markets within which to realize surplus value. The realization of surplus value is, in her view, impossible within the capitalist economy. The exact nature of imperialism, although assumed to be characterized by monopoly, finance capital, nationalism, and international rivalry, is little discussed by Luxemburg. In basic agreement with other early Marxists on the issue of the regenerative impact of foreign expansion on the noncapitalist world, Luxemburg went much further in developing a stage theory embracing the disintegration of "natural society" and the rise of industrial capitalism. The fall of capitalism occurs shortly before the total transformation of the world into capitalism and the end of external markets. International conflict, strife, and crisis lead the proletariat to overthrow capitalism for socialism.

Luxemburg's analysis of imperialism has been proven to be faulty on a number of rounds. First, Luxemburg excluded from the very beginning any possibility of expanded reproduction, so that her conclusions are no surprise. She implicitly assumed that there can be no increase in variable capital (wages) to absorb the "excess" production of Department II (means of subsistence) in her reproduction scheme. Her "mistake" is that she "misunderstood and misused" the reproduction schemes, and treated the accumulation process as an instant in time rather than a process that unfolds through time. The schemes of reproduction represent what has taken place *ex post facto*.[44]

If we treat the accumulation process dynamically, it is possible for the increased demand for constant capital and variable capital in the second phase to absorb the excess product of the first phase, and so on for each succeeding phase.[45] In fact, this solution is considered by Luxemburg and discounted as "a roundabout that revolves around itself in empty space."[46] Her objection is that it violates the purpose of capitalist accumulation, the amassing of money capital. However, she is here taking one moment of the process of expanded capital reproduction and making it the goal of the capitalist. Money capital and productive capital are separated only by the time needed to convert productive capital into commodities and then into money, so that it can again reenter the production process with fresh means of production and labor power, in order to expand it still further. It makes no difference to the capitalist what form his capital takes in this process, because it is constantly being transformed, and he cannot expand it unless it is being constantly transformed.

According to Kenneth Tarbuck, "the problem of market is largely 'solved' by capitalism itself, insofar as capitalist production provides its own best market."[47] It should be noted that this is not the same as Say's Law. Underconsumption can exist, but as a periodic phenomenon rather than a permanent affliction of capitalism. By turning it into a permanent affliction, Paul Sweezy argued, Luxemburg "proved" the impossibility of capitalism itself.[48]

Luxemburg has also been criticized for ignoring the importance of the rate of profit as an explanation of imperialism. Capitalists in foreign markets realized profits not at the normal rate, but at a higher rate than the social average profit, so it was not just a matter of realization but also higher rates of profits that attracted capitalists into foreign territories.[49]

Furthermore, Luxemburg has been criticized because she did not distinguish between the expansion of early capitalism and that of late nineteenth- and early twentieth-century capitalism. While she was aware of all the important features of the latter period—the competition between capitalist countries for colonies and spheres of influence, the rising militarism and the possibility of interimperialist wars, the system of international loans, tariff barriers, the dominant role of finance capital and trusts in international politics—she takes these as the mere data of imperialism and does not integrate them into her analysis of imperialism.[50] Hilferding and the other early Marxists make these characteristics a fundamental part of their explanation of imperialism.

Perhaps one of the most important criticisms of Luxemburg from a Marxist perspective is that in her analysis the focus on class struggle and exploitation is obscured or minimized: the basis of capitalist accumulation is not the exploitation of labor but the exploitation of "third markets." According to Tarbuck, this "means that the wage labourers of the advanced capitalist countries are no longer exploited but joint exploiters with the capitalist class!''[51] On another level, Tarbuck argues that one can interpret Luxemburg in such a way that ''surplus value is not extracted from the working class, but that capitalists extract profits by trading with the 'third' market in much the same way as merchant capital was able to do under conditions of an imperfectly organized world market, i.e., by an *unequal* exchange of values.''[52]

One final point regarding Luxemburg's central thesis is that it is not at all clear exactly how surplus value is to be realized in third markets. In order to sell in foreign markets one must also buy, which does not solve the realization problem at all but merely prolongs it. Luxemburg attempts to get around this by saying that these ''third'' markets must also produce part of the constant capital, which would mean then that surplus goods are sold from Department II in exchange for raw materials from the ''third'' market, and these raw materials are then used to expand production in the capitalist sector in order to expand capital accumulation. However, this appears to be a severely limiting condition.[53]

Luxemburg's strength was her analysis of the Third World. She offered some remarkable early insights into the process of disintegration of the existing modes of production (''natural economy'') in the backward countries as the result of capitalist penetration from the outside. Many of Luxemburg's insights did not become generally recognized until 40 years later. Perhaps the most interesting example is her discussion of the opening up of the backward countries by means of ''political, military, and economic weapons'' for the purpose of seizing raw materials, coercing labor into the service of capital, and introducing commodity exchange. This implies the necessity of a forced draft transformation of the backward countries to provide the necessary means of capitalist accumulation in the advanced countries. Foreign expansion sets in motion a process of the disintegration of precapitalist modes and the development of capitalism (primitive accumulation), a process that is governed by its own logic once capitalist penetration has begun.

However, Luxemburg's stage theory is predicated upon external forces and excludes any consideration of internal forces and contradictions within the precapitalist mode of production. The latter is necessary to a complete understanding of this process, no matter how much the descriptive detail Luxemburg brings forth seems to conform to the actual situation. Had Luxemburg taken account of these internal forces she might have seen that, depending upon the specific mode of production in existence and its productive relations, capitalist penetration took different forms.[54]

Another shortcoming of Luxemburg's analysis is her assumption that although loans to the satellite would stimulate imports from the metropolitan country, the satellites would develop industries not in the export sector but rather in the sectors producing for domestic consumption. In short, the satellite is assumed to generate its own demand for industrialization. Luxemburg had to assume this, otherwise accumulation could not take place in the metropolitan center. If the satellite increases its exports to the metropolitan center, this cancels the "third market" and blocks the realization of surplus value in the center. Although there can be a bilateral trade flow between the metropolitan center and the satellite, Luxemburg thought the exports from the latter must be raw materials to be used in the metropolitan country. However, Luxemburg was referring to industrial development in this stage of assimilation, not raw material extraction.

Her faulty analysis of the surplus realization problem, then, led to problems in explaining the causes of foreign capitalist expansion as well as the process of capitalist assimilation in the backward countries.[55] Despite this it would be several decades before Marxists again took up the issue of the impact of foreign expansion on the Third World.

Nikolai Bukharin

Exposition

Nikolai Bukharin is usually treated after Vladimir Lenin in studies of early Marxist theories of imperialism, because his *Imperialism and World Economy*, written in 1915, was not published until 1918, after the publication of Lenin's *Imperialism: The Highest Stage of Capitalism* in 1916.[56] Since Bukharin's work on imperialism was written before Lenin's, his work will be taken up first. It should also be noted that Bukharin was one of Luxemburg's most thoroughgoing critics, and some of his criticism is included in the preceding discussion. His analysis of imperialism, summarized in this section, will be an implicit critique of Luxemburg, although much of it would be made explicit in Bukharin's reply to her work.[57]

Bukharin's analysis of imperialism is similar to Hilferding's and indeed can be treated as an extension of *Finance Capital*. While his analysis is more comprehensive in scope, Bukharin did not go over the ground he thought was already covered adequately by Hilferding. And although Bukharin disagreed vehemently with Luxemburg's theory of capitalist foreign expansion, he was in general agreement with her "brilliant and masterful description of colonial exploitation" and is himself largely silent on this issue.[58]

Bukharin's approach to the study of imperialism is one of the first to outline the general features of the world economy and then show how its development is shaped by the internal changes in the structures of national economies. At the most general level Bukharin defined world economy "as a system of production relations and, correspondingly, of exchange relations on a world scale."[59] The emphasis here is on the productive relations rather than exchange relations. For Bukharin, getting beneath the surface of exchange relations, which he thought had a more persuasive appearance of commodity fetishism on a world scale than in the national economy, meant treating the world economy as a set of social relationships stemming primarily from the process of production and secondarily from the international division of labor and commodity exchange:

> One must not assume that production relations are established solely in the process of commodity exchange . . . in other words, whatever the form of connections established between producers, whether directly or indirectly, once a connection has been established and has acquired a stable character, we may speak of a system of production relations, i.e., of the growth (or formation) of a social economy.[60]

This means that one treats world economy as a set of relationships "between human beings engaged in the process of production," where "connections are established both between workers and the capitalists of two countries."[61]

A common theme in Bukharin's work is that while capitalism produces a tendency toward the internationalization of capital, it also creates by the same process of expansion the nationalization of capital, i.e., the preservation of its national identity. This was an important theme for the early Marxists, because they thought it was impossible for capitalism to exist without imperialism, i.e., to exist in universal harmony. The whole structure of Bukharin's work is centered around these contradictory centrifugal and centripetal forces within capitalism.

The exchange relations in the world economy are based upon the differences in natural endowments and, more importantly for Bukharin, differences of a social nature, namely the level of development of the productive forces in any particular country. This latter is subject to the laws of uneven development. One particular manifestation of this is the reproduction of the internal separation of town and country (noted by Marx) on an international scale, with some countries appearing as industrial countries and others as agrarian countries.[62]

Bukharin attributes the extraordinary growth of the world economy in the late nineteenth and early twentieth centuries to the rapid growth in the productive forces of the world economy. Such growth was brought about by technological progress where

> labour is applied to preparatory operations for the production of the means of production; the production of the means of consumption, on the contrary, is limited to a relatively diminishing portion of society's labour as a whole.[63]

In other words, the working out of Marx's law of the increase in the organic composition of capital was in Bukharin's time expressed in the growth of heavy industry.

Heavy industry has a twofold significance for Bukharin. First, it leads to an increase in the demand for raw materials, which means an increasing need to import raw materials, and thus growth in the exchange between national economies; and second, because of the tremendous increase in the social productivity of labor and mass production, "old markets could not have absorbed a hundredth part of what is now absorbed by the world market every year."[64] Bukharin also notes that the growth of world trade is dependent upon the level of development of the technology in transportation and communication. Dramatic changes in these sectors at the turn of the century, such as transoceanic cables, bound the various national economies more closely together so that the "slightest change in one part is immediately reflected in all."[65]

The growth in the world economy also created the "international movements of populations" in response to the rising demand for labor power by capital in the "New World." Bukharin argues that this outflow "absorbs the 'superfluous population' of Europe and Asia, from the pauperised peasants who are being driven out of agriculture, to the 'reserve army' of the unemployed in the cities." The international flow of labor is regulated by the equalization of wage rates.[66]

The movement of capital is for Bukharin one of the "most essential elements in the process of internationalizing economic life, and in the process of growth of world capitalism." Bukharin notes that capital can be interest- or profit-bearing. He identifies five different forms of capital export: (1) state loans, necessary because of the need to militarize a nation if it is to exist as a power in the world economy and the need for extensive social overhead capital associated with the growth of industry and large cities; (2) buying stock of one enterprise by another for the motive of participation; (3) direct financing of foreign branch plants; (4) private unspecified lending; and (5) buying stock for holding purposes rather than for motives of participation.[67]

The "transfusion" of capital from one national sphere to another not only binds national capital together, but also through the international expanded reproduction of capital "widens over and over again the sphere of its application; it creates an ever-thickening network of international interdependence."[68]

The direction of the movement of capital is determined, according to Bukharin, by differences in the rates of profit or interest between countries. These rates will vary according to the level of the development of the productive forces. Bukharin argues that

> the more developed the country, the lower is the rate of profit, the greater is the 'overproduction' of capital, and consequently the lower is the demand for capital and the stronger the expulsion process. Conversely, the higher the rate of profit, the lower the organic composition of capital, the greater is the demand for it and the stronger the attraction.[69]

Leaving aside the incompleteness of Bukharin's analysis of the falling rate of profit, and relative versus absolute demand for "capital," it would appear from this statement that capital would flow only in the direction of less-developed countries. However, Bukharin qualifies this in his discussion of the outflow of capital, in his reply to Luxemburg:

> Non-capitalist economic forms, especially those far away from the center of developed capitalism, are the main attraction, as they guarantee a maximum profit (even including higher transport costs). The gaining of a colonial "surplus profit" explains the direction of capitalism expansion. *That does not mean that the struggle only goes or only can go in that direction.* On the contrary, the further it develops . . . the more it will become a struggle for the capitalist centers as well. In this case, too, the movement of profit is the main reason (for example, the connection of French iron with the Ruhr coal guarantees an enormous increase in profit).[70]

Thus importance is given not only to differentials in the rate of profit resulting from differences in the level of development, but to differences in the rate of profit resulting from monopolistic advantages in other developed capitalist countries. For Bukharin, then, capital will not only flow into backward areas but will be cross-invested in other developed capitalist countries as capitalists try to achieve monopolistic advantages in each other's markets.

The structure of the world economy was characterized by anarchy, Bukharin thought, despite the fact that the monopoly structure of "national economies" was being duplicated in the world economy. The process of concentration and centralization, according to Bukharin, takes place in several stages, each of which carries competition to a new higher level, from competition between large-scale enterprises to "the most stubborn competition between a few gigantic capitalist combines." With the formation of combines between industry and banking syndicates, which form a "state capitalist trust," "competition reaches the highest, the last conceivable state of development. It is now the competition of state capitalist trusts in the world market." Bukharin goes on to say that competition is "reduced to a minimum" within the confines of the nation.[71]

At this level, imperialism is for Bukharin the replacement of the internal competitive struggle over markets and market shares by the international competitive struggle between rival state capitalist groups. He argues that once the competition within the national economy nears its end, i.e., results in monopoly, then the only sphere left open to capital is the foreign sphere, where "the centre of gravity is shifted to the competition of gigantic, consolidated, and organized economic bodies possessed of a colossal fighting capacity in the world tournament of 'nations.'"[72]

Bukharin observes the same tendencies toward centralization and concentration that Hilferding noted—the formation of trusts, cartels, and combinations—reproducing themselves on an international scale. Behind these forms "stand the enterprises that finance them, i.e., primarily the banks," which have "called into being a very considerable internationalization of banking capital (by financing industrial enterprises), and insofar as it thus forms a special category: finance capital." This "all-pervading form of capital rushes to fill every 'vacuum,' whether in a 'tropical,' 'sub-tropical,' or 'polar' region, if only profits flow in sufficient quantities."[73]

Bukharin differs from Hilferding in the meaning he attaches to "finance capital." Bukharin refers to the "concrescence of bank and industrial capital"; while recognizing the predominant role of banks, he does not place bankers in control of finance capital. In Bukharin's words:

> Corresponding to this unique economic tie between the various production branches and the banks, is a special form of higher management of both. As a matter of fact, the representatives of the industrialists manage the banks, and vice versa.[74]

In Bukharin's view, a new division of labor was taking place between financial capital and industrial or productive capital, and the role of the former was becoming more important by way of its dominance over productive capital. Class control was not passing, however, from industrial capitalists to bankers; rather, industrial capitalists and bankers were being transformed into financial capitalists. Finance capital rules along with the capitalists who control it (bankers and industrialists), and it matters little whether financial capital is flowing through banking institutions or through an industrial enterprise in the form of retained earnings.

Imperialism, according to Bukharin, is the policy of finance capital, a policy that results from the structural changes in capitalism and the level of development of the forces of production. These two factors create a need for finance capital to realize surplus value in foreign markets, to obtain cheap raw materials abroad, and to find profitable outlets for the investment of surplus value abroad. These needs form the

> three roots of the policy of finance capitalism [which] represent in substance only three facets of the same phenomenon, namely of the conflict between the growth of the productive forces on the one hand, and the "national" limits of the production organization on the other.[75]

We now turn to Bukharin's analysis of these "national" limits.

First, Bukharin argues that markets must be continually expanded in order to absorb the increased output created by the production of surplus value on an extended scale. This stems from the very nature of capitalism and the expanded reproduction of capital. Bukharin follows quite closely Marx's analysis of the necessity for markets to constantly expand, blending underconsumption and disproportionality as the underlying causes of market expansion with his own analysis of the "law of mass production" and economies of scale. In addition, Bukharin cites monopoly as a restriction on quantity sold in domestic markets as a force behind foreign market expansion to realize economies of scale at home.[76]

Another explanation offered by Bukharin for "commodities to overstep the boundaries of state" is that commodities sold in foreign markets can often be sold at a price that yields a super-profit. A country with a higher level of development of productive forces, because of its higher social productivity of labor, can sell its products at a price that is below the value of the same goods produced in backward countries, or in countries where the level of development has reached as high a state, but at a price which is higher than the social (world) value of the commodity. Bukharin adds that monopoly itself is a form of obtaining super-profits and that monopoly exists not only in the national economy but in the world economy as well.[77]

Super-profits are important in Bukharin's explanation of expansion, because it "is thus obvious that not the impossibility of doing business at home, but the race for higher rates of profit is the motive power of world capitalism." He goes on to say that a "lower rate of profit drives commodities and capital further and further from their 'home,' and that this process is going on simultaneously in various sections of world economy. The capitalists of various "national economies" clash here as competitors; and the more vigorous the expansion of the productive forces of world capitalism, the more intensive the growth of foreign trade, the sharper is the competitive struggle.[78]

It was the acceleration of the competitive struggle on an international level that explained for Bukharin the scramble for colonies that took place after 1870. Once a colonial area was taken, tariff walls were thrown up to create protected spheres of influence, to keep out competitors. Frequent tariff wars sometimes escalated into armed conflict.[79]

The second factor in the foreign expansion of capitalism is the need for cheap raw materials. Bukharin notes that in the sphere of production there is a tendency for the demand for raw materials to rise faster than the supply, driving up the prices of raw materials. The rapid increase in raw material demand was occurring in Bukharin's time because of the "intensive growth of productive forces" and because the "trans-oceanic countries . . . have developed their own industry, and consequently their own demand for an ever growing amount of agricultural products [raw materials and foodstuffs—C.B.]."[80]

The competitive struggle over world market shares is then supplemented by a struggle over sources of raw materials, whose availability and cheapness are vital to profitable capital accumulation. Industries that become vertically integrated not only have a cost advantage over their competitors but also can deny their competitors access to raw materials. In the world arena "the way out" of this dilemma in the "impeccable logic" of world competition is "the decisive moment of imperialist policy—war."[81]

The third and final element in Bukharin's theory of imperialism is the outflow of capital in search of profitable investment. Capital flows abroad in the first instance because, in Marx's words, "it can be employed at a higher rate of profit in a foreign country." Noting that capital export has existed throughout capitalist history, Bukharin goes on to state that "it is only in the last decades that capital export has acquired an extraordinary significance, the like of which it never had before."[82]

Bukharin cites two sets of forces that are at work here. First, because of the "unusually rapid tempo" of capital accumulation,

due to large-scale capitalist production accompanied by incessant technical progress which makes gigantic strides and increases the productive
power of labour . . . the volumes of capital that seek employment have
reached unheard of dimensions. On the other hand, the cartels and trusts,
as the modern organization of capital, tend to put certain limits to the
employment of capital by fixing the volume of production.[83]

The necessity for capital to find profitable investment opportunities
outside of its national sphere of production is the result.

The second cause of capital export is high tariffs that place "obstacles in the way of commodities seeking to enter a foreign country. Mass
production and mass overproduction make the growth of foreign trade
necessary, but foreign trade meets with a barrier in the form of high
tariffs." In order to overcome this barrier capitalists establish production inside the protected market increasing their profits by at least the
amount of the tariff. A further advantage, Bukharin notes, is that once
inside the tariff wall, foreign capital is protected in the same way that
indigenous capital is.[84]

Capital export is also stimulated by the oganizational form of world
capitalism, i.e., monopoly. Bukharin argues that

capital export is nothing but a seizure and a monopolization of new
spheres of capital investment by the monopoly enterprises of a great
nation or—taking the process as a whole—by the organized "national"
industry, by "national" finance capital. Capital export is the most conve-
nient method of the economic policy of finance groups; it subjugates new
territories with the greatest of ease.[85]

In short, capital export is part and parcel of the worldwide competitive
struggle between national monopolies.

Capital export in the form of state or municipal loans brings special
advantages to the creditor country. These loans are "tied loans,"
which ensure that the money will be used to buy commodities from the
creditor country and that certain concessions will be made to the creditor country, such as contracts for the construction of railroads. In
addition, Bukharin notes that loans can also be used to get favorable
trade treaties.[86]

In concluding his analysis of capital export, Bukharin notes once
more that the capitalist's "stake" is a large one and that they are

therefore willing to go to almost any lengths to guard their property and the privilege of further accumulation. As with raw materials and commodity export markets, the "internationalization of economic life here, too, makes it necessary to settle controversial questions by fire and sword."[87]

Bukharin is left, after his analysis of imperialism as the policy of finance capital, with the problem of whether the centralization process extended on a world scale will lead to the formation of a "world trust, a single world state obedient to the finance capital of the victors who assimilate all the rest."[88] Based on the logic of Bukharin's own analysis of the centralization process and the extension of the fundamental contradictions of capitalism on a wider and wider scale, such a world trust is a theoretical possibility, as is abolition of the anarchy of capitalist production.

However, Bukharin goes to great lengths to argue that in reality "the socio-political causes would not even admit the formation of such an all-embracing trust."[89] His argument is based on the instability of trust and cartel agreements and the shifting patterns of competitive advantages brought about because of the uneven development of productive forces between different capitals. Even the costs of militarization do not dampen imperialism, since, as Bukharin thought, these costs were primarily borne by the working class. He also thought it unlikely that the tendency toward nationalism would be overcome even by the growing trend toward "participation in and financing of international enterprises," i.e., what we would now call the global corporation.[90]

Bukharin argues, therefore, that "finance capital cannot pursue any other policy than an imperialist one," so there is no possibility for the formation of single world trust.[91] In this way, Bukharin is able to evade the reformist conclusion that is inherent in his theoretical analysis, i.e., that imperialism is the last *antagonistic* stage of capitalism: that it would give rise to a single world trust, which, by ending competition, would eliminate the "fundamental contradictions of capitalism." But, although Bukharin cannot accept the reformist implications of his own analysis at the international level, like Hilferding he accepts them at the national level.

Summary and critique

Bukharin's analysis of imperialism, with its emphasis on finance capital, monopoly, state capitalist trusts, and the international competitive struggle carried out in economic, political, and military policies, is in many ways similar to Hilferding's. However, Bukharin's analysis goes much deeper, taking into account uneven development and the forces of production, the organic composition of capital, the falling rate of profit, and underconsumption. Thus the Marxist theory of imperialism has been advanced significantly.

The reason Bukharin was able to do this was that he recognized from the outset the importance of going beyond exchange relations and examining the production relations on which they are based. This was one of the fundamental shortcomings of Hilferding's theory, and even Bukharin can be criticized for the mechanical and incomplete way in which he linked exchange and production. His treatments of the organic composition of capital, falling rate of profit, and underconsumption are all highly controversial even today.

On another level we are still left with the unresolved issue of monopoly and competition. For Bukharin monopoly is the negation of competition and would lead, with the rise of finance capital, to what Bukharin was later to call "organized capitalism."[92] Again one notes the reformist implications of Bukharin's theory, though he did not explicitly draw them until later. Unlike Hilferding, however, Bukharin goes beyond a sociopolitical explanation and brings in economic factors to explain why the formation of a world trust was an impossibility. Of importance here are the shifting patterns of competitive advantage and the uneven development of the forces of production for different capitals. Just how these are negated at the national level, but not the international level, is an unresolved problem in Bukharin's work.

Vladimir Lenin

Exposition

Vladimir Lenin's theory of imperialism is considered by many to be *the* Marxist theory of imperialism, the "official" word.[93] This status seems to have been accorded not only on account of the power of Lenin's ideas but also in recognition of his eventual role in the October Revolution and his leadership of the first country to adopt socialism. Lenin's theory draws heavily upon the work of Hobson (a liberal critic of imperialism) and that of Hilferding, and is in many ways similar to Bukharin's analysis. But it is more than just a rehash of others' ideas: although Lenin did not intend his work to be a definitive one, he does offer some original insights.

Lenin wrote *Imperialism: The Highest Stage of Capitalism* not as a purely academic exercise but as a theoretical guide to proletarian revolution. In Lenin's words:

> Not the slightest progress can be made toward the solution of the practical problems of the Communist movement and of the impending social revolution unless the economic roots of this phenomenon are understood and unless its political and sociological significance is appreciated.[94]

When Lenin wrote this there was in his opinion no satisfactory theoretical analysis of imperialism. Bukharin's work had not been cleared by the tsarist censor, and Lenin thought that Hilferding's work suffered from errors. Lenin intended his brief pamphlet to fill the void, to "show the connection and relationships between the *principal* economic features of imperialism."[95] It is important to keep this background in mind because, in spite of what some of Lenin's followers and detractors have claimed, he did not intend this work to be definitive. In fact, Lenin is careful to note that his work is provisional and not intended to encompass more than a "general picture of the world capitalist system," which could "never include all the concatenations of a phenomenon in its complete development."[96]

For Lenin, the turn of the century was a time of transition from "capitalism to a higher social and economic system." In this period capitalism manifested in compound fashion all of its inherent contradictions. It was no longer progressive but rather "parasitic and decaying," even though it was still capable of rapid economic growth. The "definite victory of world finance capitalism" was a key feature of the period.[97]

Lenin refers to this stage of capitalist development as "monopoly capitalism," the "highest stage" of capitalist development. It is in this stage that capitalism's fundamental attributes begin to be transformed into their opposites.

> Economically, the main thing in this process is the substitution of capital-

ist monopolies for capitalist free competition. Free competition is the fundamental attribute of capitalism, and of commodity production generally. Monopoly is exactly the opposite of free competition; but we have seen the latter being transformed into monopoly before our very eyes, creating large-scale industry by still larger-scale industry, finally leading to such a concentration of production and capital that monopoly has been and is the result: cartels, syndicates, and trusts, and merging with them, the capital of a dozen or so banks manipulating thousands of millions.[98]

Lenin is careful to note that centralization and concentration are not an aberration in capitalism but the result of the "immanent laws of capitalism," the law of increasing concentration and centralization of capital which Marx had derived sixty years earlier.

Lenin's analysis follows both Hilferding and Bukharin up to a point. Lenin adopts Hilferding's notion of "finance capital" and defines it as the "bank capital of a few big monopolist banks, merged with the capital of the monopolist combines of manufacturers."[99] On the rise of banking, and its role, Lenin writes:

As banking develops and becomes concentrated in a small number of establishments the banks become transformed, and instead of being modest intermediaries they become powerful monopolies having at their command almost the whole of the money capital of all the capitalists and small businessmen and also a large part of the means of production and of the sources of raw materials of the given country and in a number of countries. The transformation of numerous modest intermediaries into a handful of monopolitists represents one of the fundamental processes in the transformation of capitalism into capitalist imperialism.[100]

The concentration of banking gave banks specific kinds of power over industrial concerns:

They can, by means of their banking connections, by running current accounts and transacting other financial operations, first *ascertain exactly* the position of the various capitalists, then *control* them, influence them by restricting or enlarging, facilitating or hindering their credits, and finally they can *entirely determine* their fate, determine their income, deprive them of capital, or, on the other hand, permit them to increase their capital rapidly and to enormous dimensions, etc.[101]

For Lenin the growth of banking marks the end of the "domination of capital in general" and the beginning of the "domination of finance capital." There are some ambiguities in these phrases. Paul Sweezy claims that by "domination of finance capital" Lenin did not mean the same thing as had Hilferding, who argued that "capital was controlled by banks and utilized by the industrialists."[102] Sweezy places the entire burden of this interpretation on Lenin's use of the words "merging" or "concrescence" of banking and industrial capital, which implies a union of bankers and industrialists rather than the dominance of bankers over industrialists. However, Lenin also refers to the "terrorism" of banks over industrial and commercial enterprises, and to prove the point he cites a case where one of Germany's largest banks "terrorizes" a large German cartel.[103] One can argue whether this was the general case, but there can be no doubt that Lenin thought that banks were in charge.

There is another more important difference between Lenin's analysis of monopoly and finance capital and both Hilferding's and Bukharin's analyses. Monopoly and the rise of finance capital do not negate competition or the contradictions of capitalism, but rather heighten competition and intensify the contradictions:

> When monopoly appears in *certain* branches of industry, it increases and intensifies the anarchy inherent in capitalist production *as a whole*. The disparity between the development of agriculture and that of industry, which is characteristic of capitalism, is increased. The privileged position of the most highly cartelised industry, so-called *heavy* industry, especially coal and iron, causes a "still greater lack of concerted organisation" in other branches of production. . . . The increased risk is connected in the long run with the prodigious increase of capital, which overflows the brim, as it were, flows abroad, etc. At the same time the extremely rapid rate of technical progress gives rise more and more to disturbances in the co-ordination between the various spheres of national economy, to anarchy and crisis.[104]

By the same token Lenin argues that the formation of international trusts and combines leads to the intensification of "unevenness and contradictions inherent in world economy." Thus, though there may be a tendency toward the state capitalist trust and the world trust, there was, according to Lenin, no theoretical possibility for this to occur.

This represents a substantial theoretical difference between Lenin and Bukharin and Hilferding.

Central to the expansion of capitalism on a world scale in the era of monopoly capitalism is the export of capital, rather than the export of commodities: "Under the old capitalism, when free competition prevailed, the export of goods was the most typical feature. Under monopoly capitalism, when monopolies prevail, the export of *capital* has become the typical feature."[105] This represents for Lenin a qualitative change in capitalism, but not one that changes in any sense the fundamental laws of motion of capitalism.

The conditions for capital export are created, Lenin thought, by the law of uneven development, "the uneven and spasmodic character of the development of individual enterprises, of individual branches of industry and individual countries."[106] Noting the inevitability of uneven development in capitalism, Lenin goes on to argue that though England, the first capitalist country, had adopted a free trade policy based on its monopoly of manufactured goods, it soon lost its preeminent position as other countries established capitalist states and challenged British supremacy.

Lenin thought that the accumulation of capital had reached such "gigantic proportions" in the advanced capitalist countries that a "superabundance of capital" existed and that this provided the basis for capital export.

> The necessity for exporting capital arises from the fact that in a few countries capitalism has become "over-ripe" and (owing to the backward state of agriculture and the impoverished state of the masses) capital cannot find "profitable" investment.[107]

Rather than using this surplus capital to develop agriculture or raise the standard of living of the masses, which would lower profits, Lenin thought capitalists would export this capital abroad to backward countries where "profits are usually high, for capital is scarce, the price of land is relatively low, wages are low, raw materials are cheap."[108]

Although it is possible to interpret Lenin here as an underconsumptionist, given his emphasis on the "impoverishment of the masses" as one of the causes of capital export, this is a very puzzling point, because Lenin in his other writings comes down explicitly against underconsumption. Because of the incompleteness of Lenin's argument here it is hard to second guess exactly what he meant; however, it seems safe to assume, based on his earier writings, that he was not here making an underconsumptionist argument.

Using Hobson's statistics, Lenin concludes that capital export "provided a solid basis for imperialist oppression and the exploitation of most of the countries and nations of the world; a solid basis for capitalist parasitism of a handful of wealthy states!"[109] In Lenin's view capital was exported not only to the colonies but also to Russia, Europe, and America; however, capital export to the backward countries was a major attraction because super-profits could be had there.[110] The form of capital varied from industrial undertakings to capital in the form of government loans.

Lenin, like the other early Marxists, thought that capital export would accelerate the development of capitalism in the backward countries, while "to a certain extent arresting development in the countries exporting capital."[111] Though Lenin does not specify what he means by "arresting" the development of the capital-exporting countries, he probably had in mind that if this capital could have been profitably invested in its home country, the domestic rate of capital formation would have been greater. In another context, when referring to this phase of capitalism as decadent, Lenin notes that he does not mean that capitalism stops growing; in fact he suggests that it can even speed up its growth.[112]

The export of capital allows finance and monopoly capital to obtain certain advantages which make this epoch peculiar. Using monopolistic methods, finance capital is able to establish "connections" everywhere and "almost literally, one might say, spreads its net over all countries of the world. Banks founded in the colonies, or their branches, play an important part in these operations."[113]

After establishing the importance of the export of capital in this phase of capitalist development, Lenin argues that the whole world is divided up among different capitalist combines:

> Monopolist capitalist combines—cartels, syndicates, trusts—divide among themselves, first of all, the whole internal market of a country, and impose their control, more or less completely, upon the industry of that country. . . . But under capitalism the home market is inevitably bound

up with the foreign market. Capitalism long ago created a world market. As the export of capital increased, and as the foreign and colonial relations and the "spheres" of influence of the big monopolist combines expanded, things "naturally" gravitated towards the formation of international cartels . . . super-monopoly develops.[114]

Like Hilferding and Bukharin, Lenin thought that the division of the world would not be a permanent one. Rather it would be constantly subject to redivision as the "result of uneven development, war, bankruptcy, etc."[115]

Colonies play a particularly important role in Lenin's theory of imperialism. Lenin uses the term "colonial territories" rather loosely to refer both to formal colonies and to informal dependencies, which he refers to as "semi-colonies," "enmeshed in the net of financial and diplomatic dependence."[116] Colonies did not originate with this period of capitalist development, yet it is in this period that the "boom in colonial annexations begins, and the territorial divisions of the world become extraordinarily keen."[117]

Lenin argues that colonial policy differs under finance capital:

Colonial possession alone gives complete guarantee of success to the monopolies against all the risks of the struggle with competitors, including the risk that the latter will defend themselves by means of a law establishing a state monopoly. The more capitalism is developed, the more the need for raw materials is felt, the more bitter competition becomes, and the more feverishly the hunt for raw materials proceeds throughout the whole world, the more desperate becomes the struggle for the acquisition of colonies.[118]

Colonial possessions are also necessary for the export of capital, as Lenin thought it would be easier to eliminate competition and ensure the "necessary connections" for commodity exports. Finally, the noneconomic superstructure that stands upon finance capital creates a politics and ideology that stimulate the drive for colonial conquest.[119] However, Lenin does not attempt to delve any further into these noneconomic aspects of imperialism.

This completes Lenin's analysis of imperialism and it is at this point that he comes up with his famous definition of imperialism, a list of its five essential features. Lenin is careful to qualify the conditional nature of his definition and to warn his readers of using such definitions. In the briefest possible form, Lenin defined imperialism simply as the monopoly stage of capitalism. More specifically, its essential features are:

(1) The concentration of production and capital developed to such a high stage that it created monopolies which play a decisive role in economic life.

(2) The merging of bank capital with industrial capital, and the creation, on the basis of this "finance capital," of a "financial oligarchy."

(3) The export of capital, which has become extremely important, as distinguished from the export of commodities.

(4) The formation of international capitalist monopolies which share the world among themselves.

(5) The territorial division of the whole world among the greatest capitalist powers is completed.[120]

Summary and critique

The concentration and centralization of capital constitute for Lenin the most important and predominant tendency explaining the rise of imperialism. This tendency gives rise to monopoly and finance capital, which heightens the competition and contradictions of capitalism. One such contradiction is the uneven development of different branches of production and different nations. Capital is driven from the branches and countries that are most developed and where the rate of profit is the lowest, to those branches and countries where the rate of profit is highest. The competition between monopolies on a world scale intensifies and leads to a renewed surge of colonialization and redivision of the world among the monopolies of the most powerful countries. The export of capital is in this period the leading edge of foreign expansion, alongside the continued drive for foreign markets and the renewed drive for raw materials to feed the huge industrial combines of this period.

The distinguishing characteristic of Lenin's analysis of imperialism is his emphasis on capital export as the unique feature of capitalist imperialism; the other early Marxists place capital export on an equal footing with market expansion and raw material extraction. Furthermore, Lenin is the only early Marxist who correctly saw that monopoly heightened competition at the national as well as the international level. Thus, Lenin did not come to reformist conclusions concerning the fate of monopoly capitalism. For Lenin, the contradictions of capitalism were imbedded in its productive relations and could not be superseded except by a change in those relations, that is, by revolution.

From a theoretical point of view, Lenin's analysis is more descriptive than analytical, despite his important understanding of the inner nature of capitalism, missed by the other early Marxists as well as later Marxists (as will be seen in later chapters). The usefulness of Lenin's work is the particular way he pulled together the various aspects of imperialism, noted by the other early Marxists, and the way he emphasized particular aspects over others to give monopoly capitalism a particular imperialist cast.

Perhaps the greatest theoretical shortcoming of Lenin's work is his analysis of the causes of the superabundance of capital and capital export. It is not clear what he means by "over-ripeness" of capitalism or the "impoverished state of the masses" or the backwardness of agriculture as the causes of the superabundance of capital (I am purposefully avoiding calling this a "surplus of capital," which has a different meaning). Many Marxists have interpreted Lenin not as an underconsumptionist but as arguing here that the capital outflow was due to the tendency for the rate of profit to fall.[121] Strangely, however, Lenin never refers to this well-known law derived by Marx, and had he really had this in mind he surely would have evoked the law. Lenin leaves us then with a very incomplete understanding of the ultimate causes of imperialism.

Lenin has been subjected to more criticism than any other Marxist theorist on imperialism, both by Marxists and by non-Marxists.[122] One problem concerns the export of capital as an outlet for the "plethora of capital" that Lenin thought existed in the most advanced capitalist countries. It has been argued that capital export did not play this role because most of the capital export during this period was actually reinvestment of the surplus value produced by previous foreign investment. Britain, for example, had a net inflow of capital during this period, due to the return flow of profits and interest from capital already placed abroad.

Lenin can hardly be criticized for this, for such information was not available.[123] It is true that Lenin did not analyze the process of the expanded reproduction of capital on a world scale. This is a theoretical shortcoming for all the early Marxists. However, the inflow of capital does not refute the surplus capital argument by itself. For example, it could simply mean that there are limits within which the export of capital can act as an outlet beyond which capital cannot be absorbed. It is likely that Lenin assumed that the surplus value generated by foreign investment abroad would be absorbed within the backward countries, where in his view industrialization was being promoted. However, Lenin along with Marx and the other early Marxists (except Luxemburg), were proven wrong on this point by subsequent history.

Another criticism concerns the problem of the timing of imperialism. Lenin tied imperialism not only to a particular period of history, but also to such factors as the appearance of monopoly, export of capital, and acceleration of colonial expansion. Many of the characteristics that Lenin, as well as the other early Marxists, associated with this phase of capitalism were present in some countries but absent in others. Lenin explicitly warned his readers against assuming that these characteristics appeared everywhere at the same time. He was not developing a rigid deterministic model of imperialism but instead was trying to trace out the main features and interrelationships of a complex phenomenon. In this task he did pick out the predominant features of the period; if these features did not all appear at the same time, it was not long afterwards that they appeared everywhere. Timing is a problem only if one tries to reduce Lenin's work to a deterministic and overly rigid model.

A final criticism frequently made by non-Marxists is that Lenin did not analyze noneconomic forces, although he certainly recognized their importance. Some of these critics argue that imperialism is at base a political phenomenon, not one rooted in the economic sphere. Certainly the political sphere has played an important role and one that Lenin did not adequately analyze; nevertheless, it is hard to believe that the structural economic changes that occurred during this period and the heightened international competition among monopolies did not form a fundamental context within which international politics was played out. Political determinism is even less satisfying than narrow economic determinism, which neither Lenin nor the other early Marxists ascribed to, their detractors to the contrary.[124]

Conclusion

The development of the theory of imperialism by the early Marxists was a major advance in Marxist thought. Although at the time Marx was writing the international aspects of capitalism could be safely pushed aside, by the turn of the century foreign expansion was of paramount importance. The early Marxists provided a more comprehensive understanding of the working out of the tendency toward the concentration and centralization of capital, predicted by Marx. The analysis of monopoly and the rise of finance capital form the underlying basis for the outward thrust of capitalism beyond its national frontiers—in a word, imperialism.

Imperialism was seen not so much as the exploitation of backward nations by advanced capitalist ones, but as the economic, political, and military consequences of monopoly competition raging among countries on a world scale. Imperialism was seen as more than a policy that could be reversed in Hobsonian fashion, but as a policy that was an inevitable outgrowth of monopoly capitalism and essential to the interests of monopoly and finance capital. Although in the opinion of Hilferding and Bukharin, capitalist contradictions (with the exception of class conflict) could be overcome within the confines of capitalist production relations at the national level, all agreed that the contradictions of capitalism on a world scale would necessitate a socialist revolution. This systemic nature of imperialism differentiates Marxist theories of imperialism from non-Marxist theories.

Despite the significant advances, there remain several unresolved issues and problems. Although there were in many cases earnest attempts to integrate the theory of imperialism with the laws of motion and contradictions of capitalism derived by Marx, these efforts proved inadequate, leaving a wide gap between Marx's analysis and that of the early Marxists. Bukharin's work was the most explicit effort to bridge this gap, but even he fails to bring about a synthesis, a synthesis that even today has not been completed. Perhaps the greatest theoretical shortcoming of the early Marxists was their inability to combine descriptive analysis and the analysis of exchange relations more formally with the process of capital accumulation and production relations.

Another unresolved issue is the impact of monopoly on competition, as well as on the laws of motion of capitalism more generally. In the contemporary period this is one of the major theoretical issues confronting Marxists. Yet another problem is the relationship between foreign expansion and the tendency of the rate of profit to fall, underconsumption, and the tendency toward economic crises. Just how the laws of capital accumulation are changed once the accumulation process is internationalized also remains a problem. Finally, there is a great need for a systematic analysis of the process of capitalist development in the backward countries, once penetrated by foreign capital. The impact of such expansion needs to be analyzed in terms of its impact on existing modes of production, the primitive accumulation of capital, and the process of capital accumulation.

In subsequent chapters we will explore how contemporary Marxists have dealt with, or avoided, these questions.

3

Monopoly Capital and
Imperialism I:
Surplus Absorption

The "monopoly capital school" represents the major strand of postwar Marxist economic thought. The original ideas of its founders, Paul Baran and Paul Sweezy, gained widespread acceptance by other Marxists. Paul Sweezy's book *The Theory of Capitalist Development*, published in 1942, was received as an authoritative interpretation of Marx's economics and became for many the definitive text on Marx. Paul Baran, in *The Political Economy of Growth*, published in 1957, laid the foundation of what was later to become, with Sweezy's collaboration, a "neo-Marxist" theory of monopoly capitalism. The synthesis of their ideas took place in a joint work entitled *Monopoly Capital*, published in 1966. The authors claimed that this work took up where Marx and the early Marxists left off: that while Marx's analysis held for the era of competitive capitalism, a fresh approach was needed to account for the changed nature of capitalism in the contemporary era of monopoly capitalism.

Because the monopoly capital school's approach and analysis represent such a critical departure from Marx, a brief discussion of Baran and Sweezy's theory of monopoly capitalism will be presented here. This will provide the basis for the subsequent discussion of imperialism in this chapter and in Chapter 4.

In the second part of the present chapter the monopoly capital theory of foreign expansion, especially as developed in works by Baran and Sweezy (cited above), James O'Connor,[1] and Harry Magdoff,[2] will be discussed and analyzed. The following chapter will focus on the monopoly capital school's theory of underdevelopment and particularly the work of Paul Baran and Andre Gunder Frank, the two primary architects of "dependency theory."

Baran and Sweezy's theory
of monopoly capital

The Baran and Sweezy analysis of monopoly capitalism represents a significant break with Marx, although they see it more as a continuation of the early Marxist work. They were dissatisfied with the progress that Marxist social science had made since Lenin:

> Important works of Marxian social science have been rare in recent years. Marxists have too often been content to repeat familiar formulations, as though nothing really new had happened since the days of Marx and Engels—or of Lenin at the latest. As a result Marxists have failed to explain important developments, or sometimes even to recognize their existence.[3]

They cite what they think is the principal cause of this failure:

> The stagnation of Marxian social science, its lagging vitality and fruitfulness, cannot be explained by any simple hypothesis. . . . But there is one important factor which we believe can be identified and isolated and hence (at least in principle) remedied: the Marxian analysis of capitalism still rests in the final analysis on the assumption of a competitive economy.[4]

In reference to Marx, Baran and Sweezy note that while he recognized the trend toward concentration and centralization, he never attempted to analyze what would then have been a hypothetical system of large-scale enterprise and monopoly. It should be noted that Marx did provide an analysis of monopoly in Volume III of *Capital*, which proceeds along lines totally different from those taken by Baran and Sweezy, and that they make no reference to Marx's analysis.

Baran and Sweezy recognize the contributions made by Lenin and the other early Marxists who "gave full weight to the predominance of monopoly."

> It remains true that neither Lenin nor any of his followers attempted to explore the consequences of the predominance of monopoly for the work-

ing principles and "laws of motion" of the underlying capitalist economy. There Marx's *Capital* continued to reign supreme.[5]

In short, Baran and Sweezy argue that Marx and those who followed stopped short of analyzing the impact of monopoly on the fundamentals of Marxian economic theory."

They claim that "the time has come to remedy this situation and to do so in an explicit and indeed radical fashion," explaining:

> If we are to follow the example set by Marx and make full use of his powerful analytical method, we cannot be content with patching up and amending the competitive model which underlies his economic theory. We must recognize that competition, which was the predominant form of market relations in nineteenth century Britain, has ceased to occupy that position, not only in Britain but everywhere else in the capitalist world. . . . In an attempt to understand capitalism in its monopoly stage, we cannot abstract from monopoly or introduce it as a mere modifying factor; we must put it at the very center of the analytical effort.[6]

Competition is nowhere defined by Baran and Sweezy, although it appears that they were using a neoclassical notion of competition, i.e., the number of sellers in a particular market.

Whereas Marx's emphasis was on productive relations, Baran and Sweezy emphasize exchange or market relations.

> Overall, monopoly capitalism is as unplanned as its competitive predecessor. The big corporations relate to each other, to consumers, to labor, to smaller business *primarily through the market.* The way the system works is still the unintended outcome of the self-regarding actions of the numerous units that compose it. *And since market relations are essentially price relations, the study of monopoly capitalism like that of competitive capitalism, must begin with the workings of the price mechanism.*[7]

This is a crucial difference between the monopoly capital school and Marx. Marx started from an analysis of the sphere of production, derived the law of value, and then determined what took place in the sphere of circulation, i.e., in the market. Baran and Sweezy start (and end) with the sphere of circulation and replace the relation between capital and labor in the sphere of production with the relations between corporations and consumers and labor in the market. Their analysis is an attempt to derive the laws of motion of monopoly capitalism from these relations between buyers and sellers.

The central concern in Baran and Sweezy's analysis of monopoly capitalism is the generation and absorption of economic surplus under conditions of monopoly capitalism. Surplus is a concept that originated with Paul Baran and bears no theoretical relationship to Marx's concept of surplus value. There are two variants of the concept that are important here. First, there is the actual surplus, which is defined by Baran as

> the difference between society's *actual* current output and its *actual* current consumption. It is thus identical with current savings or accumulation, and finds its embodiment in assets of various kinds added to society's wealth during the period in question; productive facilities and equipment, inventories, foreign balances, and gold hoards.[8]

Later, in *Monopoly Capital*, actual consumption is determined by all those necessary costs incurred to produce actual output. When these costs are subtracted from the total revenue, what remains is the actual economic surplus.[9]

There is a tendency to interpret surplus as total surplus value or surplus product. However, Baran differentiates surplus from these concepts:

> It comprises obviously a lesser share of total output than that encompassed by Marx's notion of surplus value. The latter, it will be recalled, consists of the entire difference between aggregate net output and the real income of labor. The ''actual economic surplus'' as defined above is merely that part of surplus value that is being *accumulated*; it does not include, in other words, the consumption of the capitalist class, the government's spending on administration, military establishment, and the like.[10]

Economic surplus then is not only different from surplus value, but also has no relationship to the labor theory of value or to the law of value that Marx derived from his analysis of ''competitive'' capitalism.

In addition to actual surplus, there is what Baran refers to as potential economic surplus. It is defined as the

difference between the output that *could* be produced in a given natural
and technological environment with the help of employable productive
resources, and what might be regarded as essential consumption. Its
realization presupposes a more or less drastic reorganization of the production and distribution of social output, and implies far-reaching
changes in the structure of society.[11]

This variant of economic surplus is important to Baran and Sweezy
because it establishes, along with actual surplus, the basis for concluding that monopoly capitalism is an irrational system that should be
replaced by socialism. Potential surplus is particularly useful, according to Baran, because "it transcends the horizon of the existing social
order, relating as it does not merely to the easily observable perfor-
mance of the given socioeconomic organization, but also to the less
readily visualized *image* of a more rationally ordered society."[12] Thus
surplus is an ahistorical concept which applies equally well to any mode
of production and has no specific relationship to any particular social
relations of production.[13]

The fundamental law of motion of monopoly capitalism is the tendency for the economy surplus to rise both absolutely and relatively
over time. Baran and Sweezy derive this law from an analysis of the
market behavior of large-scale monopoly enterprises based on the "traditional monopoly price theory of classical and neo-classical
economics."[14]

Two trends in the market behavior of monopoly enterprise are important to Baran and Sweezy. First, as price competition is eliminated,
prices become downwardly rigid and firms seek to avoid price wars,
which could destroy all the firms in an industry. Second, competition is
not eliminated but limited to nonprice forms of competition, or to what
Baran and Sweezy refer to as the sales effort. The latter takes the form
of product differentiation and advertising. A firm can only increase its
profits by increasing its market share (by nonprice competitive means),
extending the market, or adopting cost-reducing innovations. In fact,
on the cost side competition under conditions of monopoly seems to be
heightened:

> that with regard to the cost discipline which it imposes on its members the
> monopoly capitalist economy is no less severe than its competitive prede-
> cessor, and that in addition it generates new and powerful impulses to

innovation. There can therefore be no doubt about the downward trend of production costs under monopoly capitalism.[15]

Competition would seem still to be a predominant force even in monopoly capitalism, albeit in modified form.[16]

If these two trends, falling costs and downwardly rigid prices, combine, continuously widening profit margins result. From here it is but a small step to arguing that this results in a tendency for the economic surplus to rise, both absolutely and relatively. This tendency acts as the absolute law of monopoly capitalism, and replaces Marx's tendency for the rate of profit to fall.[17]

Having established their case for the tendency for the surplus to rise under monopoly capitalism, Baran and Sweezy proceed to analyze the ways in which this rising surplus is absorbed or utilized in monopoly capitalism. This appears to be analogous to realizing surplus value. From the outset it is assumed that consumption in monopoly capitalism rises at a slower rate than the potential productive capacity of the economy.[18] The problem for Baran and Sweezy is how monopoly capitalism absorbs an ever-increasing economic surplus. First, they discount the possibility of rising capitalist consumption as a possible outlet. Second, both domestic and foreign investment are discounted, because on the one hand all investment gives rise to expanded capacity and even more surplus, which makes absorption more of a problem later; on the other hand, while foreign investment provides an outlet, it simultaneously acts as a siphon pumping surplus out of the underdeveloped countries into the countries where monopoly capitalism is highly developed. In short, the surplus flowing back into the country as a result of foreign investment is larger than the initial outflow, which means even more surplus to absorb.[19]

Baran and Sweezy conclude their analysis of the normal outlets for surplus absorption with the following statements:

> Twist and turn as one will, there is no way to avoid the conclusion that monopoly capitalism is a self-contradictory system. It tends to generate ever more surplus, yet it fails to provide the consumption and investment outlets required for the absorption of a rising surplus and hence for the smooth working of the system. Since surplus which cannot be absorbed will not be produced, it follows that the *normal* state of the monopoly capitalist economy is stagnation.[20]

This could be interpreted to mean that stagnation is the result of the lack of effective demand (consumption and investment), along the lines of Keynesian analysis. However, it is not the lack of effective demand that causes stagnation in their analysis, but rather the lack of only one component of demand, consumption. In other words, Baran and Sweezy's stagnation thesis rests on the implicit assumption of underconsumption, which is prior to their consideration of the absorption of surplus.[21]

Baran and Sweezy argue that "left to itself . . . in the absence of counteracting forces which are not part of what may be called the 'elementary logic' of the system . . . monopoly capitalism would sink deeper into a bog of chronic depression,'' yet there are countervailing forces at work.[22] These forces are classified as "powerful external stimuli'' and include epoch-making innovations (e.g., railroads, automobiles, etc.), not to be confused with innovations generated by a system's internal logic. The other important counteracting force is war and its aftermath.[23]

Baran and Sweezy argue that in the contemporary period we are unlikely to see any new epoch-making innovations, because of the tendency of monopoly capitalism to stifle innovations that would destroy (make obsolete) large investments in fixed plant and equipment.[24] Therefore, such innovations cannot be counted on to bring the system out of stagnation in the future.[25]

The absorption of the surplus in the postwar period is accounted for by Keynesian macroeconomic policies plus the external stimuli of the aftermath of the war and the second great wave of automobilization. However, each alone was incapable of absorbing the entire surplus, which was absorbed only by the combined effect of all these factors, according to Baran and Sweezy. A discussion of the new demand policies of business and government is important for an understanding of Baran and Sweezy's analysis of surplus absorption in postwar monopoly capitalism and the implications for continued future absorption.

The more sophisticated policies of business are those referred to as the "sales effort,'' which include advertising, product differentiation, planned obsolescence, and credit schemes. Whereas expenditures associated with the sales effort are treated as costs by businesses, Baran and Sweezy argue that in reality they are part of the surplus because they are not necessary costs of production, no matter how necessary they seem in monopoly capitalism. These "costs'' are offset by an increase in the price of consumer goods, so that income is shifted from productive workers to unproductive workers in the sales effort. This, according to Baran and Sweezy, represents an addition to the surplus, as real wages are reduced so that the difference between aggregate output and real wages is larger. Further, some of the selling expenses are borne by capitalists and other unproductive workers, because of the higher prices that they must pay for consumer goods. This, however, does not represent an increase in surplus but rather the redistribution of surplus from one unproductive group to another.[26]

The sales effort has both direct and indirect impacts on the economy. The direct impact is similar to government spending financed by tax revenue and measured by the balanced budget multiplier. In this case, aggregate income and output are increased by the amount of the original outlay and are ''associated with higher employment of unproductive workers in advertising agencies, advertising media, and the like.''[27]

An equally important indirect effect of the sales effort is its impact on the division of income between consumption and saving, or what Keynes called the propensity to consume. According to Baran and Sweezy, the sales effort maintains and increases the propensity to consume, thus increasing effective demand. This stimulates investment in plant and equipment which otherwise would not take place. Therefore, the sales effort both directly absorbs part of the surplus and indirectly promotes the absorption of another part of the surplus.[28]

The second new policy, and by far the most important according to Baran and Sweezy, is government stimulation of effective demand. Their analysis is strictly Keynesian.[29] On this basis they argue that government spending is the major factor in the postwar period that explains the absorption and creation of surplus.

There are certain limitations on government spending, however. First, civilian purchases and transfer payments are limited both by the ideology of capitalism and by powerful private interests who would oppose any spending programs that interfered with those interests and the maintenance of capitalist hegemony. Although civilian spending has absorbed a portion of the postwar surplus, it has not accounted for an increasing share. What has increased dramatically has been military spending, and it is argued that this form of spending is ideologically acceptable and does not encroach upon dominant private interests.

Furthermore, it is argued that militarism is necessary for the containment of the socialist world and the protection of monopoly capital interests abroad. According to Baran and Sweezy, military expenditures account for the lion's share of surplus absorption in the postwar period.

There are also, however, limitations on government military spending itself. On the one hand, the military industry is subject to rapidly declining costs per unit of destructive power, which places a limit on military spending as an outlet for the growing surplus. On the other hand, the growth in destructive force produces a counteracting force in the form of a disarmament movement, which also limits the expansion of military spending. Therefore, it is argued that military spending cannot continue to absorb the increasing surplus.

Baran and Sweezy conclude that the system must again return to its natural state of stagnation. Despite the theoretical possibility of overcoming the deficiency in aggregate demand, reality places certain insurmountable obstacles in the path of monopoly capitalism that prevent it from overcoming its tendency toward stagnation. The ultimate irrationality of the system is its tendency to underutilize its resources, causing unemployment and excess capacity. However, even when capacity is utilized and the surplus absorbed, it is done so irrationally, producing waste and destruction, rather than in ways that meet social and human needs. These contradictions can only be overcome with the replacement of monopoly capitalism by a rational socialist system.

Baran and Sweezy's concept of surplus and their theory of monopoly capitalism gained widespread acceptance in the 1960s and early 1970s. It provided a generation of Marxists (the New Left), particularly in the United States, with a theoretical approach and understanding of monopoly capitalism. It is from this foundation that the contemporary Marxist theory of imperialism was built. But before we proceed, a brief evaluation is in order.

On the positive side, Baran and Sweezy's development of the concept of surplus and analysis of monopoly capitalism have produced an awareness and understanding of waste and irrationality in capitalism not present before. The concept of economic surplus has been particularly useful here. Their analysis of the behavior and market practices of monopoly enterprises is also masterful. However, the analysis is superficial and not without serious problems: (1) the tendency for surplus to increase relatively over time has not been convincingly established either theoretically or empirically; (2) stagnation as the natural state of capitalism, due to underconsumption, is highly questionable and denies the dialectical relationship between expansion and contraction, as well as the systemic nature of both; (3) the concept of surplus (as opposed to surplus value) is an ahistorical concept and theoretically unrelated to class, exploitation, or the accumulation process in capitalism; (4) it is highly questionable that the law of value and Marx's analysis of the laws of motion of capitalism are dependent on the neoclassical assumption of perfect competition; (5) the methodology and analysis are limited to the sphere of exchange and ignore production relations, exploitation, and class struggle. (See Appendix I for an extended critique.)

Monopoly capital and the theory of foreign expansion

The monopoly capital school's approach to the study and analysis of monopoly capitalism underlies what until recently was the dominant view of imperialism. The contemporary literature has tended to focus on the impact that capitalist foreign expansion has had on the backward countries; much less emphasis has been placed on the causes of expansion and interimperialist rivalries, which, it will be recalled, were the primary concern of the early Marxists. For many in the contemporary period imperialism has come to mean the "exploitation" of the backward countries by the industrialized capitalist countries.[30]

In this section the discussions of capitalist foreign expansion will be taken up, to show how foreign expansion is tied into the notion of economic surplus and the problem of surplus absorption. This analysis was begun by Baran and Sweezy[31] and later refined and expanded by James O'Connor.[32] Harry Magdoff, although considered part of the monopoly capital school, will be treated separately from Baran, Sweezy, and O'Connor.

Paul Baran, Paul Sweezy, and James O'Connor

Baran, Sweezy, and O'Connor generally agree that the early Marxist theory of imperialism needs to be abandoned, or at least modified, to take into account the changes capitalism has undergone since World War I. O'Connor argues that Lenin's theory of imperialism is no longer useful as an explanation of contemporary imperialism for the following reasons:

> In the first place, the advanced capitalist economies have become mass consumption societies; secondly, savings have become concentrated in the hands of the goverment, financial intermediaries, and trust funds, as well as a relatively few giant corporations; thirdly, the concept of "the" rate of profit is out-of-date. In the overcrowded competitive sector of the advanced capitalist economies, the profit rate remains a datum, a given, but in the oligopolistic sector, profit margins are themselves determined by corporate price, output, and investment policies.[33]

No further elaboration is offered by O'Connor. He goes on to say that Baran and Sweezy have "proposed an alternative approach of identifying the important economic contradictions in advanced capitalist societies."[34]

Baran and Sweezy contend that the Marxian theory of imperialism is outdated because it rests on the notion that capital export "is . . . supposed to provide a crucially important outlet for the surplus of the rich countries," which they maintain is not true today.[35] Furthermore, since World War I, "certain changes in the characteristics of the ruling classes in the dominant countries have taken place which need to be taken into account in the development of the theory [of imperialism]." More specifically, today giant multinational corporations are the "basic units of monopoly capitalism in its present state; their (big) owners and functionaries constitute the leading echelon of the ruling class," rather than the finance capitalists (bankers) of the earlier period.[36] They further note that "such a huge and complicated institutional 'capitalist' can hardly be assumed to have exactly the same attitudes and behavior patterns as the industrial or finance capitalists of classical Marxian theory."[37]

In *Monopoly Capital* Baran and Sweezy's analysis of capitalist expansion is limited to a very brief discussion of foreign investment as an outlet for surplus and a source of militarism. They argue that except for relatively brief periods, when the export of capital is high, foreign investment acts as a siphon that pumps surplus out of the underdevel-

oped countries. It is, therefore, "far from being an outlet for domestically generated surplus," but is rather "a most efficient device for
transferring surplus generated abroad in the investing country." Thus,
foreign investment aggravates rather than solves the surplus absorption
problem.[38]

The question that arises immediately is, why, if it makes the problem
worse, do firms invest abroad? Baran and Sweezy do not raise this
question, but it is clear from their analysis, and has been explicitly
argued by O'Connor, that though it is a problem for the system as a
whole, from the standpoint of the monopoly enterprise the "price" of
even more surplus next year (after disposing of this year's surplus by
investing abroad) is hardly any price to pay at all. This is one of the
contradictions of monopoly capitalism. A problem is created for all
capitalists at the macro level by the search for profits at the micro level
by individual capitalists.[39]

Baran and Sweezy describe the international capitalist system as
consisting of a hierarchy of nations linked by a complex set of
exploitative relations. This is the forerunner to Andre Gunder Frank's
structural analysis of the world capitalist system. Each nation exploits
those nations below it; those at the very bottom have no one to exploit.
Each nation strives in this system to be the lone exploiter of as many
countries as possible. The glue that holds this system together is outright force, which gives rise to militarism as each nation vies with all
the others to maintain and improve its position within the system.[40]

The three most important characteristics of the contemporary imperialist period are, according to Baran and Sweezy, the emergence after
World War II of the United States as the undisputed dominant power
and leader of the world capitalist system, the threat of socialist expansion posed to capitalists' interests, and the growth of the giant multinational corporation.[41]

The elevation of the United States to the pinnacle of power in this
period and the corresponding extension of its business interests to every
corner of the world have given rise to the need for a vast military
apparatus to maintain this empire. The chief factor accounting for the
rise of U.S. militarism has been, it is argued, the need to "prevent the
expansion of socialism, to compress it into as small an area as possible,
and ultimately to wipe it off the face of the earth," in order to maintain
and increase the opportunities for U.S. businesses to profit from doing
business with and in the rest of the world.[42]

While these political and military forces establish the broad parameters within which contemporary imperialism operates, the basis for a proper understanding of imperialism in this period lies in understanding the "behavior and interests" of the chief economic actors on the international stage. In Baran and Sweezy's view, these actors have undergone fundamental changes, which have altered the very functioning of imperialism. More specifically, the change responsible for this alteration has been the transformation of the national monopoly corporation into the multinational corporation with branch plants in several countries around the world, vertically integrated and horizontally well diversified.

As a result of the rise of multinational corporations, business interests in this period have changed from having commerce with other countries to actually producing in other countries. These corporations seek monopolistic control over foreign markets and sources of supply. This enables them to do business on privileged terms and to shift orders and sources of supply from one country to another to take advantage of the best tax rates, lowest wages, and other beneficial policies affecting profits.[43]

The true *differentia specifica* of the multinational corporation is, according to Baran and Sweezy, the fact that its managers make decisions concerning marketing, production, and research based on worldwide alternatives. This gives rise to specific economic interests that are "variegated and complex, often contradictory rather than complementary," and that differ substantially from the primary interests of the turn-of-the-century industrialist and banker to export commodities and capital. They argue, based on empirical evidence, that these giant corporations are net importers of capital and that branch plants are taking the place of commodity exports.[44]

Baran and Sweezy note that, although it is difficult to generalize about the "variegated and complex" interests of these corporations,

they will seek a solution [to their problems] which maximizes the (long-run) profits of the enterprise as a whole. And this of course means that whenever necessary to the furtherance of this goal, the interests of particular subsidiaries and countries will be ruthlessly sacrificed.[45]

What Baran and Sweezy are trying to establish here is the separation of national interests from the interests of multinational corporations; it is no longer possible, they think, to speak of national policies of finance capital in the sense that the early Marxists did. Baran and Sweezy do note, however, that there are

> common interests and desired general policies, but that for the most part they are not narrowly economic in nature. The multinational companies often have conflicting interests when it comes to tariffs, export subsidies, foreign investment, etc. But they are absolutely united on two things: First, they want the world of nations in which they can operate to be as large as possible. And second, they want its laws and institutions to be favorable to the unfettered development of private capitalist enterprise.[46]

Baran and Sweezy do little more than trace some of the changed characteristics of contemporary imperialism. Their two major points are that the rise of socialism threatens capitalism and that the rise of the multinational corporation makes it difficult if not impossible to speak in terms of the interests of national capital, when capital has global interests.

O'Connor extends Baran and Sweezy's analysis of imperialism. He cites five main features of the contemporary imperialist system that serve to update Lenin's definition of imperialism. These features are:

> (1) The further concentration and centralization of capital, and the integration of the world capitalist economy into the structures of the giant United States based multinational corporations, or integrated conglomerate monopolistic enterprises; and the acceleration of technological change under the auspices of these corporations.
> (2) The abandonment of the "free" international market, and the substitution of administered prices in commodity trade and investment; and the determination of profit margins through adjustments in the internal accounting schemes of the multinational corporations.
> (3) The active participation of state capital in international investment; subsidies and guarantees to private investment; and a global foreign policy which corresponds to the global interests and perspective of the multinational corporation.
> (4) The consolidation of an international ruling class constituted on the basis of ownership and control of the multinational corporations, and the concomitant decline of national rivalries initiated by the national power elites in the advanced capitalist countries; and the internationalization of the world capital market by the World Bank and other agencies of the international ruling class.

(5) The intensification of all of these tendencies arising from the threat of world socialism to the world capitalist system.[47]

There are major differences between this description and Lenin's. The rise of the multinational corporation was only dimly perceived by the early Marxists, and the threat of world socialism did not yet exist. The abandonment of the ''free'' international market is certainly not new, although intrafirm pricing on an international scale is. The active participation of the state, while not new, has been developed to a higher degree with the creation of multilateral lending institutions. In O'Connor's view, the active role of the state in granting ''subsidies and guarantees'' to private foreign capital contradicts Baran and Sweezy's notion that on the economic level there is little common interest between the state and the multinational corporations. In reference to the consolidation of the international ruling class and the end of national capitalist rivalries, O'Connor gives no further justification or explanation for leaving hanging a position that Lenin argued had no theoretical possibility, although Bukharin and Hilferding admitted such a possibility. The issue of rivalries today is an open question.[48]

Where Baran and Sweezy are implicit, O'Connor is explicit, concerning the increasing inability of monopoly capitalism to absorb its growing economic surplus. Foreign investment becomes increasingly more important as a source of surplus absorption. O'Connor argues that U.S. multinational corporations are under ''unceasing pressure'' to expand their operations outside U.S. borders and that it is precisely this expansion, along with military spending, that accounts for postwar economic prosperity.[49]

However, global expansion does not eliminate or weaken the contradiction between the generation and absorption of surplus, but creates, according to O'Connor, forces that intensify it. Where Baran and Sweezy emphasize the influx of economic surplus pumped out of the underdeveloped countries as the result of foreign investment, O'Connor argues that capitalist expansion tends to diminish the capacity of the backward countries to absorb continuously increasing amounts of economic surplus. This intensifies the surplus absorption problem in the metropolitan countries.

It is argued that capitalist expansion sets in motion certain forces in the backward countries which produce anticolonial and national independence movements. The success of these movements does not prevent the inflow of foreign capital into the backward countries, because the local bourgeoisies are anxious to participate with foreign capital in profitable investment activities. Second, the pressure for social and economic development in these countries is great, while local sources of surplus, wasted in luxuries, speculation, and in the absence of fundamental reforms, cannot be mobilized. This drives the ex-colonies toward actively seeking foreign investment. Third, those areas that are incorporated into currency blocs have no choice but to seek foreign capital from the country whose currency it is dependent upon. Finally, those countries that are dependent upon primary exports have difficulty in distributing and marketing these commodities without the participation of foreign capital.[50]

The success of these movements, though not discouraging foreign capital inflows, does produce, according to O'Connor, three tendencies that limit the absorption of metropolitan surplus by backward countries:

> first, increased collaboration between foreign and local capital; second, the shift in the composition of foreign investments against primary commodity sectors and in favor of manufacturing and related activities; and third, the shift in the composition of capital exports against private investment and in favor of state loans and grants.[51]

In the first case, pressures for local participation force multinational corporations increasingly to mobilize local savings and capital instead of using metropolitan sources of finance capital. This reduces the capacity to absorb the economic surplus of the metropolitan country.[52]

In the second case, there is a direct reduction in the absorptive capacity of the agricultural and raw materials sectors in the backward countries because of the development of synthetics, the inelastic demand for foodstuffs, a reduction in the mineral component of production, and metropolitan tariffs on imported raw materials.[53] There is also a reduction in these sectors' ability to effect surplus absorption indirectly by lowering the costs of labor and raw materials in the metropolitan countries, as occurred in the nineteenth century. These sectors are today highly monopolized and subject to decreasing returns to scale. Thus, one of the indirect expansionary effects of foreign investment in these sectors is blocked, according to O'Connor, and surplus absorption correspondingly diminishes.[54]

In O'Connor's view, the increased growth in foreign investment in manufacturing is unlikely to compensate for the decline in the absorptive capacity of the primary sectors. First of all, it is claimed that most of these investments are of the tariff-hopping kind and do not absorb more surplus, but merely represent a change in the location of production facilities from the metropolitan countries to backward countries. Secondly, foreign investment in manufacturing is limited in the backward countries because of the lack of effective demand. And finally, the foreign investment in other advanced countries, not limited by effective demand, is mostly of the tariff-hopping or export-competing kind, which O'Connor argues is self-defeating in the long run. O'Connor concludes that surplus absorption in both advanced and backward countries will be limited to "replacement demand," together with a modest flow of new investments necessary to keep pace with expanding incomes abroad.[55]

In the third and final case, O'Connor notes that there has been a tendency for public capital flows to replace private foreign capital flows in the postwar period. These public and international loans are used to build up the infrastructure of the backward countries and stimulate the flow of private foreign investment. In the case of infrastructure investments there are clearly limits beyond which further expansion cannot take place. On the other hand, the stimulation of private investments is subject to the same limitations discussed above concerning the limits of foreign capital flows into the primary and manufacturing sectors of the backward economies. Therefore, O'Connor reaches the same conclusion: the limited ability of the backward countries to absorb metropolitan surplus.[56]

Despite these tendencies, O'Connor notes that the opportunities for profitable investments in the backward countries do not appear to be weakening. The reasons given are that multinational corporations are able to "penetrate, control, and dominate" the economies of the backward countries with smaller amounts of capital by "mobilizing and utilizing" local capital, by controlling technology, and by the active participation of the home state. Another reason for continued profitability is that the multinationals tend to use a large share of their retained earnings for "modernization" investments, which lower costs and thus raise profits. Finally, these corporations are more "integrated and diversified," thus minimizing risk and uncertainty.[57]

However, for the system as a whole the disposal of this year's surplus means more surplus next year and an ever-increasing surplus disposal problem. Therefore, O'Connor argues, the metropolis is compelled to follow the policies of a "militant, expansive imperialist power." More specifically:

> The United States government, the European powers, and the United States-dominated international agencies are thus under growing pressure by the international monopolies to formulate and implement political-economic policies which will create an "attractive" investment climate abroad, in particular in the underexploited countries.[58]

O'Connor delineates the major differences between these policies and the imperialist policies in the nineteenth century. First, informal control (neocolonialism) is substituted for formal political control (colonialism) of the backward countries. The former economic and political ties are maintained by "closed currency zones, preferential trading systems, military alliances, and political-military pacts." Other policies include "economic, political, and cultural missions, labor union delegations, joint military training programs, military grants, and bribes to local ruling classes in the form of economic 'aid,' which substitute for direct colonial rule." The "instruments of coercion and force" are used when indirect policies fail.[59]

The second difference is the increase in the financial and thus political autonomy of present imperialist states. O'Connor argues that this signifies that the contemporary imperialist state no longer depends on the private capital market and can be more flexile in its foreign policy to absorb the economic surplus abroad without a *quid pro quo*. He cites as examples the Marshall Plan, military aid and grants, and low-cost loans to the backward countries. In evaluating these policies, O'Connor states that the capacity for this type of surplus absorption is unlimited, with two exceptions. First, these grants and loans compete with private loans and are resisted by private capitalist interests; and second, "economic strings" attached to these grants and loans serve to discipline the satellites. Further, state loans financed from private capital sources have to earn a rate of return high enough to cover the interest of the original loan plus the cost of administration. As mentioned above, these loans are restricted in the first place because of the limited opportunity for profitable investment in the backward countries.[60]

Finally, it is argued that the absence of significant conflict between the national and foreign interests of the nineteenth-century imperialist countries has given way to modern conflict. In the United States, for example, there is a conflict between national capitalist interests and the need to strengthen the international capitalist system. More specifically:

> Policies [in the backward countries] which aim to recruit new members for local comprador groups, stimulate the development of capitalist agriculture and the middle farmers, reinforce the dominance of local financial and commercial classes, and reinvigorate local manufacturing activities. . . .[61]

These policies, according to O'Connor, directly threaten the interests of U.S. national capitalists. These policies help to keep the backward countries in the imperialist camp in the short run; but local capitalist interests, which these policies foster, may demand their independence from U.S. imperialism in the long run.[62]

Harry Magdoff

Harry Magdoff's major work, *The Age of Imperialism*, perhaps the most widely read Marxist work on imperialism, appeared in 1969.[63] It has been followed by several articles and another book, *Imperialism from the Colonial Age to the Present* (1978).[64]

Magdoff's analysis of imperialism, though not directly built on Baran and Sweezy's analytical foundation, is included in this chapter because he is considered part of the monopoly capital school. For the most part his work represents a descriptive analysis of the capitalist imperialist network. On a more theoretical level, Magdoff does deal somewhat with the causes of capitalist foreign expansion, but he is not concerned with the causes of underdevelopment. Nevertheless, it is clear from his works that he supports the view of underdevelopment put forth by the monopoly capital school, as presented in the next chapter.

The Age of Imperialism is primarily devoted to an in-depth analysis of the ways the postwar international monetary system, U.S. financial operations, military expenditures, and foreign aid are used to achieve, maintain, and increase the concentration of U.S. economic power for the major economic and financial sectors of the economy. The key factor in achieving this goal is control over the environment in which these sectors operate, which is "necessary for the safety of the capital invested and as an important source of increased profits." In the age of monopoly capitalism, the "imperatives of control and profit growth involve extensions of economic activity beyond national borders: to control and influence raw material sources, to control and influence markets, and to obtain higher profit rates through cheaper labor and other inputs."[65]

The circumstances following World War II and the political, economic, and military activities of the United States have produced a situation where U.S. institutions dominate the capitalist world system. Magdoff argues that

> The great prosperity of the United States during the postwar years is rooted in this dominating role. The maintenance of the military establishment and its activities has been a major source of direct and indirect business activity and profits. Industry and finance profitably expanded abroad under the protection of this globe-striding military force. The military, financial, and industrial foreign expansion supported the U.S. assumption of world banking leadership and the domination of the dollar as a world currency. In turn, the central role of the U.S. money market has been instrumental in financing military operations abroad, the international expansion of industry and banking, and the use of foreign aid as a means of controlling and dominating the imperialist network.[66]

It is the "complex web of interdependence" between these factors in forming the imperialist network that captures most of Magdoff's attention, in what is probably the best and most complete descriptive work on imperialism in the postwar period. Magdoff offers here a wealth of material showing how each part of this network works to maintain and extend control and to facilitate imperial industrial and financial foreign expansion in order to increase profits.

However, for immediate purposes, neither this descriptive material nor the inner workings of the imperialist network is of concern here, but rather the explanation Magdoff offers of just exactly why imperialism occurs and takes the particular form that it does. Here Magdoff takes what he sees as an essentially Leninist position, arguing that with the rise of monopoly capitalism we see the concomitant rise of imperialism. He notes two decisive factors behind the rise of imperialism: the rise of a small number of large integrated industrial and financial firms (finance capital), and the appearance of rival industrial powers.

The key to expansion, according to Magdoff, is the struggle of competing monopoly enterprises for "survival and growth." This is accomplished through controlling the business environment in the following ways: first, by gaining control over as many of the sources of raw materials as possible, wherever these sources may be, in order to "limit new competition and to control production and prices of the finished products";[67] second, by the conquest of foreign markets, to provide "the growth rate needed to sustain a large investment of capital and to exploit new market opportunities" in the face of pressure from foreign competitors;[68] third, by investing abroad, external markets can be created and protected from rivals;[69] finally, by political control, such as protective tariffs, "threats, wars, colonial occupation," as well as bribes, loans, and alliances to ensure imperial domination.[70]

These developments in the monopoly capitalist period form, according to Magdoff, a "new network of international economic and political relations," which are subject to changes in shape and emphasis "as the result of wars, depression, and differential rates of industrialization." This system is under "continuous ferment as a result of the battles among giant corporations over the world scene . . . along with their state governments, to maintain domination and control over weaker nations."[71]

Magdoff comments on Lenin's theory of imperialism:

> The special value of Lenin's theory is the highlighting of all the principal levers that have moved international economic relations. These levers are the ones associated with the new stage of monopoly and the essential ways monopoly operates to achieve, wherever and whenever feasible, domination and control over sources of supply and over markets. The fact that these are still the principal levers explains why the theory is still relevant. But the particular forms in which these factors operate and become adapted to new conditions requires continuous re-examination.[72]

Although Magdoff treats Lenin with reverence, he also tries to distance himself from classical Marxism and fails to note the distinctiveness of Lenin's theory of imperialism, e.g., the primacy of export capital. Magdoff rejects the superabundance or surplus of capital as the cause of the export of capital and argues that this did not play a principal role in Lenin's theory of imperialism.[73] However, Magdoff is clearly wrong on this point concerning Lenin and it is not necessary here to go back over Lenin's theory to prove this.

Magdoff's rejection of surplus capital as the cause of capital export is based on empirical data which show that only a small percentage of the finance capital for foreign investment actually comes from the investing country. Most of this capital is supplied by local sources in the foreign country. Magdoff concludes from this data, as many critics of Lenin have, that foreign investment can hardly be the result of the pressure of a superabundance of capital.[74]

While Magdoff is willing to concede that "domestic opportunities may have lagged in some places and at some times," he argues that the primary cause of capital export "was not the pressure of surplus capital but the utilization of capital where profitable opportunities existed, constrained of course by the technology of the time, the economic and political conditions in the other countries, and the resources of the home country."[75]

It should be noted that Magdoff has misinterpreted Lenin, who along with Marx argued that capital would be exported, not because it was absolutely impossible to invest in the home market, but because it could obtain a higher rate of profit abroad. The variance of profits existed ostensibly because of the uneven development of capitalism, where capitalism had become "overripe" in some countries. Lenin would not disagree with Magdoff's contention that capital flows where profitable opportunities exist, nor does this counter the superabundance of capital argument. Capital was superabundant, Lenin thought, because the conditions of profitability were being undermined in the advanced capitalist countries (though Lenin did not analyze these conditions adequately).

It should also be noted that the use of foreign sources of finance and the import of capital into the imperialist countries do not necessarily contradict the superabundance of capital thesis, as was shown in Chapter 2. It may just mean that capital is becoming superabundant on a world scale.

In another context, Magdoff's data on sources of finance would seem seriously to qualify the whole notion of the tendency for the economic surplus to rise and the problem of surplus absorption, although Magdoff tries to sever the two issues completely in order to defend Baran and Sweezy's theory. It will be useful to quote Magdoff on this point.

> A distinction needs to be made, however, between the question posed by Baran and Sweezy and the one we are examining here. In fact, they deal with the concept of "economic surplus" and not "surplus capital." The term "economic surplus" does not necessarily imply "two-muchness" of capital. It is simply a surplus over necessary costs of production, and whether any of it is also surplus in the sense of theories which relate surplus to capital export is a totally different and even unrelated question.[76]

This appears to be an attempt by Magdoff to "protect" Baran and Sweezy's analysis from criticism, because Magdoff certainly knows that while it is true the concept of economic surplus does not imply the "two-muchness of capital," Baran and Sweezy devote the major part of their analysis to trying to prove that monopoly capitalism generates too much economic surplus, more than it can profitably utilize, and that this is very much related to the question of surplus capital and the export of capital.

Magdoff also disputes two other arguments that attempt to explain foreign economic expansion. First, in reference to the falling rate of profit thesis, Magdoff argues that under conditions of monopoly this law is no longer valid, because monopoly prevents the tendency toward the equalization of profits from being realized. There are instead "discrete" rates of profit, not one average rate of profit toward which individual profit rates tend, because competing capitals are no longer interchangeable.[77] However, Magdoff's argument is not completely clear, because he limits his discussion to the market rate of profit, and the tendency for the rate of profit to fall is based on an analysis of *value*, which is not the same as the *money* rate of profit.

Magdoff does not think that the average rate of profit is an important consideration. First, the outflow of loan capital is dependent upon the rate of interest, which is considerably below the industrial rate of profit.[78] Second, Magdoff argues that although investment in raw materials is often motivated by higher profits, in most cases it is motivated not by profits but by geology. Even though raw materials are in many cases highly profitable, Magdoff argues that in these cases the decisive factor is not the falling rate of profit. [79]

The final argument against the importance of the tendency for the rate of profit to fall is in reference to foreign investment in manufacturing. Here Magdoff argues that it is not comparative average rates of profit that matter but rather "a comparison of the profitability of additional (marginal) investment in industry at home and industry abroad." It is this gap in marginal profitability that gives rise to foreign investment in manufacturing, and Magdoff asserts that this "has no necessary connection with any fall in the average profitability of investment at home." [80]

Magdoff refutes the argument that economic crises have caused imperialist expansion. Here Magdoff claims that they might have speeded up the birth of imperialism, but the "roots of imperialism go much deeper than any particular crisis or the reaction of any government to the crisis." [81] In fact, Magdoff suggests that crises and imperialism are the outcome of the same forces: the rapid transformation of capitalism in the late nineteenth century. Magdoff is willing to admit that crises act to "remind laggard governments of their 'duty' and prod them into action"; however, "the policies and practices of economic and political imperialism are as much part of prosperity as of depression." [82]

For Magdoff, the main drive for capital export is found in the "imperatives of capital operating under monopoly conditions." It is the essence of "business" behavior to control its own markets and operate "as if the whole globe were its preserve," and this had been so from the very beginning of capitalism. For Magdoff, capitalism is inherently a world system; when monopoly and rival industrial nations impinge upon this world system, forces are created that give rise to capital export and imperialism. With the advent of monopoly, the possibility of control becomes a reality for businesses and it becomes "essential for the security of the firm and its assets." Once capital operates on a world scale, "the competitive struggle among giants for markets stretches over large sections of the globe." Capital export arises out of this competitive struggle for the control of raw materials and the control and expansion of markets. In short, the export of capital and imperialism are the result of monopoly competition on a world scale.[83]

It should be noted that it is not the foreign expansion of capitalism itself that gives rise to imperialism, according to Magdoff; rather this need to operate on a world scale meets with certain obstacles, namely the "recalcitrance of natives and the rivalry of other capitalist states," and it is this which gives rise to imperialism.[84] This is very close to the early Marxist view of imperialism.

Magdoff argues that these primary determinants of imperialism remain today, plus several new features: first, the shift from an emphasis on rivalry in carving up the world to a struggle to keep the system from contracting due to "the inroads made by the growth of socialist societies and the spread of national liberation movements which seek to remove their countries from the imperialist trade and investment network";[85] second, the transfer of power to the United States as "leader and organizer of the world imperialist system";[86] and finally, the development of new technologies in transportation, communications, and armaments, which have bound the system closer together and altered fundamentally some of the ways control is exercised.[87]

Because of these new features, the "retention of influence and control by the metropolitan centers in the postcolonial period has therefore required special attention" and new policies. These policies fall into the following categories:

> (a) Where possible, formal economic and political arrangements to maintain former economic ties. These include preferential trade agreements and maintenance of currency blocs.
>
> (b) Manipulation and support of the local ruling groups with a view to keeping the special influence of the metropolitan centres and to preventing internal social revolution. . . .
>
> (c) Establishing influence and control over the direction of economic development and, as much as possible, over government decisions affecting the allocation of resources. Under this heading fall bilateral economic aid arrangements and the policies and practices of the World Bank and International Monetary Fund. These activities, in addition to influencing the direction of economic development, tend to intensify the financial dependence of aid recipients. . . .[88]

The United States has played the predominant role in reestablishing stability in the imperialist system since World War II, and its greatest gain, according to Magdoff, has been the dominant position of the U.S. dollar as an international currency and the location of the main international banking center in New York. This facilitated the extension of U.S. business interests by expanding exports, capital investment, and international banking into all parts of the world that had previously been untapped or were the special preserve of other imperialist countries. Equally important were the establishment of U.S. military bases all over the world and the heavy reliance on the United States for military and economic aid by the former colonial powers and former colonies alike. This "global military presence" and the threat of its use "provide the substance of the political force which maintains the imperialist system in the absence of colonies."[89]

Summary and critique

The postwar Marxists surveyed in this chapter offer a theory of imperialism that both updates the early Marxists and alters fundamentally the Marxist theoretical basis. Their efforts to tie foreign economic expansion directly to monopoly capitalism as a systemic necessity represent a continuation of earlier efforts, although based on a different set of assumptions and theoretical framework. Their most important contribution has been to update our understanding of imperialism with a new empirical analysis of the changed nature of the post-World War II imperialist system. This has included analysis of the rise of multinational corporations, the development of a complex of financial institutions, the decline of colonialism, and the existence of rival socialist nations.

On a theoretical level all four of the theorists have distanced themselves from "classical" Marxist analysis. Their rationale for such a break rests on the belief that contemporary monopoly capitalism is subject to new laws of motion based on conditions of monopoly, whereas Marx's laws of motion were based on the assumption of competition. What emerges is an entirely new analysis of the laws of motion and contradictions of capitalism which some have labeled neo-Marxist. The major conclusions of the theory are that monopoly capitalism is inherently stagnationist and that its major contradictions are irrationality, militarism, and imperialism.

Although influential for a whole generation of radicals, the theoretical basis of the monopoly capital school has been subjected to far-reaching criticism both in terms of its own theoretical consistency and in terms of certain features of the political economy that it ignores but which are of importance to Marxists.

To the extent that the theory of imperialism has been built on the monopoly capital foundation, it too is subject to the same criticisms. This includes the work of Baran and Sweezy and O'Connor, who see foreign capitalist expansion as an outgrowth of the system's tendency to generate more economic surplus than it can absorb through normal institutional channels. Imperialism is at best a temporary expedient, because the inflow of surplus tends to be greater than the outflow, thus compounding the surplus absorption problem. Magdoff does not dispute this analysis but argues, unlike the others, that it cannot be the cause of imperialism precisely because it does not work to absorb the surplus but makes the problem worse. For him the cause of foreign expansion is monopoly competition over markets, raw materials, and investment outlets. His analysis is reminiscent of Bukharin's eclecticism, although Magdoff prefers to cite Lenin.

Magdoff also distances himself from Marx and the early Marxists on the issues of the superabundance of capital, the falling rate of profit, and economic crises as causes of imperialism. It is clear from his treatment of these issues, particularly the falling rate of profit, that he agrees with the notion that monopoly calls into question Marx's analysis of capitalism, thought to rest on the assumption of competition. Magdoff's analysis of these issues is not without problems, however, as noted above.

Magdoff's strength lies not with his theory, which is in any event peripheral in his work, but with his masterful descriptive analysis of the American Empire and the complexities of imperialist control in the postwar period. His work is instrumental to an understanding of the rise and workings of U.S. imperialism.

In comparing Magdoff's work to that of Baran and Sweezy and O'Connor, we find that the different causes of imperialism (surplus absorption vs. monopoly competition) lead them to different conclusions concerning the issue of interimperialist rivalry. Magdoff, in agreement with Lenin, argues against international capitalist unity and argues that even U.S. economic and political hegemony over the rest of the world is not permanent. O'Connor on the other hand sees an international class of financiers and industrialists associated with multinational banks and corporations who no longer have separate national interests but instead have common international interests. More than ten years later, O'Connor's thesis still seems to be farfetched, with present circumstances more closely resembling interimperialist rivalry. Sixty years after the early Marxists, there are still major disagreements over this fundamental question.

On a methodological level the monopoly capital school is consistent with Marx's emphasis on the material base of society as well as the systemic nature of capitalist contradictions. However, they also deviate significantly from other aspects of Marx's method, namely his emphasis on the sphere of production. There is nothing wrong *per se* with an analysis that focuses on exchange relations and empirical descriptions. However, as argued earlier, to ignore the sphere of production is to ignore the crucial system-defining basis of capital, its class nature as well as the labor process and thus the working class.

Such omissions leave pretty large holes in the monopoly capital school's analysis of monopoly capitalism and imperialism. Although the theorists examined in this chapter have analyzed imperialism from the perspective of the advanced capitalist countries, it remains to be seen what others within this school of thought have said about the impact of foreign expansion on the Third World. This is the subject of the next chapter.

Monopoly Capital and
Imperialism II:
Dependency Theory

The persistence of backwardness, or what has come to be called underdevelopment, has been a major issue for contemporary theorists. Some Marxists have argued that capitalist penetration into the economies of backward countries *prevents* industrialization and capitalist development there rather than promoting it. This theory—known variously as the theory of underdevelopment, the surplus extraction model, or simply dependency theory—has been the major focus of attention for Marxists studying imperialism in this period.[1]

Dependency theory was pioneered by Paul Baran in the 1950s and by Andre Gunder Frank in the 1960s and early 1970s. Their basic argument is that underdevelopment in the backward countries is the result of the expropriation by the advanced capitalist countries of the economic surplus generated in the backward countries, and the advanced countries' appropriation of this surplus for their own development. In other words, imperialism is defined as the exploitation of Third World countries.

This chapter will begin with a discussion of Baran's pioneering work, *The Political Economy of Growth* (1957), which is devoted primarily to a theory of economic backwardness. This work was later refined and extended, most importantly by Andre Gunder Frank. Many others have made significant and noteworthy contributions, but the discussion in the second part of this chapter will be limited to Frank's works, as they are the most representative of this group and provide the theoretical base from which most of the others operate. Finally, Frank and Baran will be compared and dependency theory evaluated.

Paul Baran and the problem
of economic backwardness

Paul Baran argued that to understand the forces blocking the progress of the backward countries along lines similar to those of the advanced capitalist countries, one must first examine the salient features of the decomposition of feudalism and the rise of capitalism in Western Europe. Baran noted four crucial factors: the rise in agricultural output; the massive displacement of peasants, which created the potential for an industrial proletariat; the extension of the division of labor, which created a class of merchants and artisans located in the towns; and the accumulation of capital in the hands of the rising class of merchants and wealthy peasants.[2]

The confluence of these factors established the preconditions for the emergence of capitalism in Western Europe; however, according to Baran, the fourth factor, "the primary accumulation of capital," was of "strategic significance." Primary accumulation has been singled out by Baran as the most important, because the other conditions of transition were "maturing nearly everywhere," albeit at different times and paces. However, in Western Europe there was a difference. The "scope and speed of the accumulation of merchant capital and of the ascent of the merchant class" were greater and played a major role in setting the stage for the demise of feudalism and the rise of capitalism. In this fashion Baran distinguished Western Europe from the rest of the world. It should be noted that Baran did not think that the rise of a merchant class and merchant capital automatically led to the development of capitalism; the rise of a merchant class could reinforce feudalism.[3]

Western Europe was the first world area to develop capitalism; however, according to Baran, the conditions for transition obtained in many other societies that were also experiencing internal tensions.[4] That Western Europe left the rest of the world behind, Baran argues, was due not so much to the fact that it was first, but to the way in which capitalism spread from its original centers of accumulation. In areas where capitalist penetration from Western Europe met with very little resistance, because of "more or less complete societal vacua," capitalism established itself from the onset "unencumbered by the fetters and barriers of feudalism." Indeed, the new bourgeois societies in North

America, Australia, New Zealand, etc. very early became strong enough to overthrow the yoke of foreign domination and to create political systems that fostered the growth of capitalism.[5]

In contrast, when Western European expansion involved primitive and tribal societies and where "general conditions" precluded the mass settlement of Europeans, European interests sought to "extract the largest possible gains" from these countries by "outright plunder or in plunder thinly veiled as trade, seizing and removing tremendous wealth from the place of their penetration," which flowed back to the metropolitan country.[6]

This "transfusion" of wealth and the methods by which it was implemented "violently jolted [the backward country's] entire development and affected drastically its subsequent course."[7] What occurred in the backward countries was accelerated destruction of precapitalist structures, the breaking up of the existing patterns of agricultural economy, and a reallocation of resources away from domestic food production to the production of export crops. The self-sufficiency of these economies was destroyed and the scope of commodity circulation extended. Moreover, the seizure of peasant-occupied land for use as plantations and other foreign enterprises, and the destruction of rural handicrafts, which were subject to "withering competition" from foreign industrial imports, created a large pool of pauperized labor. Capitalist penetration "advanced the evolution of legal and property relations attuned to the needs of a market economy and established administrative institutions required for their enforcement." In addition, such penetration forced the use of some of the backward country's economic surplus for improving the economic infrastructure, e.g., railroads, harbors, and highways.[8]

However, in Baran's view, while capitalist penetration accelerated the creation of some of the conditions for the successful development of capitalism, it also blocked the development of others. The primary accumulation of capital in the backward countries was set back by the "removal of a large share of the affected countries' previously accumulated and currently generated surplus." The "ruinous competition from abroad" smothered their "fledging industries." Although the expansion of commodity circulation and the creation of a potential industrial proletariat "provided a powerful impetus to the development of capitalism, this development was forcibly shunted off its normal course, distorted, and crippled to suit the purpose of Western imperialism."[9]

Baran concludes this preliminary discussion of the roots of backwardness with the following statement:

> Thus the peoples who came into the orbit of Western capitalist expansion found themselves in the twilight of feudalism and capitalism enduring the worst features of both worlds, and the entire impact of imperialist subjugation to boot. . . . They were thrust into extensive contact with the advanced science of the West, yet remained in a state of the darkest backwardness.[10]

The backward countries, in Baran's view, are mired between feudalism and capitalism and suffer from the worst aspects of both systems. Disagreement over this point is one of the major differences between Baran and Frank.

The absence of the "classical conditions" for growth blocked the development of a healthy capitalism in the backward countries. On the one hand, consumption had been pushed down to or below the minimum subsistence level by foreign penetration (creating an economic surplus that is large relative to total output); on the other hand, this surplus was either drained away to the advanced capitalist countries (promoting development there) or was unproductively utilized in the backward countries.

There are four major sectors that generate and utilize economic surplus in the underdeveloped countries: the rural sector, the service sector, the industrial sector, and the state. The most important single sector in terms of the generation and utilization of the economic surplus is the rural sector. Baran estimates that the surplus generated in this sector accounts for roughly half of the total national product in the underdeveloped countries. The surplus is squeezed out of the peasantry, tenant farmers, and laborers by the landowners, moneylenders, and merchants.

However, the rural surplus is not utilized in a productive way to expand agricultural output; instead it is devoted to excess consumption by the landed aristocracy. This unproductive utilization of the surplus is the result of both certain social conventions, which are a carry-over from earlier times, and the objective economic conditions in the underdeveloped countries, which make it unprofitable and risky to mechanize agriculture. Baran cites as barriers to productive utilization the high price of imported machinery, the slow materialization of returns to fixed assets, high interest rates, cheap labor, agricultural price fluctuations, and landowners' difficulties in capturing increases in productivity on tenant-occupied lands. Furthermore, there is no incentive for small holders or tenants to increase their productivity, because of the smallness of their plots.[11]

Baran goes on to argue that

> while a large share of the economic surplus produced in agriculture remains *potential* surplus that could be used for investment if excess consumption and unproductive expenditures of all kinds were eliminated, what *actual* surplus there is becomes imbedded in the economic pores of the backward societies making but little contribution to increase productivity.[12]

The only way out would be an agrarian revolution and counter-agrarian revolution, as occurred in Western Europe. However, the conditions for this to take place are absent in the underdeveloped countries, according to Baran, because of the limited development of an indigenous bourgeoisie and the control of the state by the landed aristocracy, which benefits from maintaining the existing modes of exploitation.[13]

In the service sector a large part of the economic surplus in the underdeveloped countries is appropriated by the merchants, moneylenders, dealers, peddlers, trading stand operators, and "people with nondescript occupations crowding the streets, squares, and coffeehouses." The size of this parasitic "socioeconomic stratum," whose income for the most part represents a transfer of surplus from other classes or a diversion of surplus that would otherwise be available to other classes, is very large. Baran argues that this situation results in a significant drain on capital accumulation without any significant compensating social contribution. The portion of the economic surplus appropriated by the service sector tends to remain within this sector and does not enter the sphere of industrial production, because there are "formidable obstacles barring the entry of such mercantile accumulations."[14]

As for the industrial sector, Baran argues that under capitalism, industrial expansion tends to create its own internal markets and thus is largely self-expanding. In the underdeveloped countries, however, whatever internal markets were created by capitalist foreign expansion into the backward countries became appendages to the metropolitan economy. This stimulated investment and growth in the metropolitan economy and extinguished the spark that might have ignited industrial expansion and investment in the underdeveloped countries. The lack of investment became self-perpetuating and the markets in the underdeveloped countries remained narrow. When the possibility for investment was created due to tariffs or other government concessions, it was usually undertaken by foreigners. However, the narrow markets became monopolistically controlled and monopolistic price and output policies prevented the widening of these markets and the expansion of these enterprises.[15]

Investment in industry serving the internal market and investment in the export sector barely stimulate the rest of the domestic economy, because most of the linkages are external rather than internal to it. By and large the inputs for these industries are purchased abroad and much of the skilled labor (whose incomes are spent mostly on imported goods) is also imported. The income accruing to the indigenous population is generally limited to the low wages of unskilled labor and is spent on the "acquisition of the most elementary wage goods that are produced in agriculture, by local craftsmen, or imported, and therefore cannot possibly form a market encouraging the development of industrial enterprise."[16]

The economic surplus generated in the industrial sector is estimated to be quite large by Baran; however, much of it flows back to the metropolitan country as repatriated profits, royalty payments, and other forms of disguised foreign remittances. The portion of the surplus appropriated by the local bourgeoisie is used for luxurious living and is spent on the construction of urban and rural residences, servants, and luxury consumption, and invested in land, mercantile activities, usury, and speculation, when it is not invested abroad as a hedge against currency depreciation and social and political unrest.[17]

In addition to limiting further expansion, on account of the outflow or unproductive use of surplus, foreign domination "strengthens the sway of merchant capitalism." Indirectly, it influences the creation of a group of merchants who thrive within the "orbit of foreign capital." These merchants form an element of the native bourgeoisie who are dependent upon the operations of foreign business. Further, the native industrial monopolists who are "interlocked and interwoven with domestic merchant capital" are also dependent on foreign enterprise. They too "depend on the maintenance of the existing economic structure," and their "monopolistic status would be swept away by the rise of industrial capitalism." The result is a "political and social coalition of wealthy compradors, powerful monopolists, and large landowners dedicated to the defense of the existing feudal-mercantile order."[18]

The final mode of surplus utilization is state expenditures. The appropriation of surplus by the state represents a transfer of surplus from other groups, as well as an addition to surplus in those cases where it is obtained by a corresponding reduction in consumption. For the most part Baran argues that the use of surplus by the state represents a tremendous waste, because such large sums are squandered on the "maintenance of sprawling bureaucracies and military establishments" whose function is to maintain the power of "comprador regimes."[19]

Even in countries with "New Deal"-type governments (such as India, Indonesia, and Burma), the state has been unable to bring about industrial expansion. The fate of attempts to bring about an indigenous industrial capitalism under conditions of underdevelopment depends, in Baran's words,

> on the economic and political strength of the national bourgeosie, on the quality of its leadership, on its determination to dislodge the feudal and compradore elements from their position of dominance, on the intensity of the resistance on their part, and on the extent to which the international constellation permits the elimination or considerable weakening of the support given to these strata by the world's imperialist powers.[20]

However, the popular bourgeois, democratic, antifeudal, and anti-imperialist movements that brought these governments to power in the underdeveloped countries tended to create at the same time the danger of social revolution from below by labor and peasant groups. This "destroyed whatever chances there were of the capitalist classes joining and leading" these popular movements. Baran goes on to note:

> Whatever differences and antagonism existed between large and small landowners, between monopolistic and competitive business, between

liberal bourgeois and reactionary feudal overlords, between domestic and
foreign interests, were largely submerged on all important occasions by
the overriding *common* interest in staving off socialism.[21]

In short, the possibility for the bourgeoisie to undertake its historic
mission and clear away the obstacles to the development of industrial
capitalism is thwarted; it is driven into a coalition with the very elements of society that oppose such a development. Baran concludes that
if the underdeveloped countries fail to bring about capitalist development, a new "social ethos" will arise which will become the spirit and
guide for a new age of economic planning and social collectivism, i.e.,
socialism.[22]

Andre Gunder Frank and the development of underdevelopment

Andre Gunder Frank's principal thesis is that the evolution and expansion of capitalism produce both development and underdevelopment,
which are opposite sides of the same coin.[23] The underdevelopment of
the backward countries is the inevitable result of the development of
capitalism and its internal contradictions.

According to Frank, the internal contradictions of the capitalist
system include the expropriation of economic surplus from the majority
and its appropriation by the few; the polarization of the capitalist
system into a metropolitan center and peripheral satellite countries; and
the continuity of this structure throughout the expansion and evolution
of capitalism, so that these contradictions are reproduced and maintained everywhere and at all times.[24]

The expansion and evolution of capitalism generate and maintain
underdevelopment in one part of the world, where the economic surplus is expropriated, by another part of the world, which appropriates
this surplus for its own development. Thus, according to Frank:

> Economic development and underdevelopment are not just relative and
> quantitative, in that one represents more economic development than the
> other; economic development and underdevelopment are relational and
> qualitative, in that each is structurally different from, yet caused by its
> relation with, the other. Yet development and underdevelopment are the
> same in that they are the product of a single, but dialectically contradic-
> tory, economic structure and process of capitalism.[25]

In other words, capitalist development requires its opposite, capitalist underdevelopment: you cannot have one without the other.

Frank notes four important characteristics of this world capitalist system:

> (1) Close economic, political, social and cultural ties between each metropolis and its satellites, which result in the total integration of the farthest outpost and peasant into the system as a whole . . .
>
> (2) Monopolistic structure of the whole system, in which each metropolis holds monopoly power over its satellites; the source of the monopoly varies from one case to another, but the existence of this monopoly is universal through the system.
>
> (3) As occurs in any monopolistic system, misuse and misdirection of available resources throughout the whole system and metropolis–satellite chain.
>
> (4) As part of this misuse, the expropriation and appropriation of a large part or even all of and more than the economic surplus or surplus value of the satellite by its local, regional, national or international metropolis.[26]

These characteristics arise from the evolution and expansion of capitalism into the backward countries of the world; indeed this expansion is necessary to capitalist development.

More specifically, Frank argues that the capitalist system has spread from fifteenth-century Western Europe to "all corners of the earth." Capitalist expansion produced a "commercial network" that extended over the "entire face of the globe" and incorporated the world into a "*single, organic* mercantilist or mercantile capitalist and later also industrial and financial capitalist system and whose peripheral satellites underdeveloped on all the remaining continents."[27] The purpose of this expansion was "to extract the fruits of [the backward countries'] labor through monopoly trade." In order to accomplish this the metropolitan countries had to destroy or totally transform the once viable social and economic systems in the backward countries and incorporate them into the "metropolitan dominated worldwide capitalist system."[28]

Frank argues that the penetration of capitalism into the backward countries did not result in a dualistic or semifeudal social and economic structure, but rather in the complete integration, from the fifteenth century onwards, of the "farthest outpost and peasant" into the worldwide metropolis–satellite structure of capitalism.[29] In Frank's view, both the developed and underdeveloped parts of this system are equally capitalist, part and parcel of the same worldwide system.

The structure of this system extends beyond the so-called "export enclaves" of the backward countries into the interior of these countries, reaching every peasant. This structure is characterized by a constellation or chain of metropolises and satellites which extends from the U.S. and European metropolitan centers to the farthest "outposts" in the backward countries. In between are various submetropolises, with varying degrees of monopoly power, that are satellites of those above them in the chain, and metropolises in relation to those below them. Thus for example, the national capital and export enclave of the underdeveloped country is a satellite of the world metropolis and at the same time a submetropolis or national metropolis over regional, provincial, and rural satellites within the backward country.

With the establishment of this metropolis–satellite structure on a global scale, the laws of motion of the backward satellites are determined by the evolution and development of the world metropolis. As the needs of the center change, corresponding changes are forced upon the satellite. These changes produce certain structural changes in the satellites, but they do not alter any of the basic structural characteristics of dependency. This process of change in the backward countries in response to the changing needs of the metropolis results in what Frank refers to as the development of underdevelopment.

The history of the development of underdevelopment begins in the colonial period, when the stage is set and the fate of different regions of the world fixed, Frank argues. Where the wealth for exploitation was the greatest, the "poorer and more undeveloped" that region is today, while by contrast, the less endowed regions are today the "richer and more developed." The key is Frank's assertion that in areas that lacked the "geographical and climatic conditions and the indigenous populations necessary for the establishment of an export economy," such as in the northern regions of North America, the structure of underdevelopment was not established. Where such conditions did exist, a colonial class structure was established that permitted "ultra-exploitation."[30]

During the Age of Conquest these colonial regions were placed "in a situation of growing subjection and economic dependence, both colonial and neo-colonial, in the single world system of expanding commercial capitalism.''[31] This is a crucial point in Frank's analysis. He is contending that capitalism arises because of the extension of the market. The extension of the market in some cases gives rise to developed capitalism, as in Western Europe, and in other cases to underdeveloped capitalism, as in Latin America. He argues that in the fifteenth and sixteenth centuries commercial expansion from Western Europe was essentially capitalist, and that therefore the structures it imposed upon the rest of the world were also capitalist. The basis for this claim is that the original commercial forces were motivated by profit maximization, and that the productive structures of the backward countries were reorganized for ultra-exploitation of the direct producers, whose product became a commodity exchanged on the world market. Thus, in Latin America the *encomienda*, *catequil*, *latifundium*, and *hacienda* are all considered capitalist forms of production and exploitation, because they are geared to production for exchange and individual gain.[32]

The subjection of the backward countries to this colonial and neocolonial relationship transforms the domestic class structure; it becomes dominated by a bourgeoisie that is dependent for its existence and livelihood on the world metropolis. In Frank's words:

> This process of production imposed upon Latin America necessarily gave rise to a resident commercial *and productive* bourgeoisie, which directed this process and shared its benefits in economic ad political alliance with the metropolis. In the resulting Latin American economic and class structure, the fruits of the vast majority of labor were immediately appropriated by the small commercial and productive bourgeois minority. Being subordinate and dependent bourgeoisie from the very start, the latter remitted a major part of these fruits in the form of capital transfers to the metropolis overseas, where they were eventually invested in metropolitan economic development.[33]

This class then acts as the agent of imperialism in the satellites and actively maintains the metropolis–satellite structure and promotes a ''policy of underdevelopment in the economic, social, and political life'' of the satellite.[34]

Once this colonial and class structure is imposed upon the backward countries, the process of the development of underdevelopment begins. The history of this process can be explained, according to Frank, first by the strength of the ties between the metropolis and its satellites, and second by the changing needs of the metropolis. Referring to the former, Frank argues that the weakening of ties (for example, during wars or depressions) between the metropolis and its satellites produces in the satellites either passive involution and severe stagnation, or active involution and limited development based on internal colonialism and imperialism. These outcomes are determined by the particular circumstances and the previous economic and class structures in the satellite. When ties are renewed between the metropolis and its satellites, the generation of underdevelopment is also renewed, and any development that took place is either "strangled or misdirected." Frank derives a series of hypotheses based on the strength of these ties, and in two masterful cases studies, of Brazil and Chile, Frank shows the power of dependency theory to enhance the understanding of underdevelopment.[35]

In addition to the strength of the ties between the metropolis and its satellites, the changing needs of the metropolis dictate changes in the satellites. As capital accumulation proceeds and development occurs in the metropolis, its needs change. More specifically, as capitalism advanced in the metropolitan countries, its monopoly advantage over the satellites changed to more advanced branches of production:

> During the mercantilist era, the metropolitan monopoly lay in commercial monopoly; in the era of liberalism, the metropolitan monopoly came to be industry; in the first half of the twentieth century the metropolitan monopoly switched increasingly to capital goods industry. . . . In the second half of the twentieth century the basis of metropolitan monopoly seems to be switching increasingly to technology.[36]

As development proceeded in the metropolis, the satellites were allowed to produce in those areas previously denied by the metropolitan country. This does not mean that development in the satellites lags only one step behind the metropolis. Quite the contrary, while some "development" does take place in the satellite, the metropolitan–satellite hierarchy is still maintained, due to the superiority of the metropolis in the most modern or advanced branches of production. This gives the metropolis continued monopoly power over its satellites and allows it to continue to expropriate the economic surplus generated in the satellite economy and appropriate that surplus for continued development in the metropolis.

Despite periods of respite in the history of the development of underdevelopment, the possibility of capitalist development in the satellites does not exist. Frank argues that even though some autonomous industrialization occurred in Brazil, Chile, Mexico, and other satellite countries during the period 1930-1953 (when the metropolitan countries were preoccupied with economic crisis and war, and metropolis-satellite ties were weakened), these conditions gave rise to what Frank calls "bourgeois-nationalist industrialization." Previously imported industrial goods were produced domestically in the satellite countries. According to Frank, two constraining factors limited industrialization to import substitution in these countries:

> First, bourgeois reformers had to begin with the existing income distribution and demand structure. This meant that they had to concentrate on consumer goods, particularly for the high-income market. Without a major change in the class structure and income distribution, the internal market could not expand fast enough to sustain the import substitution process indefinitely. Second, for this reason, the industrialization programs did not produce enough industrial equipment or producers' goods, which had increasingly to be imported from abroad in order even to keep the import substitution process going.[37]

Faced with increasing difficulty in earning foreign exchange to obtain the imported inputs necessary to maintain autonomous industrialization, the satellites were forced to turn back to the metropolitan countries after World War II and "welcome foreign investment, which supplied the needed semiprocessed material, equipment, and technology. The price, of course, was increased de-Latin Americanization of industry and satellitization of the Latin American economy and bourgeoisie."[38]

The renewal of metropolis–satellite ties in the postwar period choked off autonomous industrialization in the satellites and gave rise to the continued development of underdevelopment, or what Frank in his later work calls "lumpen-development." This period is characterized by a new policy of foreign investment that results in "neoimperialism and neodependence." Such a policy is the result of the changed needs of capital accumulation in the metropolis for maintenance of a high rate of technological growth and high monopoly profits, needs that are dictated by the gigantic monopoly enterprises in the era of monopoly capitalism.[39]

In order to fulfill the needs of monopoly capital the satellites become outlets for obsolete equipment and technology, "where it may still be used without competing with the output" of the metropolis, and "where it will still produce a profit."[40] Therefore, in the postwar period

> the metropolis is no longer interested in exporting the actual finished goods, since the metropolitan bourgeoisie can now achieve greater economic control and earnings at home and abroad by exporting the equipment and technology which is its new source of monopoly power, as well as financial control.[41]

The result is the production of some finished goods as well as means of production in the satellites by subsidiaries of metropolitan multinational corporations and by domestic enterprises in "partnership" with foreign monopolies. In underdeveloped countries where this process of industrialization had already been started, it was taken over by the metropolis once the ties between it and the satellite were renewed following the war.

The reestablishment of the metropolis–satellite relationship restricts even further the ability of the satellites to develop economically and socially. As in previous periods when ties were maintained, the economic surplus is drained out of the satellites into the metropolis, as evidenced by the net outflow of capital and other forms of surplus outflow from the satellites. In fact, Frank notes that one of the most important characteristics of the postwar period is that the metropolis has increased the outflow of surplus while minimizing its own financial contribution. It has accomplished this by utilizing the financial resources of the satellites to finance over 90 percent of metropolitan operations in the satellites. Much of this satellite finance has gone to pay for obsolete and overpriced equipment and technology imported from the metropolis. The utilization of the satellites' financial resources has been made possible by the takeover of their banking and financial institutions by metropolitan multinational banks. Coupled with the metropolitan monopoly of producers' goods and technology, financial control has enabled the metropolis to funnel increasing amounts of surplus into the metropolis for its own development, while at the same time risking very little of its own resources.[42]

The resatellization of these countries results in an economic and class structure that reestablishes the conditions for the ultra-exploitation of labor and high rates of unemployment. Dependence fosters a highly unequal distribution of income, which limits the purchasing power of the majority and concentrates income in the hands of a small minority. Therefore, in the postwar period industrialization is still severely limited to the production of luxury goods, as it was in the previous period of bourgeois-nationalist industrialization. Limited markets result in increased production costs, because of under-utilization of plants and higher selling prices, which in turn further limits the process of industrialization.

Foreign and domestic enterprises channel domestic savings not only into luxury goods production, but also into capital goods and equipment industries. However, these supply the durable consumer goods industries rather than the needs of economic development, so that the satellites fail to develop the capacity to supply more than a limited amount of their own means of production.[43]

These contradictions of the world metropolis–satellite capitalist structure then result, according to Frank,

> in [the] underutilization of national resources, improper use of resources which might have been more adequately employed in promoting self-sustaining economic development, deepening inequalities in the distribution of income, and the creation of . . . vested economic, social, and political interests which are committed to continuing policies of underdevelopment. All this has an unfavorable effect on other existing industries and on the national economy as a whole.[44]

The bourgeoisie and enlarged middle class, beneficiaries of the ultraexploitation of the majority and the metropolis–satellite structure of dependency, join an "alliance for the progress of imperialism" as junior partners. According to Frank, no satellite nation has escaped this metropolis–satellite structure or achieved economic development except by "abandoning the imperialist and capitalist system altogether and going over to socialism."[45] The possibility of successful capitalist development is thus in Frank's view foreclosed.

Summary and critique

Despite many differences in their analyses, Paul Baran and Andre Gunder Frank agree that the principal cause of underdevelopment or persistent backwardness is the extraction of economic surplus from the backward countries by the advanced capitalist countries. Both also

agree that the inflow of surplus is a necessary prerequisite for successful capitalist development in the metropolitan countries, although
Baran does not place as much emphasis on it as Frank does. What Frank
has added to Baran's analysis is a more clearly defined worldwide
structure of imperialism within which surplus extraction takes place, as
well as a more exhaustive and updated analysis of the history of
underdevelopment.

As long as Third World countries remain dependent appendages of
the advanced capitalist countries, both Baran and Frank see no possibility for their successful capitalist development. However, when it comes
to specifying the barriers to development, they disagree. Baran argues
that the development of a capitalist economic and class structure is
incomplete in the satellites; conversely, Frank argues that these structures have been fully capitalist since the Age of Conquest. Thus for
Frank, the successful development of capitalism in the periphery is not
a question of the incompleteness of capitalism, but a question of whether countries were initially integrated into the world capitalist system as
satellites or metropolises. If satellites, they became fully capitalist but
underdeveloped, and there is no chance for successful capitalist development.

Frank argues that once a satellite-type economic and class structure
has been imposed on a backward country, its fate is sealed, and its
structure continues to generate underdevelopment even when the satellite is freed from metropolitan ties. The inherent laws of motion of
underdevelopment push the bourgeoisie of these "independent" countries back into dependency on the metropolis, in an effort to overcome
internal contradictions as well as maintain their vested interests. Capitalist development is thus an impossibility.[46]

For Baran, however, the integration of the backward countries into
the international capitalist network of imperialism leads to a partial
disintegration of precapitalist modes of production and the incomplete
development of capitalist economic and class structures, which leaves
them "semifeudal." This is an important difference, for in Baran's
analysis, just as the extraction of surplus is the principal cause of
underdevelopment, so the incomplete development of the capitalist
mode of production is an additional internal obstacle to successful
development. Whether or not successful capitalist development can
take place hinges on whether a country, once it has managed to escape
the clutches of imperialism, can overcome the internal barriers re-

straining full development. In order to overcome these internal obstacles, the capitalist class and its allies must overthrow the feudal and the reactionary elements. As was shown earlier, Baran thought that this was not likely and that therefore successful capitalist development was highly unlikely in the Third World.

The basic difference in views here stems from the very different ways in which Baran and Frank conceptualize capitalism. Frank conceptualizes capitalism as a system subjectively determined by individual maximization of gains and objectively determined by markets and monopoly control. In contrast to this market-based conceptualization, Baran views capitalism as a mode of production objectively determined by the existence of wage labor, capital, and commodity production. Dependency theorists have not, however, followed Baran's lead. They have utilized Frank's conceptualization of capitalism as a system, rather than a mode of production, and analyzed it in terms of exchange relations rather than exchange and productive relations. These differences will be discussed in more detail below.

Dependency theory represents a major advance in the Marxist theory of imperialism. In contrast to the early Marxist theory (except as developed by Rosa Luxemburg), dependency theory provides a comprehensive analysis of the impact of capitalist penetration into the Third World. This analysis is carried out within a theoretical structure that treats capitalist development and underdevelopment within a unified framework of mutual cause and effect. The view of metropolitan dominance and control over the economic, social, and political structures of the satellite, while similar to the early Marxists', is profoundly different in that such control is seen to prevent satellites from achieving successful capitalist development even after national liberation. Far from creating the conditions for successful development, capitalist penetration has created the conditions for capitalist underdevelopment. Indeed, such penetration creates the conditions for successful development only in the metropolitan center. This outcome is the result of capitalism's inherent contradictions. It is dependent not upon direct political control (i.e., colonialism), but economic control, through the forces of neocolonialism.

Dependency theory thus conforms more closely to the post-World War II experience in the Third World. It has provided an analytic structure that has furthered our understanding of contemporary imperialism and the history of underdevelopment in the Third World. Dependency theorists have also provided one of the most comprehensive critiques of mainstream theories of economic development, which have tended to treat economic development without reference to imperialism or history.[47] In fact, dependency theory has profoundly affected mainstream theory, though not mainstream conclusions concerning the desirability and possibility of successful capitalist development in the Third World.[48]

Dependency theory is not without its flaws, however, and in recent years these have cast a shadow of doubt on the theory's theoretical validity, despite many years of almost unanimous acceptance.[49] The most fundamental issue is the usefulness of a conceptualization of capitalism and imperialism that is generalized at the level of a system, rather than rooted in modes of production, classes, and capital accumulation. The generalization of dependency theory at the level of a world system creates three basic problems. The first issue is the question of whether the underdeveloped countries are capitalist, feudal, or some hybrid social formation. The second problem concerns the theoretical adequacy and thus the validity of the surplus extraction thesis in explaining underdevelopment. The final problem concerns the usefulness of the concept of economic surplus for analyzing the impact of capitalist expansion on the peripheral countries. Each of these issues will be taken up separately below.

1. Frank's contention that the backward countries have been capitalist ever since they became bound up in the "organic mercantile capitalist system" was the first to be criticized. There are two problems here. First, nowhere does Frank explicitly define what he means by capitalist. It can be inferred, however, that he means a system of production for exchange, where profit is the motive and where there is exploitation of the many by the few. Exploitation seems to take place through exchange between different groups and countries, based on the degree of monopoly power held.

Such a conception of capitalism differs from that of capitalism as a mode of production. Frank's implicit definition of capitalism is not historically specific; both exchange and the exploitation of the many by the few existed prior to the capitalism, as did monopoly. The relations of production, which are for Marx the most distinguishing characteristic of any mode of production, are ignored by Frank.[50]

Second, and related to the first problem, is Frank's contention that the rise of capitalism is brought about by an extension of the market, the rise of a world commercial network.[51] In Frank's view, the extension of the market on a world scale gives rise to a "*single organic* mercantilist or mercantile capitalist and later also industrial and financial capitalist system whose metropolitan center developed in Western Europe and then North America and whose peripheral satellites underdeveloped on all the remaining continents."[52] One can infer from this that Frank believes that with the expansion of the market and commodity production the conditions are created for the emergence of capitalist productive and social relations. Such an influence is borne out by Frank's claim that the backward countries have been capitalist since the Age of Conquest in the fifteenth century. His proof consists of showing that the expansion of world commerce was based on the profit motive (individual gain) and that production was reordered in the periphery to suit the needs of the world market and was based on "ultra-exploitation." The varied ways in which production was reordered in the periphery, from slave plantations to latifundia, in response to the demands of worldwide commercial network, are all considered capitalist by Frank.[53] One critic argues that with such a wide notion of capitalism one could easily assert that there has never been anything but capitalism since the neolithic age.[54]

The argument that the extension of the market by itself gave rise to capitalist productive and social relations ignores the importance of the role that class structures and conflict play in the rise of capitalism and the transition from feudalism.[55] The extension of the market is an important force, but it is not a sufficient condition for the rise of capitalism, which depends upon previous class structures. Class structure determines, through class conflict, whether the conditions for the rise of capitalism materialize, namely the conditions for the primitive or original accumulation of capital.

History has shown that the response to the extension of the market has been varied precisely because of differences in existing class structures. These responses have varied from the intensification and entrenchment of feudalism (Eastern Europe) to slavery (North and South America) to capitalism (most of Western Europe).[56] The outcome is not automatic, nor is Frank correct in classifying any and all outcomes as capitalist. This problem is rooted in his definition of capitalism, which is so general that it lacks historical specificity and ignores the critical importance that productive and social relations play both in specifying modes of production and in determining their rise and fall.

Baran, on the other hand, does not make this mistake and explicitly notes that neither the rise of exchange nor the rise of merchant capital automatically brings about the development of capitalism. Baran begins with a more accurate conception of the capitalist mode of production and the process of transition to it from feudalism, and is thus able to show that the integration of the backward countries into the "world commercial network" does not automatically give rise to capitalism but rather gives rise to the incomplete development of capitalism. The full development of capitalism in the backward countries is blocked by the extraction of surplus and the destruction of internal productive capacity, which prevents the complete development of capitalist social forces. The backward countries thus remain partially feudal or precapitalist, not in the dualistic sense, which is how Frank interprets it, but in the sense that, despite the total penetration of the backward countries and the reordering of their production for the world market, they still remain essentially feudal or precapitalist.[57]

But Baran's analysis, though closer to the reality of backward countries, has significant theoretical problems of its own. More specifically, Baran's analysis, ostensibly rooted in "class structure," is in fact divorced from the sphere of production and any actual productive relations, particularly the relations of exploitation.[58] This shortcoming applies equally to Frank's analysis and forms the basis of a criticism of the surplus extraction thesis in the next section.

2. The absence of any analysis of class relations at the point of production has cast further doubt on the surplus-extraction theory of capitalist development and underdevelopment. Baran's and Frank's surplus-extraction thesis is derived from an analysis that is restricted to markets. The source of capital accumulation in this view is not the exploitation of labor, but the expropriation/appropriation of the economic surplus of one country, leaving it underdeveloped, by another country, which experiences development. This surplus is extracted through markets, by the country, region, or group having the greatest amount of monopoly power (market power), from those with the least amount of power.

It has been noted that, while the transfer of surplus from one country to another is certainly a characteristic of capitalism on a world scale, the "plunder of one geographic area for the enrichment *of a class* (or classes) of expropriators in another geographic area has been a characteristic of virtually all historical epochs."[59] The exploitation of one country by another "derives from domination" and "is no more characteristic of capitalism in its imperialist stage than it was characteristic of competitive capitalism or ancient Rome."[60]

Therefore, Baran's and Frank's analyses do not tell us anything specific about the capitalist mode of production and its impact on, or interrelation with, other specific modes of production. They ignore how the economic surplus transferred from one country to another in exchange is produced. This would entail an analysis of classes at the point of production and the exploitation of one class by another, i.e., the appropriation of "material surplus in natural (use-value) or money form by a class of non-producers." The specific form that this takes is determined by the way the means of production and labor are brought together, and in capitalism these are combined in the form of capital and free wage labor, the former appropriating the surplus of the latter.

Therefore, one of the central elements in the understanding of capitalism, and thus imperialism, is totally ignored by both Baran and Frank, as it was by the early Marxists, although they refer to classes in their analyses of backwardness and underdevelopment. According to Dore and Weeks:

> By ignoring the mode of production, production itself is ignored. Once the analysis loses touch with the process of production, the fundamental social axiom that all societies, save the most primitive onces, are based upon the exploitation of direct producers disappears from view. And without the mode of appropriation (and thus exploitation) at the heart of an analysis of societies, a discussion of *classes* has no scientific content. Without reference to the mode of production, the concept of *class* merely provides a taxonomy for the sphere of appearances, a more-or-less arbitrary exercise in attaching labels.[61]

This is a serious shortcoming of dependency theory and its explanation of the spread of capitalism and its impact on the rest of the world, in a word, imperialism.

3. The final theoretical issue concerns the usefulness of an analysis based on the concept of economic surplus as opposed to one based on surplus value. It has been argued by Barclay and Stengel that although surplus value is superior for analyzing exploitative class relationships within a country, economic surplus is superior for studying the "structures of dominance and subordination" between nations. Between nations the exploitative relationships of class are

mediated through international, regional, and racial structures of dominance and subordination. Thus, potential economic surplus points to the concentration of technology-intensive activities in the metropole, the canalization of forward and backward linkages by international capital, and the dependent rhythm of economic expansion and contraction in the hinterland of world capitalism. In each case, it is a matter of "output lost because of the irrational and wasteful organization of the existing productive apparatus" rather than the appropriation of surplus value from wage labor.[62]

Unlike Baran and Frank and other dependency theorists, Barclay and Stengel hold that an

> analysis and action which focuses on the extraction of potential economic surplus risks the danger of obscuring the reality of class conflict and contradictions *within* the subordinated race, region, or nation. Together the two concepts [economic surplus and surplus value] direct our theoretical and political praxis to the need for both national and social liberation.[63]

In short, it is argued that these two concepts are both useful, but for understanding or illuminating different parts of reality. Both concepts are essential to a complete understanding of imperialism and the nature of persistent backwardness. It is true that economic surplus has been a particularly powerful concept. The generation of an economic surplus is essential to economic development, and the particular ways in which this surplus is utilized are important to the economic advancement of society. As dependency theory has shown, such surplus generated in the Third World has in large part been extracted by foreigners through plunder, trade, and monopoly control, with the remainder being used in nonproductive ways that further stifle economic development.

There are two problems here. First, dependency theory does not go beyond a study of the relations of dominance and subordination between nations, i.e., it ignores exploitative class relationships. Such relationships are clearly also relations of dominance and subordination; in fact without them no surplus could be produced. Therefore, such class relations form the basis for all other relations. In short, that part of reality that is supposed to be illuminated by the concept of surplus value is ignored altogether, leaving a gap in dependency theory.

A second problem is the supposed inability of surplus value to illuminate more than exploitative class relations at the point of production. It is not clear that such is the case. For example, Marx showed how monopoly in the sphere of exchange transferred to itself surplus value produced in competitive branches of production. He also showed how surplus value could be transferred through unequal exchange by merchants on international markets. Dependency theorists obviously have not thought it fruitful to pursue an analysis of imperialism based on Marx's categories and analytical framework. The rationale for such a split has never been adequately explained by dependency theorists or the monopoly capital school in general.

These and other issues leave dependency theory with several unresolved problems, and thus with an incomplete theory of imperialism. Nonetheless, dependency theory and the work of dependency theorists represent a major step forward in understanding imperialism. Dependency theory has set the terms on which Marxists deal with imperialism in the Third World. It has provided a global framework within which to analyze the impact of capitalist foreign expansion on Third World countries, and has done so in a way that brings to the forefront foreign capitalist domination of the Third World.

5

The Theory of Imperialism and Unequal Exchange: Arghiri Emmanuel

One of the most controversial Marxist works on imperialism in the contemporary period is *Unequal Exchange: A Study in the Imperialism of Trade* by Arghiri Emmanuel. This book was published in France in 1969, and translated into English and published in the United States in 1972. The purpose of Emmanuel's work was to show, through analysis of the international price system, how unequal exchange takes place between the underdeveloped countries and the developed capitalist countries. Emmanuel attempts to prove his thesis using the labor theory of value and Marx's transformation of values into *international* prices of production, which Emmanuel sometimes refers to as "equilibrium prices."

Although Emmanuel's work focuses quite narrowly on the formation of international prices, his theory of unequal exchange forms the basis for a more general theory of imperialism. His work can be seen as an attempt to provide a more rigorous proof of the exploitation of the poor countries by the rich capitalist countries through the market exchange process, as well as an attempt to bridge the gap between contemporary Marxist analysis and Marx.

Emmanuel's theory of imperialism

Emmanuel begins his analysis of imperialism by reversing some of David Ricardo's assumptions concerning the formation of international prices.[1] First, it is assumed that labor is immobile between countries while capital is mobile. Second, it is assumed that the mobility of capital causes the equalization of rates of profit between countries. Third, Emmanuel assumes that wages are an independent variable and tend to vary from country to country because of the immobility of labor between countries. Fourth, the commodities that enter into international exchange are unique to certain countries. Emmanuel calls these commodities "irreducible use-values." Finally, the variance in wages between the center and periphery is assumed to be greater than the differences in productivities.

From these assumptions Emmanuel proceeds to apply Marx's transformation models to international exchange. He intends to show that there will be a transfer of value from low-wage countries to high-wage countries. Here is Emmanuel's example[2]:

K = total capital invested (c + v + noncirculating constant capital)

	K	c	v	s	V	Rate of profit	Profit	Price of pro-duction
Rich country	240	50	100	20	170	33-1/3%	80	230
Poor country	120	50	20	100	170	33-1/3%	40	110
	360	100	120	120	340		120	340

If exchange took place at values (direct prices) there would be an exchange of equivalents (170:170). However, with the international equalization of profit rates, value is transferred from the poor to the rich country in an unequal exchange (230:110). In other words, 60 units of surplus value produced in the poor country are transferred in exchange from the poor to rich country, leaving the latter with a profit of 80, versus 20 before exchange, and the poor country with 40, versus 100 before exchange. This, according to Emmanuel, constitutes the basis of unequal exchange and the imperialism of trade between developed and underdeveloped countries.

In the example above, the rate of exploitation (s/v) is higher in the underdeveloped country. This is due to lower real wages and a higher organic composition of capital (K - v/v) in the underdeveloped country. It is not clear why Emmanuel makes the organic composition of capital approximately five times higher in the underdeveloped countries.[3] However, it can be easily shown that with equal rates of organic composition or with a higher composition in the developed country, the transfer of value is greater in both cases with unequal rates of surplus value than with equal rates of surplus value; this need not be shown here.

According to Emmanuel, there are two forms of nonequivalence in international exchange:

> One (apparent) form arises from the mere transformation of values into prices of production, when wage rates are the same but the organic composition of capital is different. The other, which I [call] nonequivalence in the strict sense, is characterized by differences in both wages and organic composition.[4]

Only the latter qualifies as unequal exchange, according to Emmanuel, because there is a qualitative difference between them. He argues that nonequivalence in the case of unequal organic compositions alone is not peculiar to foreign trade but takes place between regions and branches of production within one country. In this case, "How could France or Guinea complain about the mere transformation of values into prices of production when this same transformation takes place inside each country's national economy?" Emmanuel goes on to say that this form of nonequivalence

> is due, among other things, to the specific technical features of the different branches. Differentiation in wages is due to imperfect competition by the labor factor, caused by distances and political frontiers, and is proportionate to the imperfection of this competition. Constant increase in organic composition is a structural necessity for the development of capitalism, whereas disparity of wage levels is an accidental feature.[5]

Therefore, because differences in the organic compositions are a "structural necessity" in capitalism, and thus correspond to a sort of "rationality" and progress with capitalist development, countries cannot "complain" about losing their surplus value in exchange with other countries. However, the differences in wage levels between countries are not a structural necessity of capitalism but, according to Emmanuel, an "accidental" feature. In this case, countries can legitimately complain about being "exploited." It is this latter form of nonequivalence that Emmanuel prefers to call unequal exchange, and it forms the basis for this theory of imperialism.

A key theoretical point here is the connection Emmanuel makes between the organic composition of capital and wages. Wages are for Emmanuel independent and thus they determine the organic composition as well as the international division of labor. Therefore, the transfer of value due to inequality of wages is primary, because it shapes the international division of labor in a way that results in a low organic composition of capital in the underdeveloped countries. Emmanuel refuses to call unequal exchange the nonequivalence that is purely the result of unequal compositions when rates of surplus value are the same. However, on the basis of Emmanuel's own assumptions it is impossible to have different organic compositions of capital between countries without also having unequal wages; that is, unequal wages are prior to everything else in Emmanuel's model. In the final analysis, Emmanuel's claim of exploitation rests on the assumption that differences in wages between countries are an accidental feature of capitalism, and this forms the *objective* base for the Third World's claim of being exploited by the industrialized capitalist countries. The whole notion of unequal exchange and what it constitutes will be taken up later.

The transfer of surplus value produced in the underdeveloped countries to the developed countries promotes the growth of the latter and retards the growth of the former. The cumulative effect in the developed countries is explained as follows by Emmanuel:

> Once a country has got ahead, through some historical accident, even if this be merely that a harsher climate has given men additional needs, this country starts to make other countries pay for its high wage level through unequal exchange. From that point onward, the impoverishment of one country becomes an increasing function of the enrichment of another, and vice versa. The super-profit from unequal exchange ensures a faster rate of growth.[6]

The "super-profit" does not accrue to the capitalist in the development countries but to the consumers. The capitalist cannot benefit in the long run from international exchange, because the competition between capital equalizes the rate of profit between countries. This leaves only the consumers (workers) in the developed countries to benefit from the deterioration in the terms of trade against the underdeveloped countries, i.e., from unequal exchange.[7]

The transfer of value to the high-wage countries promotes, through the benefits gained by consumers there,

> technological and cultural development. In order to deal with increasingly complicated production tasks, the ruling class is obliged to raise the people's educational level. The conditions favoring trade-union organization are created. . . . Little by little new forms of consumption spread everywhere and create fresh needs. The progressive enlargement of the market attracts foreign capital, and the influx of this capital speeds up development. This influx, moreover, constitutes in itself a factor tending to increase wages. The existence of already available outlets stimulates investment, and increased investment causes an increase in the organic composition of capital, which forms the source of a second transfer of value from the poorer foreign country to the richer country.[8]

Emmanuel goes on to argue that these combined forces raise wages even higher in the high-wage countries, making the inequality in wages between rich and poor countries even greater. The result is greater unequal exchange, and this works to "set all these factors in motion, which leads to the creation of new needs among workers, an increase in the value of labor power, and, finally, a fresh increase in wages. Wealth begets wealth."[9]

On the other hand, in the poor country wages continue to be tied to the "elementary physiological subsistence" level. The transfer of a large part of its surplus value to the rich countries deprives it of the means of accumulation and growth:

> The narrowness and stagnancy of its market discourage capital, which flees from it, so that despite the low organic composition and the low wages, a substantial proportion of its labor force is unable to find employment. . . . In proportion as wages increase in the other countries and the terms of exchange worsen, the value of labor power in the poor country decreases still further.[10]

According to Emmanuel, the decrease in the value of labor power in the poor countries makes it unprofitable to adopt more advanced techniques and methods, which would economize on human labor and increase investment in fixed capital. The result is an average composition of capital in the poor countries that is lower than the world average and significantly lower than the average in the industrialized economies. "This becomes," writes Emmanuel, "an additional and independent mechanism for transferring value from the poor countries to the rich ones. Poverty begets poverty."[11]

Unequal exchange, then, not only perpetuates inequality, it deepens it by promoting a spiral of higher wages and growth in the high-wage countries and depressing wages and retarding growth in low-wage countries. Emmanuel's argument concerning the blocked growth of the underdeveloped countries is an underconsumptionist one; however, it is rooted not in unequal exchange, but in low wages. Low wages have the *combined* effect of fostering unequal exchange *and* a movement of capital and an international division of labor that block the growth of the Third World countries. It will be useful to quote Emmanuel at length on this point:

> However substantial may be the transfer of value engendered by unequal exchange, and even if we take into account not merely the immediate and momentary impact this has but also its cumulative effect from year to year, *this transfer does not seem to be sufficient to explain completely the difference in standard of living and development that there is today between, on the one hand, the big industrial countries, and on the other, the underdeveloped ones.* To find the reason for this we must look at the movement of capital and the international division of labor.
>
> These two factors do indeed include forces that *block* the development of the Third World. But it so happens that *the same cause, that is, the disparity between wage levels that produces unequal exchange and thereby, indirectly, a certain unevenness of development through the draining off of part of the surplus available for accumulation, also produces, directly and independently of this draining off process, uneven development itself,* as a whole, *by setting in motion of the mechanism of these block-forces included in the movement of capital and international division of labor.*[12]

A closer look at how the movement of capital and international division of labor directly and independently block the development of the Third World reveals that the primary problem for capitalism "is not to produce but to sell." Capital is thus attracted to countries where there are extensive outlets and expanding markets. These outlets and markets are created where there is a high standard of living and not where the costs of production are low. In the poor countries the market is too narrow on account of the low level of wages there. According to Emmanuel, this accounts for the "perverse" movement of capital out of countries where capital is scarce and to countries where it is plentiful.[13]

Concerning the effect of the international division of labor and blocked development, Emmanuel argues in neoclassical fashion that firms will invest in those branches of production that absorb the largest amount of that factor of production that is relatively cheapest, and that within each branch of production the firm will adopt that technology that utilizes relatively more of the abundant and cheap factor of production. In a low-wage country this means choosing those branches and techniques with the lowest "organic compositions of capital." Emmanuel goes on to argue that in addition the firm will choose branches and techniques with the lowest "organic composition of labor," i.e., use relatively more low-skilled than high-skilled labor. He concludes by saying that "low-paid laborers keep machines and engineers out of the underdeveloped countries, while machines and engineers take the place of highly paid laborers in the advanced ones."[14]

It would appear that in the Third World there is no "incentive" for capital to revolutionize the forces of production, because labor power is so cheap that it does not pay to economize on it. Emmanuel is aware of the fact that England managed the Industrial Revolution without the "incentive" of high wages. He argues that this case only proves he is right, because in England high tariffs kept the surplus value from flowing out of the country. It remained within the country in the form of surplus rents, which were converted into industrial capital when the landed aristocracy "transformed themselves" into industrial capitalists.[15]

Yet Emmanuel argues that in the case of the Third World it is not enough just to keep the surplus value from being pumped out through unequal exchange; this is because low wages will still exist, resulting in insufficient outlets for capitalists. He is emphatic on this point: "In the last analysis . . . what determines the blocking of development in the Third World, at bottom and in the long run, is the absences there of opportunities for new investment, the lack of profitable projects. . . .

Market forces thus seem adequate to explain the 'blocking.'''[16]

Increasing wage levels in the Third World to those of the advanced countries is of course out of the question as a solution to the blocked development. Emmanuel sees only two choices open to these countries. The first is to tax exports, to transfer back to the home state the surplus value that is being transferred abroad through unequal exchange. This solution is not practical, according to Emmanuel, because it would prompt international trade wars.[17]

The second solution, preferred by Emmanuel, is the diversification of production by transferring factors of production from export industries to industries that can replace imports. Such transfers, Emmanuel argues, will "enable the national consumer to benefit from the low national wage level." Although this might be disruptive and lead to a decline in world efficiency, from the point of view of the Third World it would, Emmanuel believes, be beneficial. Such a dangerous dislocation of the established division of labor will necessitate a "national incomes policy on the international scale corresponding to what exists, however imperfectly, inside the nation."[18] Only then in this way will Third World countries be able to achieve successful capitalist development.

Summary and critique

Emmanuel's theory of imperialism is an attempt to show how Third World countries are exploited by the advanced capitalist countries through international trade. Surplus value produced in the Third World is transferred through the exchange process, leaving the Third World impoverished. The only way out, according to Emmanuel, is for these countries to diversify their economies by reallocating their resources from the export sector to the import-competing industries. The resulting disruptions of the existing international division of labor can be remedied with an international incomes policy. In other words, for Emmanuel capitalist development is possible if certain reforms are undertaken; it is not exactly clear how probable Emmanuel thinks such reforms actually are.

The great merit of Emmanuel's work is that he attempts to establish a rigorous theoretical base for the exploitation of the Third World through the ordinary process of an international trade. Emmanuel's theoretical base represents a Marxist theory of international prices based on Marx's labor theory of value and Marx's economic categories. The question of international prices and value formation has never before received any serious attention from Marxists, and Emmanuel's work must be seen as a pioneering effort. It is one of the first attempts to bridge the gap between the Marxist theory of imperialism and Marxist economic theory. Finally, the theory of unequal exchange directly challenges the theory of comparative advantage, which claims that all countries benefit from international trade and specialization.

In most respects Emmanuel's theory of imperialism stands alone, but it can be seen as an attempt to more rigorously show how surplus is extracted from Third World countries. The mechanism for extraction is much different from that posited by the monopoly capital school's dependency theory. The latter sees monopoly and dependency mediated through the extraction mechanism of economic, social, and political structures; such structures play little if any role in Emmanuel's theory. While both see underconsumption as a serious problem in the Third World, for Emmanuel this is caused by low wages, not by unequal exchange, which only exacerbates underconsumption; for the dependency theorists surplus extraction causes underconsumption. So, despite some similarities, there are significant differences both at the theoretical and methodological levels.

Although deserving of praise, Emmanuel's theory of unequal exchange is highly controversial and has been subject to a great deal of criticism.[19] Only the major points of disagreement will be touched on here. The interested reader may consult Appendix II for a more extended critique as well as an alternative formulation of unequal exchange.

One of the most serious controversies has been over the question of the independence of wages in Emmanuel's theory; for him, wages determine the structure of the international economy and the development of capitalism. This view has been challenged by Charles Bettelheim and Ernest Mandel, who both argue that wages, or the value of labor power, are not independent of the level of development of the forces of production and the relations of production. They argue that it is the uneven development of the forces of production and relations of production that determines national wage diferences, not the other way around.[20] For Emmanuel, the level of wages is prior to everything else;

this is crucial to his theory of imperialism. However, Emmanuel is not very convincing in his case for the independence of wages, and so this criticism casts a shadow of doubt over the theory of unequal exchange.

A related and equally serious problem is that Emmanuel not only asserts the primacy of wages but also the primacy of exchange over the development of the forces of production, productive relations, and the accumulation of capital. To be sure, the emphasis on market relations in the theory of imperialism has been a problem for most Marxists. However, in Emmanuel's case this problem is especially serious because Emmanuel reverses the traditional Marxian sequence from the sphere of production to the sphere of exchange. Emmanuel's treatment of wages lies at the heart of this issue, and it is analogous to the problem of the expansion of markets and the rise of capitalism discussed in the last chapter.

The sphere of production is important because the sphere of exchange obscures class relations and exploitation. At the level of markets, commodities exchange for each other as equivalents, i.e., all commodities are purchased at their full value, including labor power. The source of profit is not exchange but the exploitation of labor in the sphere of production, where it produces more value than the exchange value of labor power.

In relations between countries these relationships drop out of sight, because Emmanuel focuses on the transfer of value from poor (low-wage) to rich (high-wage) countries through the exchange process. Thus the source of exploitation is exchange rather than production. Marx also noted the possibility for unequal exchange due to differences in the organic composition of capital (which Emmanuel acknowledges but refuses to call unequal exchange). Unequal exchange could also take place, according to Marx, because of international differences in the values of commodities in isolated markets. Such transfers of value Marx likened to merchants' profit. Although Marx recognized the importance of both forms of unequal exchange, this did not convince him that exchange was more fundamental than production in determining the laws of motion of capitalism. It is highly questionable that Emmanuel's theory of unequal exchange, based on wage differences, provides such a rationale. His approach and theory is similar to that of "neo-Ricardians" who have abandoned Marx's approach and method.[21]

A third problem concerns the validity of Emmanuel's determination of international prices. Emmanuel's assumption that the rate of exploitation in the Third World is higher than in the advanced capitalist economies has been challenged.[22] Crucial to such an assumption is the determination of the value of labor power in the Third World. Here the means of subsistence are produced internationally as well as locally under capitalist and noncapitalist conditions of production. The determination of the exchange value of labor power in the Third World, indeed the determination of the international exchange value of all commodities, presupposes a fully developed and articulated world capitalism. It is certainly questionable that such conditions exist, and this raises questions about the validity of the application of the law of value to determine exchange value on an international scale.

A fourth problem concerns Emmanuel's conclusion about the possibility for successful capitalist development. Without a more systematic analysis of productive structures and relations of production in the Third World it is hasty to conclude, as Emmanuel does, that a few simple reforms, no matter how difficult to bring about, will turn the tide in the underdeveloped countries. Emmanuel's reform proposals are remarkably similar to the calls for a "new international economic order" and the policies of import substitution. Import substitution turned out to be grossly inefficient, and it is doubtful that a new international order will be very successful without a new internal economic order in the Third World countries. In short, the question here concerns the causes of poverty and underdevelopment, and whether or not the causes are systemic or, as in Emmanuel's view, simply accidents of history and wage differentials.

A final problem is the political implications of Emmanuel's theory. The major beneficiaries of unequal exchange are the high-wage countries generally and workers-consumers particularly. This means that the working class has a major interest in pursuing imperialism and the policies that promote and perpetuate it. This view has created a strong reaction in Marxist circles. The debate has a long history, dating from the time Engels and Lenin raised the issue of an "aristocracy of labor" that benefited from imperialism, i.e., could be bought off with imperialist profits. However, in Emmanuel's view the working class is not bought off, but benefits directly from low-wage labor through the process of unequal exchange. One could say that to some degree workers in the advanced capitalist economies live off the fruits of low wage labor in the Third World. (For a treatment of unequal exchange that avoids such conclusions see Appendix II.)

Despite the problems in his work, Emmanuel has raised some important questions about imperialism that have not been dealt with before and he has stimulated others to work in this area. There are, however, few adherents to Emmanuel's theory of unequal exchange, although as we shall see in the next chapter, unequal exchange does play an important part in Samir Amin's theory of imperialism.

⑥
Samir Amin:
An Eclectic Synthesis

The extensive work of Samir Amin is probably the most significant body of thought concerning imperialism and underdevelopment since the work of Andre Gunder Frank. Amin's two main works, *Accumulation on a World Scale* and *Unequal Development*, appeared in English translations in 1974 and 1976, some years after their original publication in France. Notwithstanding its title, *Accumulation on a World Scale* deals primarily with what Amin refers to as the "social formations of peripheral capitalism." The second work treats imperialism more systematically, from the perspectives of both the center and the periphery. It is in part an extension of the earlier work, but also borrows from it heavily, many times word for word. For this reason, and despite subsequent writings by Amin, *Unequal Development* can be said to contain the nucleus of Amin's thought.

Amin's work is an ambitious attempt to bring together the various strands of Marxist thought on imperialism in order to establish the laws of motion of capitalism on a world scale. Amin tries to explain both capitalist foreign expansion and the impact of that expansion on the rest of the world, within a framework that focuses on the logic and needs of expanded capital reproduction. He argues that foreign expansion is an inner necessity for capitalism and at the same time blocks the full development of capitalism in the Third World.

Amin covers a great deal in his writings and it is sometimes hard to distill the essence of his work, to isolate a coherent theory of imperialism. It should be noted that at various junctures I have taken the liberty of selectively citing and interpreting Amin's sometimes ambiguous and contradictory positions.

Below I present a discussion of Amin's analysis of capitalist expansion, broken down into historical stages, and then a discussion of Amin's theory of persistent backwardness. Each part contains an evaluation of Amin's contribution. The chapter concludes with an overall assessment.

Causes of capitalist foreign expansion

The characteristic feature of central capitalist formations, in Amin's view, is that they contain only one mode of production, whereas previous economic formations contained more than one mode of production. A second feature is that the process of capital accumulation is essentially internally generated. This produces what Amin calls "autocentric accumulation." Autocentric accumulation leads to the progressive development of the forces of production, i.e., successful capitalist industrialization.

According to Amin, the external relations between the center and periphery as a whole are marginal when compared with internal relations within the center.[1] Capitalism moves forward primarily on the basis of internally generated forces (demand?) and foreign expansion plays only a secondary role.[2] It is not immediately clear whether Amin thinks that foreign expansion is dispensable to capitalism. However, as will be shown below, his analysis places a high premium on foreign expansion as a key to the laws of motion of capitalism in the core countries.

At the most general level, Amin states that external markets are sought because of the competitive search for profits, which speeds the rate of capital accumulation in capitalism. This competitive drive forces capital to seek raw materials and markets farther and farther from its original centers of accumulation. Amin's claim here is much different from that of Luxemburg, whom he criticizes.[3] The dynamic that promotes a widening and deepening of the internal market operates externally as well. According to Amin, this expansion takes place between developing capitalist formations as well as between capitalist and precapitalist (peripheral) formations.[4]

More specifically, Amin argues that foreign expansion is the result of the ultimate contradiction in capitalism between the capacity to produce and the capacity to consume. This contradiction manifests itself in a falling rate of profit, which in Amin's view, is overcome by deepening the purely capitalist internal market and by the foreign expansion of markets. The exact relationship between underconsumption and the tendency for the rate of profit to fall is not clear in Amin's work.[5]

Amin isolates three historical tendencies in capitalism's accumulation process which serve to check the falling rate of profit:

> The first, which Marx studies at length in *Capital*, is increasing the rate of surplus value; in other words, aggravating the conditions of capitalist exploitation at the center of the system, which implies relative impoverishment. The second means is spreading the capitalist mode of production to new regions where the rate of surplus value is higher and where it is therefore possible to obtain a superprofit through unequal exchange. The third means consists in developing various forms of waste: selling costs, military expenditure, or luxury consumption, making it possible for profits that cannot be reinvested owing to the inadequacy of the rate of profit to be spent nevertheless. This third means was only glimpsed by Marx, its large-scale development being a feature of our own time.[6]

These means of checking the fall in the rate of profit constitute for Amin "the three profound tendencies of this mode's dynamic of accumulation."[7] As will be shown, each of these requires the foreign expansion of capitalism.

At this point Amin develops a stage theory of capitalist development and imperialism. The stages resemble Frank's and Dos Santos's stages of underdevelopment. Historically, foreign expansion unfolds in a distinct manner, corresponding to three periods of capitalist expansion: (1) the competitive period up to 1880; (2) the monopoly period up to World War II; and (3) the post-World War II state monopoly period. According to Amin, "at each of these stages capitalism reveals its expansionist tendency: the commercial expansionism of the first phase, then imperialism (in Lenin's sense of the word),[8] and now postimperialism."[9]

Expansion in competitive capitalism

In the era of competitive capitalism (up to 1880) the check on the falling rate of profit is the increase brought about in the rate of surplus value. According to Amin, this caused a slow growth in real wages, and also caused the capacity to consume to lag behind the capacity to produce blocking autocentric accumulation. He states that, if

> real wages do not increase at the necessary rate, accumulation requires, as compensation, a steady *external* expansion of the market. This is what underlies the necessary expansionism of the capitalist mode. Throughout the nineteenth century, until the 1880's, because real wages at the center did not increase sufficiently, a form of expansionism was necessary that conferred certain functions upon the periphery.[10]

Amin appears to be making a case for underconsumption as the cause of expansion of markets in the nineteenth century. This underconsumption was brought about by the relative impoverishment of the working class, which in turn was brought on by the attempts of capitalists to overcome the falling rate of profit by increasing the rate of exploitation. The success of these attempts was contradictory, however, as the increased rate of exploitation caused consumption to lag behind productive capacity, resulting in a shortage of markets.

In another place, Amin argues that the objective need for capitalism to expand its markets externally is twofold:

> (1) the inadequacy of the market, which is essentially agricultural in the first stages, restricted by the pace and scope of the progress of productivity in agriculture; and
> (2) the requirements for maximizing the rate of profit, which imply seeking abroad for cheaper goods for popular consumption (especially cereals), so that the cost of labor can be reduced, as well as for raw materials making it possible to reduce the value of constant capital employed.[11]

Amin cites Marx in support of these two points concerning foreign trade as a counteracting tendency to the falling rate of profit.[12]

Although it is difficult to ascertain exactly what Amin is arguing here regarding the causes of foreign expansion, he would appear to mean that in this period capital resorts to both internal and external measures to increase the rate of surplus value, in order to stave off the falling rate of profit. However, internal policies to keep the rate of surplus value high (successful, Amin argues, because of the large reserves of labor and lack of working-class cohesion) cause the capacity to consume to lag behind the capacity to produce. Foreign expansion then becomes necessary not only to overcome the falling rate of profit, but to overcome underconsumption as well.

These objective needs of central capitalism during the competitive period lead to a certain set of policies carried out by central states in support of foreign expansion. These policies include:

> colonial conquest and the opening of protected markets for the benefit of the metropolitan country, destruction of crafts in the colonies, with recourse to political means for this purpose (the example of India is illuminating in this connection), encouragement of emigration and the opening of land for producing wheat and meat in the North American West and in South America, etc. In this period, the export of capital was still unknown as a means of expanding markets. This is why the predominant form it assumed, in the exceptional cases when it appeared at all, was still investment in public debt, collected at the center by the most powerful finance houses, as with the loans made to the Khedive of Egypt.[13]

The export of capital was generally unknown in this period because individual enterprises were too small to generate the size of capital or the control necessary to extend production beyond their national frontiers.

Expansion before World War II

Amin's analysis of foreign expansion in the monopoly period after 1880 is an amalgam of continued responses to a falling rate of profit, the export of capital, and unequal exchange. Although his analysis is ostensibly based on the law of value, at one point Amin argues that capitalism in this period underwent a qualitative change that negated the labor theory of value:

> For monopoly is above all a hindrance to the equalization of profit. Prices therefore cease to be determined by a general law based on values. The field of operation of the law of value contracts. There is no longer any rationality, even apparent, in the price system. Prices are determined by social relations of strength within the dominant class, between the financial groups that dominate the various sectors of economic activity.[14]

Despite this essentially neo-Ricardian position, Amin's analysis is one that is based on tendencies that were derived from the law of value. Later on even these are abandoned or drastically modified.

In the monopoly period after 1880, the expansion of central capitalism assumed new forms because, according to Amin, real wages began
to increase at a faster rate. While the actual rise in real wages was
achieved through the organization of the working class into unions, the
objective conditions for this increase were established by the appearance of monopoly. With the rise of monopoly the downward pressure
on prices could be resisted. In fact, Amin notes that after 1880–1890
there was a steady rise in prices rather than the reduction in prices
which characterized most of the nineteenth century. These rising prices
facilitated a faster "rise in incomes," both wages and profits.[15]

What is important here for Amin is that the rise in real wages slowed
or halted the increase in the rate of surplus value, negating it as a
countertendency to the falling rate of profit. This, Amin argues, was
the inevitable outcome of capitalist development. This contradiction
manifested two contrary movements within the law of the falling rate of
profit. First, the organic composition of capital tends to rise. Second,
the rate of surplus value tends to rise because technical progress induces
a surplus of labor, allowing capital to drive down the value of labor
power.

These two movements contradicted each other, the one lowering the
rate of profit and the other raising it. However, the increase in the rate
of surplus value could not go on indefinitely, because in the process of
satisfying the requirements of autocentric accumulation the rate of
surplus value tended to stabilize itself in the advanced capitalist countries, and the rate of profit had to fall in these fully developed economies.[16] Amin does not spell out clearly how the rate of surplus value
was stabilized. It seems to be related to the rise of monopolies, which
facilitated the cohesiveness of the working class and brought about
higher wages. Amin goes no further than this in his explanation.

The expansion of markets, Amin argues, is a permanent tendency of
capitalism, which was transformed qualitatively with the onset of monopolies. Monopolies themselves arose because of the inherent tendency of capitalism toward concentration and centralization. Prior to this
stage of monopoly, the typical firm was incapable of exporting capital.
Market expansion took the form of the export of goods and the political
intervention of the state. However, in the monopoly period, this tendency toward market expansion found "a new form of expression: the
export of capital."[17]

Amin emphasizes that while qualitative changes were taking place in the external sphere, the functional nature of these changes to the capitalist system was essentially the same:

> to serve the same functions so far as central capital was concerned, namely, to offset the tendency of the rate of profit to fall: (1) by enlarging markets and exploiting new regions where the rate of surplus value was higher than at the center; and (2) by reducing the cost of labor power and of constant capital.[18]

Capital is driven beyond its original centers of accumulation in search of a higher rate of profit because the rising real wages at the center put a check on increasing the rate of surplus value to counteract the falling rate of profit. The imperative of the capitalist system was to find another way of countering the falling rate of profit. The system's response, according to Amin, was monopoly and imperialism in the Leninist sense.[19] A major difference between Amin and Lenin, however, is that Lenin did not derive imperialist expansion from the law of the tendency for the rate of profit to fall.

The major outlets for the export of capital were the new centers of autocentric accumulation (other advancing capitalist countries), where the most modern technology could be used. In these countries the rate of profit was much higher, despite higher wages in many cases, on account of the higher labor productivity in these countries. In the backward countries (the peripheral social formations) the attraction for foreign capital was exactly the opposite: wages were lower there for an equivalent product, giving rise to a higher rate of surplus value.[20]

Amin argues that with the appearance of monopoly capital and the large-scale export of capital, the problem of determining international exchange value became important. Prior to this period the conditions did not exist for determining exchange value on a world scale. For that determination, according to Amin, the equalization of rates of profit between countries required a world commodity market and mobility of capital on a world scale,[21] conditions that were satisfied in the monopoly phase of capitalist expansion. Amin solves the problem of the formation of values and prices on an international scale by transforming international values into international prices of production.[22]

Following Emmanuel, Amin argues that the basis for imperialism in this stage was unequal exchange. He essentially recapitulates

Emmanuel's basic argument with a few changes.[23] He contends that if the organic compositions of capital are similar between two countries, while one country has lower real wages than the other (i.e., a higher rate of surplus value), then it can be shown there will be a transfer of value in the process of international commodity exchange from the country with lower real wages to the country with higher real wages. These conditions apply to differences between central and peripheral capitalist formations, so that unequal exchange forms the underlying basis of imperialism. It allows the center to overcome the tendency for the rate of profit to fall, simultaneously keeping wages high in the center and low in the periphery.[24]

One of the main differences between Amin and Emmanuel is over the determination of wages. For Amin, wages are not an independent variable. They are a dependent variable, determined by the specific nature of the peripheral capitalist mode of production with respect to the central one and by the level of development of the forces of production. This overcomes one of the major criticisms of Emmanuel's analysis of unequal exchange.[25] However, it does not effect the outcome. Unequal exchange occurs just the same, regardless of the source of wage differentials.

Another difference is that Amin thinks that although the transformation of values into prices of production gives unequal exchange a "scientific content" and defines the conditions that govern it (i.e., unequal wages), it is impractical and flawed because of the transformation problem. Drawing on the work of Oscar Braun,[26] Amin substitutes Sraffa's determination of prices, which he argues is more satisfactory because it is carried out in "positivistic empirical terms" and is thus amenable to the actual measurement of unequal exchange. Amin notes in passing that Sraffa's approach cannot determine causality, i.e., whether international prices cause inequality in wages or vice versa. Based on *a priori* reasoning, Amin argues that wages are prior to prices.[27]

According to Amin's estimates, the "hidden" transfer of value amounted to 15 percent of the product of the peripheral countries, which he states "is far from being negligible in relative terms, and is alone sufficient to account for the blocking of the growth of the periphery, and the increasing gap between it and the center."[28] It should be noted, however, that Amin does not think that unequal exchange was the cause of persistent backwardness, a point that will be substantiated below.

Amin further contends that this transfer of value was not negligible for the center either, as it represented 1.5 percent of its product, and that it was "especially important for the giant firms that are its direct beneficiaries."[29] Amin does not elaborate on just exactly how these firms benefited from, or how they captured the benefits of unequal exchange.

Finally, Amin argues that these relations of unequal exchange between the center and the periphery were not relations of expanded reproduction, but of primitive accumulation:

> A fresh geographical extension of capitalism's domain then became necessary (after the First Industrial Revolution). The periphery as we know it today was created by way of colonial conquest. This conquest brought different social formations again into mutual contact, but in new forms; those of central capitalism and those of peripheral capitalism in process of constitution. The mechanism of primitive accumulation for the benefit of the center reappeared in a new form. The characteristic feature of primitive accumulation in contrast to normal expanded reproduction, is unequal exchange, that is, the exchange of products whose prices of production, in the Marxist sense, are unequal.[30]

Amin concludes that, while the basis for expansion was the realization of surplus value in the competitive period, realization in the monopoly period was accomplished by rising incomes (real wages and profits). In the monopoly period, rising incomes limited the increases in the rate of surplus value as a countervailing tendency to a falling rate of profit. The export of capital to the periphery, where rates of exploitation were higher due to low wage costs, checked the fall in the rate of profit during the monopoly period through the mechanism of unequal exchange.[31]

Expansion in the postwar period

Amin argues that the law of the tendency of the rate of profit to fall signifies that crises in capitalism must worsen. Just why they should do so Amin does not say, but he notes that they tended to worsen through the 1930s.[32] In the competitive period the cycle was caused by the inability of capitalism to "plan" its investment, but in the monopoly period planning occurs with state help, "in a certain sense and within certain limits."[33]

Amin accounts for the fact that while monopolies arrived on the scene at the turn of the century, "the cycle in its classical form" did not give way to "conjunctural oscillations" (that is, a dampened, irregular cycle) until after World War II. This was because convertibility into gold had not been abandoned and the monetary authorities and the state were not yet aware of the possibility of a "concerted economy." However, after the war, the maintenance of external controls along with a heightened awareness of a "concerted economy" brought planning intended to tame the cycle in monopoly capitalism.[34]

The concerted economy (state monopoly capitalism) has been somewhat successful in controlling the cycle, at least until recently; Amin argues that the cycle is beginning to reassert itself on a world scale. In short, central capitalist formations have succeeded in overcoming capitalism's internal contradictions only to have them reappear as contradictions that plague the world system. On that plane the center cannot plan, due to the "still-national character of institutions and structures" of the center.[35] While global economic planning seems to be a theoretical possibility for Amin, he rules it out as a practical impossibility.

Amin's analysis of the cycle brings us into the third phase of capitalist expansion, now current, which began around 1945. For reasons that are not clear, Amin refers to this period as "postimperialism," perhaps to distinguish it from Lenin's imperialist stage. Amin's analysis of this period reflects a further break with Marx:

> Monopolies and imperialism are the system's response to this tendency (for the rate of profit to fall), putting an end to the equalization of profit. However, on the one hand, the 'reparation' of profits from the periphery, where capital has gone in search of a better return, and on the other, the steady decline in the rate of profit at the center, together with pursuit of the mechanisms of autocentric accumulation, aggravate the problem of how to absorb excess capital. The way in which the system overcomes this problem is through state monopoly capitalism, which organizes the absorption of the surplus.[36]

Amin's defense of this break with Marx is essentially the same as Baran and Sweezy's:

The tendency for the surplus to increase, which results from the policy of the state and of the monopolies in the epoch of contemporary monopoly capitalism, does not contradict the tendency for the rate of profit to fall—on the contrary, it is the way the latter finds expression in the system as it exists in our time.[37]

With this Amin makes the transition to Baran and Sweezy's analysis of the problem of surplus absorption. His justification for the use of the concept of surplus rather than surplus value is that surplus is "a wider concept than that of surplus value," which includes "nonproductive incomes and state revenues."[38] Of course, this is incorrect. Surplus value is shared out, according to Marx, among all sorts of nonproductive groups, including the state.

Amin essentially reiterates Baran and Sweezy's analysis. The fundamental law of state monopoly capitalism is the law of the tendency for the surplus to increase, and the fundamental problem for this system is how to absorb this surplus profitably. The absorption of surplus is facilitated through an increase in selling costs, which monopolies must incur in order to realize their monopoly profits. This reduces the rate of profit without absorbing all the surplus. Increases in civilian and military expenditures by the state absorb the rest. However, the reservation here is that not all of the "potential surplus," which is always larger than the "actual surplus," is absorbed.

This creates underutilization of capacity and chronic under-employment. According to Amin, this predicament dictates the laws of motion of present-day monopoly capitalism. More specifically, it drives the system to conquer external markets in order to provide a higher rate of profit for the export of capital. Amin notes, as do Baran and Sweezy, that the center's inflow of capital becomes much larger than its outflow; so this is no solution to the problem of surplus absorption, which must be handled through economic waste and public spending.[39]

The export of capital does not solve the problem of surplus absorption at the macro level, yet on the micro level, firms benefit from a higher rate of surplus value in the periphery than in the center. The return flow of profit takes the disguised form of the transfer of surplus value through the mechanism of unequal exchange. Superprofits are eliminated by the equalization of rates of profit on a world scale.[40]

Amin seems to ignore the fact of the large visible inflow of capital into the center countries. He does not provide substantiation for the assertion that profit rates are equalizing between center and periphery.

According to Amin, the postimperialist period has undergone several changes other than those noted above. This period, which included a period of "dazzling growth," caused in part by the modernization of Western Europe, brought with it several important structural changes:

> (1) The constitution of giant transnational firms that operate on the world scale. . . (2) The impact of a technological revolution that transfers the center of gravity of the industries of the future toward new branches (atomic power, space research, electronics), and renders obsolete the classical modes of accumulation, characterized by increasing organic composition of capital; the "residual factor"—"grey matter"—becomes the principal factor in growth, and the ultramodern industries are distinguished by an "organic composition of labor" that accords a much bigger place in highly skilled labor; and (3) the concentration of technological knowledge in these giant transnational firms.[41]

In the area of foreign expansion, control over production can be maintained by control over technology. As in the center, control over the means of production becomes less important.[42]

Again, Amin is asserting that capitalism undergoes changes that alter its fundamental basis. Here the "classical mode" of capital accumulation, increasing the organic composition of capital, no longer takes place. It is apparently not necessary to capitalism in this stage. Instead, we have an increasing "organic composition of labor" (a concept originating with Emmanuel) whereby more and more highly skilled labor is used relative to less-skilled labor. "Grey matter" becomes "the principal factor of growth." Ultramodern industries integrate the dynamic branches of production based on this "residual factor."

The postimperialist phase of capitalist development then represents profound changes in the very basis of capital accumulation. According to Amin, these can be best analyzed by using a surplus absorption approach and a neoclassical analysis of principal growth factors.

The causes of expansion:
An assessment

One has to admire Amin's weaving together of various theories to explain different stages of capitalist foreign expansion by the necessities of the capital accumulation process. On a general level, Amin seems to provide an explanation congruent with historical reality. However, the fit between theory and fact is rather loose, requiring more historical verification than Amin provides.

Amin maintains a fairly consistent theoretical focus on the expanded reproduction of capital and the contradictions that ensue from the capital accumulation process as capitalism develops. On the basis of these contradictions, he explains the need for foreign expansion as well as the various forms that expansion has taken historically.

Despite Amin's correct focus on the capital accumulation process as the key to understanding capitalism, his theoretical treatment of it is flawed by eclecticism, a lack of consistency in methodology and approach. Laws and tendencies derived at one level of analysis are applied at very different levels, and varied and inconsistent theories from within the Marxist "intellectual tradition" are combined with one another. Let me elaborate on each of these.

First, although his methodology and approach are ostensibly "Marxist," Amin utilizes Marxist, neo-Ricardian, neoclassical, and Keynesian methodologies (and theories) here and there throughout his work. This shifting back and forth makes it impossible to come up with an internally consistent theory of expansion and imperialism. Upon what grounds is one to evaluate Amin's work?

Next, Amin takes tendencies derived at one level of abstraction and under certain assumptions, such as the falling rate of profit and unequal exchange, and applies them indiscriminately at different levels. This makes it very difficult and often impossible to follow his reasoning. Perhaps such a lack of rigor and precision on Amin's part is due to the magnitude of the task he has set for himself: to explain all the history of capitalist foreign expansion and its impact on the noncapitalist world.

Finally, when all is said and done Amin offers an explanation of capitalist foreign expansion that consists of a series of tendencies and theories strung together to explain the history of expansion, without regard for theoretical consistency. Amin's "theory" of imperialism is a composite embracing the falling rate of profit, underconsumption, economic crises, unequal exchange, surplus absorption, and the organic composition of labor. Although all of these theories may exist within the Marxist tradition, nevertheless they are essentially incompatible. Some break so sharply with Marx that they are commonly labeled "neo-Marxist," as in the case of the surplus absorption thesis of the "monopoly capital school."

Amin recognizes this incompatibility and makes no attempt to argue that his explanations are consistent. Rather he tries to show that capitalism itself is inconsistent, i.e., that in its development capitalism undergoes such profound transformations that its essential nature changes over time. This necessitates different theories to explain different stages of capitalist development and expansion. Nevertheless, Amin has not argued convincingly (as will be shown below) that the fundamental elements of capitalism upon which Marx derived his laws of motion have been changed in any way.

The usefulness of Amin's analysis of foreign expansion depends upon the validity of the various theories he has strung together to explain different stages of capitalist foreign expansion. My criticisms will be twofold. First, although many of these theories have been seriously challenged on various grounds, Amin usually accepts them uncritically. The theory of surplus absorption has already been evaluated in a previous chapter, where it was shown to have serious theoretical problems (see Chapter 3 and Appendix I). Amin professes to have ended the debate over the controversial theory of unequal exchange; however, serious problems remain.[43] A second criticism concerns Amin's contention that capitalism has undergone a series of profound transformations in its development, which have altered its essential nature so that different approaches and theories are necessary to explain its laws of motion at different historical junctures, is ill-founded if not false.

Amin's treatment of underconsumption and the tendency for the rate of profit to fall is inadequate and faulty. The relationship between the two tendencies is not clearly specified: it is unclear whether underconsumption is prior to the falling rate of profit, or the other way around, of if they exist simultaneously on the same plane. Amin ignores completely the theoretical controversy[44] surrounding both of these tendencies, yet he evokes them to explain the internal and external laws of motion of capitalism. Furthermore, Amin uses these tendencies in such a way that he severs them from their theoretical base, which he does not establish. He jettisons the law of value after the "competitive" phase of capitalist development, yet continues to invoke the tendency for the rate of profit to fall as the underlying cause of foreign expansion. This is a particularly damaging criticism, because underconsumption and the tendency for the rate of profit to fall are central to Amin's arguments about foreign expansion; they provide one of the few common threads tying his "theory" together.

Amin argues that the classical mode of accumulation and exploitation has been replaced. In his treatment change in the "organic composition of labor" in favor of higher skill leads to an increase in surplus value and thus capital accumulation. Amin seems content to analyze highly skilled labor as a "factor of production" rather than as a producer of exchange value in the context of the extended reproduction of capital.

Amin correctly emphasized the contemporary importance of advanced scientific knowledge. However, such knowledge has always been important. Marx emphasized the importance of science to the capitalist mode of production from the very beginning. It is true that this knowledge more recently has taken different forms and been produced in different ways. However, Amin does not tell us how it is different. His omission does not negate the importance of technology or the importance of control over technology, which firms in the center have and which they can use to appropriate surplus value produced in the periphery, by licensing and other methods. However, Amin has not shown how this negates the "classical mode" of capital accumulation: he provides no basis for the assertion.

Causes of persistent backwardness

What makes Amin's analysis of underdevelopment somewhat unique is that he tries to conduct it within the context of the process of capital accumulation and social/productive relations. In this he differs from surplus drain theorists such as Baran and Frank. But, notwithstanding such differences, Amin's work obviously has been influenced by Marxists, dependency theorists, and structuralists, although the intellectual heritage of this amalgam is not always clear.

Amin's principal thesis is that capitalist foreign expansion into the periphery causes an extreme disarticulation of the peripheral economy, blocks autocentric accumulation, and creates extraverted accumulation. The result is the blocked development of these social formations as they are held in a peripheral position in the world capitalist system. The peripheral societies are characterized by more than one mode of production, with their specific forms determined by the nature of their precapitalist modes of production and the particular phases of capitalist development in which they were integrated into the world capitalist system.[45]

According to Amin, the essential difference between the periphery and the center lies in the extraverted nature of the peripheral economies, which subjects them to a dynamic emanating from the center. The periphery has been integrated into a world system in a way that suits the center's needs. The process of development in the periphery is influenced by competition with the center, which determines the periphery's "distinctive" structure. Such competition promotes three distortions in the development of peripheral capitalism by contrast with the development in the center. These are:

> (1) a crucial distortion toward export activities, which absorb the major part of the capital arriving from the center;
> (2) a distortion toward tertiary activities, which arises both from the special contradictions of peripheral capitalism and from the original structures of the peripheral formations; and
> (3) a distortion in the choice of branches of industry, toward light branches, together with the utilization of modern techniques in these branches.[46]

Export distortion

Initially, the distorted expansion of export activities is the most crucial factor. The orientation of the periphery toward export activities means that financial and human resources are allocated in a way that "gives extraversion a qualitative dimension and asserts the dominance of the exporting sector over the economic structure as a whole, which is subjected to and shaped by the requirements of the external market."[47]

The requirements of the external market are for raw materials and foodstuffs at prices lower than those of comparable or substitute commodities at the center.

Amin argues that the transformation of a natural subsistence economy into a commodity-producing society does not take place by simple economic mechanisms (although Amin seems to grant that the transformation of feudalism to capitalism in Western Europe did so) because the "traditional social structures hinder the spread of commodity exchange."[48] This, Amin argues, results in the use of violence and force as methods of primitive accumulation, to reorganize the peripheral social formations to meet the needs of the center and give them an export orientation.

The growth of the export sector does not promote a transition to capitalism but rather a transition to *peripheral* capitalism. The transition to a commodity economy in the periphery is not accompanied by an advance in productive forces, such as occurred in the central capitalist formations. Nevertheless, the transition produces "specific distortions . . . altering the original society and depriving it of its traditional character."[49]

The analysis here follows Baran's quite closely, though it focuses on the process of capital accumulation. The periphery is forced into a "mercantilization of precapitalist relations": people must obtain money, and so must either become commodity producers or sell their labor power. The land itself tends to become a commodity, and ground rent makes its appearance. In agriculture the reorientation toward the needs of the export sector leads to a regression in agricultural technique, a concentration of landownership, and an increase in rent, which "dooms agriculture to stagnation, sometimes even to retrogression."[50]

Further retrogression occurs when local craftsmen are destroyed in the competition with manufactured goods imported from the center. Amin contrasts this with the progress brought about by the destruction of crafts in the center: "Whereas in Europe society found a new equilibrium that ensured employment for its labor forces, what we see here is a regressive equilibrium that casts a part of the labor force right out of the production system."[51]

Capital export by the center to the external relations of commodity exchange does not alter the extraversion of the periphery. Foreign capital flows initially into the primary sector and later into luxury consumer goods as import substitutes. However, due to the now all too familiar leaks, very little internal demand is generated. Profits are repatriated abroad. Local capital, insufficient in size and scale, cannot compete with foreign monopolies. It is forced into sectors that do not compete with the center but are complementary, such as trade and services. However, some of the industrial capital is from local sources. The need to keep the wages of labor low requires the maintenance of local "parasitic social groups" (e.g., latifundia owners, kulaks, compradore trading bourgeoisie, and the state bureaucracy), so that the added internal demand is mainly for the luxury consumption of these groups.[52]

The internal demand leads to a partial industrialization of the periphery, promoted by a policy of import substitution. However, peripheral industry is restricted to the production of luxury goods. This in turn further distorts and reproduces the conditions of extraversion. Industrialization in the periphery begins with the "end instead of the beginning." It begins with the production of consumer durables, commodities associated with the advanced stage of capitalist development. This results in a distortion in the allocation of resources toward those sectors producing consumer durables and away from the production of nondurable consumer goods. Amin notes that production of nondurables "will attract no financial or human means to make its modernization possible" because there is little demand generated for these commodities.[53]

According to Amin, industrialization followed a different path in the central capitalist economies, where all branches of industry developed simultaneously or else descended "from the heavy equipment-producing industries to the consumers-goods industries downstream"[54] As a result of the very different kinds of industrialization that occur in the periphery, the conditions for unequal exchange are reproduced: an abundant supply of labor, due to a lack of adequate labor absorption, and consequently, low wages. In these ways import substitution opens up new opportunities for foreign capital while leaving extraversion intact.[55]

The growth and spread of the multinational firm after World War II did not alter the extraverted accumulation process. According to Amin, it just carried the process of distorted development one step further. Whereas before, the international division of labor was materialized in commodity exchange, with the arrival of the multinational corporation a new division is reproduced inside the firm. This, Amin states, leads to a new form of inequality between nations: the software, the "grey matter," and the production of the most complex equipment are reserved for the center, while the periphery specializes in the production of the hardware. According to Amin,

> This division reinforces the functions of the centralization of decision-making authority and technological innovation. Thereby it reproduces its own conditions, splitting the world labor market into watertight national markets with big differences in rewards. It deepens unequal exchange by internalizing this in the firm.[56]

Amin does not develop his point about the multinational firm's internalization of unequal exchange. One cannot tell whether transfer pricing provides the new mechanism for unequal exchange, nor how this might modify unequal exchange.

The new inequality deprives the periphery of any control over its own development and adds to the visible transfer of value from the periphery, whether in the form of profit remission or payments for software. These firms employ little labor, prevent the transformation of agriculture and the other backward sectors, and accelerate the disarticulation of the peripheral formation.[57] Furthermore, according to Amin, they create a "semi-aristocracy of labor," which ensures the docility of the proletariat. At the same time, it blocks the development of a national bourgeoisie while creating "a middle class of salaried professionals"—executives, engineers, office staff—who cleave to the patterns of consumption and ideology of the world system to which they organically belong."[58]

Amin contrasts this situation with the spread of multinationals among the center countries, where, he argues, it has "set in motion a wave of progress and technological innovations." We cannot equate that advance in the center with the "asymmetrical processes of domination and dependence that characterize the relations between the center and periphery."[59] Any unevenness among countries in the center is the result of uneven development, rather than the result of the unequal international division of labor and unequal exchange which characterize the relations between the center and periphery. Amin's distinction between the uneven development of the forces of production and the unequal international division of labor is an interesting one.

Amin's analysis thus far does not really take us much further than Baran's or Frank's. Amin differs from Frank in not arguing that the periphery is capitalist through and through. In Amin's view, the periphery is characterized by blocked capitalist development and co-existing modes of production. However, Amin does not really go beyond Baran in specifying the class nature of these modes or their interaction.

Tertiary sector distortion

Amin states that the initial distortion, which orients the peripheral economy toward export activities, brings in its train the "hypertrophy" of the tertiary sector. Amin argues that the rise of the tertiary sector in the center can be explained by the problem of surplus absorption in monopoly capitalism. However, in the periphery it arises because

> of the limitations and contradictions characteristic of peripheral development: inadequate industrialization and increasing unemployment, strengthening of the position of ground rent, etc. A fetter on accumulation, this hypertrophy of unproductive activities, expressed especially in the excessive growth of administrative expenditure, is manifested in the Third World of today by the quasi-permanent crisis of government finance.[60]

Although Amin says no more than this, still the analysis is interesting. It is reminiscent of O'Connor's *Fiscal Crisis of the State*, only here the focus is on the underdeveloped state.

Extraversion in the accumulation process

The final distortion in the periphery's development is the culmination of all of the others. Extraversion, unequal specialization, and a marked propensity to import combine to transfer the "multiplier mechanisms connected with the phenomenon known as the 'accelerator' from the periphery to the center."[61] Amin cites three reasons for this: (1) the profits on foreign investment are exported; (2) wages are low while techniques are advanced, making it impossible to achieve an equilibrium between the capacity to produce and the capacity to consume; and

(3) investment induced via the accelerator effect is absent in the periphery because the unequal international division of labor assigns intermediate branches of production to the center.[62]

In short, the peripheral economies do not have the convergent mechanisms (linkages) that can spread progress from one point in the system to the rest of the economy. Instead, in the extraverted economy progress at any one point is largely transferred abroad. The transition to peripheral capitalism, instead of producing mechanisms for convergence, produces an increasingly disarticulated economic system.[63]

Amin explains how the introduction of an export and its eventual demise affect the center and the periphery very differently.

> The areas interested in an export product that is comparatively important for the development of capitalism at the center experience brilliant periods of very rapid growth. But because no autocentric integrated entity is formed, as soon as the product in question ceases to be of interest to the center, the region falls into decline: its economy stagnates, or even retrogresses. . . . When the iron ore of Lorraine is eventually worked out, this may create a difficult reconversion problem for the region, but it will be able to overcome these difficulties, for an infrastructure of integrated industries has been formed on the basis of the mineral, which could be imported from elsewhere. But when the iron ore of Mauritania is worked out, that country will go back to desert.[64]

Amin claims that unequal exchange "is alone sufficient to account for the blocked growth of the periphery." However, he does not fall back on this to *explain* blocked growth. Here Amin stresses the need of central capital to overcome its internal contradictions. In the context of international competition, capital at the center imposes upon the rest of the world a division of labor that distorts the peripheral economies. It ensures the reproduction of those conditions that meet the needs of the center and block the growth of the periphery. One of those conditions is the maintenance of low real wages, the fundamental condition of unequal exchange. Preventing the outflow of value from the periphery through unequal exchange will not produce a transition to capitalism, because it is not the *cause* of blocked growth in the periphery.

The cause of underdevelopment for Amin is the threefold distortion, outlined above, which means, in economistic terms, the transfer from the periphery to the center of the multiplier mechanisms, which cause accumulation at the center to be a cumulative process. From this transfer results the conspicuous disarticulation of the underdeveloped economy, the dualism of this economy, and in the end, the blocking of the economy's growth.[65]

Extraversion must be overcome before peripheral development can proceed.

Amin's theory of backwardness: An assessment

Amin makes a real theoretical contribution to the understanding of blocked development. The extraversion/disarticulation thesis goes further than either surplus drain or unequal exchange theories to explain underdevelopment. Amin relies heavily on a multiplier/accelerator analysis, which partakes of the left Keynesianism characteristic of several other post-World War II Marxists. His analysis also bears many similarities to the work of the structuralists in the field of economic development, such as Hirschman (linkages), Nurkse (balanced growth), Rosenstein-Rodan (big push), and Murdal (backwash/spread effects).[66] Although it is less eclectic than his analysis of capitalist expansion, Amin's analysis of blocked development does mix concepts and methods of analysis from distinctly different paradigms.

Although Amin's analysis is in many ways an improvement over the works discussed above, it also shares many of their shortcomings. It too is basically a demand-led model. It falls short of any real analysis of the process of capital accumulation in the periphery, despite Amin's constant reference to that process. In short, Amin restricts his analysis to the sphere of circulation; there is no "supply-side" analysis.

Therefore, Amin does not specify the modes of production in peripheral social formations in a way which lays bare class forces and exploitation. Without these, one cannot specify developments on the production side that would give rise to capitalism and "autocentric" capital accumulation. Along with Frank (and others), Amin assumes that market expansion gives rise to capitalism, but Amin holds that the market is not strong enough to induce the complete development of capitalism. This chain of causality has been questioned in previous chapters.

The implication of Amin's disarticulation thesis is that
"autocentric" accumulation can be brought about in the periphery by a
policy of rearticulation, i.e., internalizing foreign linkages.[67] Although Amin does not come to such a conclusion, it seems to follow
logically from his analysis. Such a conclusion is not much different
from liberal mainstream economists' calls for Third World export
promotion, diversification, and growth with equity. It is not that the
distortions Amin cites as blocks to the successful development of capitalism in the periphery are unimportant. Clearly such distortions must
be eliminated before capitalism can progress. However, it may be that
before such distortions can be removed or eliminated more fundamental changes in class structures, the nature of exploitation, and the form
of the surplus will have to take place.

Conclusion

Amin's extremely ambitious work yields many valuable insights into
imperialism. One must admire his ambition to explain both capitalist
foreign expansion and the impact of that expansion on the rest of the
world as well as his attempt to synthesize the various theories of
imperialism advanced by Marxists. His attempt to establish the laws of
motion of capitalism on a world scale in a way that links imperialism to
the capital accumulation process, class exploitation, and class forces is
a significant improvement over previous theory.

Although Amin's work does not completely accomplish this task, he
does take us part way. His most significant contribution is his distinction between "autocentric accumulation" in the advanced capitalist
countries, which promotes the expanded reproduction of capital and
capitalist development, and "extraverted accumulation" in the peripheral countries, which does not. The extraverted accumulation concept
represents a refinement of dependency theory in that it is tied explicitly
to the process of capital accumulation.

Although Amin's work must be seen as a significant advance, his
analysis fails to take into account the nature of exploitation and class
forces. A related and serious flaw is Amin's severe eclecticism. He
mixes different paradigms and modes of analysis to suit his conve-
nience. This leads to a great deal of inconsistency, contradiction,
vagueness, and confusion in his work. Amin mixes terms and concepts

drawn from different paradigms (including neoclassical economics) that are often not reducible or translatable from one into the other.

Amin's eclectic approach mars what might have been a more useful explanation of the history of capitalist expansion, its ebb and flow. Although Amin deftly combines Marx, Lenin, Baran, Sweezy, Frank, and Emmanuel to explain different periods of history, the result raises more theoretical questions than it answers. While all of these theorists certainly fall within the Marxist tradition, there are significant differences between them. Without resolving them, one is left with a historical stage theory of capitalist expansion that does not quite hang together. Nonetheless, Amin must be congratulated for his attempt to explain the entire history of imperialism; few others have attempted it in as much detail.

Like many of the others Amin limits his analysis to one moment of what Marx treated as an organic whole. Although Amin focuses on capital accumulation, he really never gets into the productive moment. He restricts himself to what Marx called the "sphere of appearances" (circulation). Marx chastised the classical economists for this error; his purpose in *Capital* was to pierce the "veil of appearances." Amin is not alone among those who have followed in Marx's footsteps but slip back into classical habits. In the analysis of imperialism, for example, Hilferding, Bukharin, O'Connor, Frank, and Magdoff make the same error. In general, most contemporary Marxists have done the same.[68]

Amin's eclectic synthesis marks a turning point in the development of the Marxist theory of imperialism. Perhaps the greatest contribution of Amin's failed synthesis is that by bringing together the various strands of Marxist thought on imperialism, it revealed their incompatibility and thus their inherent weaknesses. It remains in the final chapter to examine the recent currents of Marxist thought on imperialism and to see what directions such thought has taken.

7
Recent Currents in Marxist Theory of Imperialism

Recent currents of Marxist theory have for the most part been critical of previous thought on imperialism. The opening salvo against Marxist dependency theory was perhaps fired by Bill Warren, who in 1973 wrote in *New Left Review* that underdevelopment was a myth and that imperialism was a progressive force bringing capitalist development to the Third World.[1] Marshaling statistical evidence, Warren tried to show that, contrary to the claims of Marxist dependency theorists, many Third World countries were well on their way to successful capitalist industrialization.

Warren's ideas were not well received and the evidence he provided to support him claims proved weak and contradictory.[2] No further work of his was published until after his death in 1978. Warren left behind a rough draft manuscript, which has been published under the title *Imperialism: Pioneer of Capitalism*. In this work Warren provides a much more developed critique of dependency theory and again tries to show empirically that capitalist industrialization is taking place rapidly in many Third World countries and that imperialism is declining. The evidence provided, although illustrative, is not very convincing, and theoretically Warren does not advance the theory of imperialism or the theory of capitalism in the Third World. He too restricts his analysis to the level of markets and he does not provide the theoretical links between the growth of exchange brought about by the forces of imperialism and the rise of capitalism in the Third World.

Although Warren does not advance the theory of imperialism, he did raise some important questions concerning the validity of dependency theory. Perhaps Warren's most significant contribution was to provide a thorough and provocative ideological and political critique of the contemporary Marxist position on imperialism:

Marxism's involvement in and theoretical characterization of the anti-imperialist movements . . . has led Marxism into the morass of a subjectivist voluntarism according to which socialism can be achieved almost irrespective of objective economic or cultural conditions, provided anti-imperialist fervour remains white-hot. Above all, Marxism . . . has acquired a dual social character: the philosophy simultaneously of socialism . . . and of modernizing nationalism, whose basic historical function is pre-socialist and, for much of humanity, specifically bourgeois.

The consequent intellectual dilution of Marxism may well have been necessary for its survival and spread, and thus for its future intellectual renewal. . . . But whatever the gains of Marxism's profound involvement in the anti-imperialist movement, the reassertion of its role as the philosophy of socialism and the working class requires re-examination of this involvement and of its theoretical and historical foundations.[3]

Warren provides much in the way of such a historical reexamination, but it remained for others to reassess and extend the theoretical foundations.

The tone and tenor of Warren's work set the stage for what has become the dominant trend in recent Marxist thought on imperialism. The major exception to this critical trend has been the world systems theory of Immanuel Wallerstein, which represents a logical derivation and continuation of dependency theory.[4] In fact, the more recent work of Andre Gunder Frank extends dependency theory in this same direction.[5] The primary unit of analysis in world systems theory is the capitalist world economy, an economic system that has a logic of its own, to which the parts are subservient. The parts of this world system are tied together through the workings of a single market, mediated by the structure of nation states. The system is divided into core, semiperiphery, and periphery, which correspond to different levels in the appropriation of surplus. The relationship of the parts in this world system are defined in terms of the division of labor and the role that a particular country plays in the world system. Uneven development is determined by the particular period of time that a society is integrated into the world system. Internal class contradictions and struggles are explainable as responses to the relative advantages or disadvantages of a particular country *vis-à-vis* the world system; that is, class struggle is global and determined by the particular role of a country in the world system.

The advantage of world systems theory is that it focuses on capitalism as a global system rather than an expanding national system colliding with other national systems, capitalist and precapitalist. Unfortunately, such a theory, while it might be insightful in terms of global dynamics, does not overcome or surmount the problems of dependency theory.[6] In fact, in many ways world systems theory exacerbates these problems by moving the analysis to yet a higher level of generalization. At this level of analysis it is even more difficult to bring into the analysis relations of production, capital accumulation, and modes of production.

This chapter focuses on recent Marxist currents of thought that head in the opposite direction from world systems theory (hereafter referred to as "dependency-world systems theory"). This critical literature has grown rapidly in the last several years and many new studies have been published. The new literaure represents several different and sometimes disparate currents. However, several commonalities are identifiable. First, the recent literature reflects a more general trend among radical leftists to return to Marx. The restudy and reinterpretation of Marx's analysis and methodology have in some cases been no more than a return to a rigid orthodoxy.[7] However, in many other cases it has produced a richer, more insightful understanding of Marx as well as a fuller appreciation of the complexity of the task Marx set for himself. In many respects, much of the recent advance in Marxist theory can be attributed to those Marxists who have been focusing on imperialism.[8]

A second common trend is that much of the current Marxist thought on imperialism represents efforts to ground the theory of imperialism in a more explicitly Marxist framework that includes historical materialism, class struggle, the mode of exploitation, articulation of modes of production, the state and capital accumulation, the internationalization of capital, and the law of value. These efforts, while critical of previous thought, have yielded many fresh insights into the nature of imperialism. However, since the theoretical advances have been on several different fronts, the literature is diverse and somewhat fragmented.

The purpose of this chapter is to review the major currents of this recent thought on imperialism. Six more or less distinct currents are identified, each associated with the work of one or more theorists. These do not necessarily represent distinct schools of thought and there is some overlap. Each of the following sections will contain a summary and brief assessment. An overall assessment will be made in the concluding section, placing these recent currents of thought within the history of Marxist intellectual thought on imperialism.

The origins of capitalism, class struggle, and the mode of exploitation

One of the major current controversies is over the nature and origins of capitalism. Andre Gunder Frank's view, it will be remembered, is that once the backward countries were subjected to the commercial pressures of the world market they became capitalist. The defining characteristics of capitalism, according to Frank, were production for exchange, individual gain, and the exploitation of the majority of direct producers by a minority of nonproducers. It has already been noted that such a definition of capitalism is so general that it can be used to define virtually any mode of production and is thus not specific enough to capture the essence of the capitalist mode. This criticism of previous theory has been made by several theorists.[9] One of the most comprehensive critiques has been made by Robert Brenner, whose work will be discussed here. Brenner's work is an attempt to define the nature of capitalism as a mode of production, establish the origins of capitalism, and then to assess the nature of the impact of capitalist penetration into noncapitalist areas.

Brenner argues that capitalism does not arise from the extension of the market, which he claims is Adam Smith's view, and in the hands of Frank and other Marxists gives rise to what Brenner calls ''neo-Smithian Marxism.'' The origins of capitalism must be sought in the origin of the capitalist social-productive relations underlying the expanded reproduction of capital. It is Brenner's contention that these relations do not evolve automatically with the extension of the market.

Brenner's central thesis is that ''production for profit via exchange'' will not promote the continued accumulation of capital and development of the forces of production unless it expresses ''a system of free wage labor.'' It will be useful to quote Brenner at length here in order to establish exactly under what conditions to expect these results:

> Only where labor has been separated from possession of the means of production, and where laborers have been emancipated from any direct relations of domination (such as slavery or serfdom), are both capital and

labor power "free" to make possible their combination at the highest *possible* level of technology. Only where they are free, will such combination appear *feasible* and *desirable*. Only where they are free, will such combination be *necessitated*. Only under conditions of free wage labor will the individual producing units (combining labor power and the means of production) be forced to sell in order to buy, to buy in order to survive and reproduce, and ultimately to expand and innovate in order to maintain this position in relationship to other competing productive units. Only under such a system, where both capital and labor power are thus commodities—and which was therefore called by Marx "generalized commodity production"—is there the necessity of producing at the "socially necessary" labor time in order to survive, and to surpass this level of productivity to ensure continued survival.[10]

In short, only under capitalist class relations is it possible and are the inherent forces such that the extended reproduction of capital takes place, the forces of production develop, and the productivity of labor increases.

According to Brenner, in precapitalist societies these conditions and forces are absent, so that there is no possibility of developing their forces of production and the productivity of labor, even when there is widespread trade present. This is a crucial contention by Brenner. The major part of his work is devoted to a logical and historical proof of this contention. He tries to answer the questions concerning the origins of capitalism and the prerequisites for capitalist development.

According to Brenner three conditions must be present before capitalist development can take place:

(1) the potential "mobility of labor power" in response to the market—which is, however, bound up with the degree of freedom/unfreedom and with that of economic dependence/independence of the direct producers;

(2) the potential for developing the productivity of labor through separation and specialization of tasks—which is, however, bound up with the possibilities for developing co-operative labor in connection with growing means of production;

(3) the potential for enforcing continuing pressure to develop labor productivity—which is, however, bound up with the survival and reproductive needs of the direct producers and exploiters in relation to their access to the means of subsistence and production.[11]

However, according to Brenner, the potential for achieving these conditions is blocked in precapitalist modes of production because the systems of surplus extraction and property, i.e., class structures, act as fetters. In the first case, the direct forceful controls over the producers (through which surplus is extracted) prevent the mobility of the producers in response to the market. Second, the possibilities for the achievement of cooperative labor are limited when producers have direct access to their means of subsistence, as in serfdom and slavery. This places definite limitations on the effectiveness of using direct force to develop cooperative labor processes. Third, there is no pressure for the continued development of the forces of production in precapitalist societies because exploiters and direct producers are both tied to their means of subsistence and means of production. Therefore, the survival and reproduction of these classes do not depend on the sale of their products in the market, and there is no pressure to compete with each other in terms of productivity. In fact, it is argued by Brenner that where surplus extraction is the result of direct force, there may be pressures that lead to use of surplus for the purposes of increasing the use of force (e.g., military) rather than for productive purposes.[12]

Is it not possible, as some Marxists argue,[13] that with the extension of the market, the possibility for a more rational productive structure was created and that the precapitalist ruling classes, seeing this opportunity, seized it in growing numbers based on the individual incentives held out by such possibilities? Brenner doubts this, because the ruling classes did not have any choice in the matter; they were not free to select the method by which they could exploit the direct producers. Brenner shows both theoretically and historically that where precapitalist relations existed in Europe, the ruling classes reacted to market pressures by forcibly squeezing the peasantry for more surplus, i.e., by increasing the absolute surplus labor, rather than by increasing relative surplus labor.[14] Given the social class structure, this ruling-class response was logical and rational.[15]

The origins of capitalism lie not in the rise of trade by itself, according to Brenner, but in the class transformations and class struggle that emerge from the contradictions in the precapitalist modes of production. More specifically, the origins of capitalism are determined by the historical processes by which serfdom was dissolved and peasant property undermined. Both outcomes ensured the elimination of direct, forceful methods of surplus extraction and paved the way for the accumulation of land, labor, and the means of production. Brenner considers these developments "inexplicable as the result of ruling-class policy or ruling-class intention." He goes on to argue that these two developments are

> the outcome of processes of class formation, rooted in class conflict. Peasant resistance had broken serfdom in Western Europe, in spite of landlord attempts to maintain it. But in Eastern Europe, the landlords prevailed and prevented this outcome. Correlatively, the application of landlord power had foreclosed the emergence of widespread peasant proprietorship following the downfall of serfdom in England. But elsewhere on the continent the peasantry succeeded in gaining the land. It is these contrasting outcomes of processes of class conflict—dependent in turn on contrasting evolutions of class society and disparate balances of class forces at different points in time—which are at the heart of the original transition from feudalism to capitalism, and which require to be understood if the onset of capitalist economic development is to be fully comprehended. [16]

The extension of Brenner's analysis to the development of capitalism in the backward countries yields interesting results and directly confronts previous Marxist analyses, specifically the work of Baran, Frank, and Amin. The expansion of the world commercial network in the sixteenth and seventeenth centuries created opportunities in the backward countries for increasing the surplus product to be sold on the growing world market. Brenner argues that the form this surplus extraction took depended (as in Europe) upon the specific class structures that existed in the backward countries. Because these structures varied from country to country at the time the demand for specific commodities increased, the forms of labor exploitation varied. In almost all areas of expansion the existing class structure necessitated the use of the existing precapitalist class structure to directly squeeze more surplus labor out of the direct producers. In some cases this was accomplished by imposing other forced labor systems, such as slavery, to expand the absolute surplus labor for the production of commodities to be sold on the world market.

The result was not the development of capitalist social and productive relations of production, but rather the intensification of existing precapitalist relations or the imposition of other forced labor systems. Both were based on the extension of absolute surplus labor time rather than relative surplus labor. Such outcomes prevented the development of capitalism in most of the backward countries that were integrated into the world capitalist network. In short, the causes of under-development are to be found in the internal barriers to capital accumulation imposed by the forced labor systems, i.e., class structures, in the backward countries.[17]

In Brenner's view, the external orientation of the national bourgeoisie, the lack of effective demand, and the outflow of surplus are not causes of underdevelopment. These factors are rather symptoms of an underlying class structure and mode of exploitation that is inconsistent with the progressive development of capitalism and the expanded accumulation of capital. The response to the need for greater surplus product was to squeeze more and more absolute surplus labor out of the direct producers by lowering their subsistence levels. Since this diminished or limited the market for both consumer and capital goods, internal investment opportunities were limited.[18]

Contrary to Frank, Brenner does not contend that all the backward countries that were integrated into the world commercial network as exporters of raw materials became underdeveloped. This depended upon the class structure in place at the time of increased demand for surplus to satisfy the world market. In the case of the mid-Atlantic region of North America, the large export of grain in the colonial period did not result from the use of a forced labor system based on "ultra-exploitation." In this case, according to Brenner, the increased demand for grain conflicted with a class structure characterized largely by small family subsistence farms where the means of production and the means of subsistence were in the hands of the direct producers. The surplus for the world market came from those farms that were large enough to produce a surplus over and above their subsistence and reproduction needs. This did not lead to the development of much specialization or new techniques, because of the nature of small subsistence farming. Brenner notes that

> a greater output would have been possible with specialization. Had it been possible to reduce these farmers to tenancy, this specialization might have been accomplished. As it was, however, their very control over the land

made them largely invulnerable to takeover by competition. On the other hand, they appear to have possessed the class power to prevent any direct attempts at expropriation.[19]

Here we have a case that directly contradicts Frank's thesis and appears explicable only in terms of the class structure with which the rising world commercial network came in contact. Brenner discusses other historical cases that also contradict Frank's thesis and show the inadequacy of the dependency approach and method of analysis. An analysis of the penetration of capitalist expansion in the backward countries that takes into account the social and productive relations offers a much more logical explanation of the outcome of such penetration. It also seems to provide a much more historically accurate account.

Although most of Brenner's analysis is restricted to the colonial period he does advance a few ideas concerning contemporary underdevelopment. He does not believe that bourgeois revolutions are "on the agenda":

> International capitalists, local capitalists and neo-feudalists alike have remained, by and large, interested in and supportive of the class structures of underdevelopment. Nevertheless, these structures have kept significant masses of use values in the form of labor power and natural resources from the field of capital accumulation. Until recently, of course, the class interests behind "industrialization via import substitution" have not, as a rule, been strong enough to force the class structural shifts that would open the way to profitable investment in development.[20]

In short, Brenner sees little hope for successful capitalist development in the Third World.

Brenner's work makes a significant contribution to Marxist economic thought on the origins and nature of capitalist development. The emphasis on the importance of class structure and dynamics to achieve the necessary conditions or prerequisites for the steady accumulation and development of capitalism provides a richer understanding of the "development process" as well as the ways in which this development is blocked in the underdeveloped countries. Most other Marxists have analyzed class structure and class dynamics as an abstract and mechanical process rather than as the real responses of certain classes of people whose choices at certain times and in certain situations are limited by their social and productive relations.

Of the contemporary Marxists discussed so far only Baran comes anywhere close to having a sense of the importance of class structure in the underdeveloped countries and its role as a blocking force; however, his analysis is based on a very abstract notion of class (i.e., it is not rooted in the production of surplus product), whose shortcomings have already been noted and are now more clearly evident. For the others, class is either peripheral to their analyses or else mechanistically imposed as it was by Frank and other dependency theorists.

One shortcoming of Brenner's analysis is that its application is for the most part restricted to the colonial period of penetration in the backward countries. This leaves a large span of history unexplained. Brenner's analysis needs to be extended to the history of underdevelopment. A much more detailed analysis of class forces and the objective needs of capital accumulation are needed as well. This said, Brenner's analysis remains an important contribution.

The articulation of modes of production

The nature and laws of capitalist development have been the focal points of many recent attempts to extend the Marxist theory of imperialism. In particular there is a group of Marxists who have sought to explain the various linkages through which the capitalist mode of production has been articulated with other modes of production in its development. The work of Pierre-Phillipe Rey laid the foundation for what has come to be called the articulation of modes of production approach. Barbara Bradby has summarized and extended Rey's ideas, and more recently, Aidan Foster-Carter has surveyed the issues and the literature on the articulation of modes of production.[21] Of Rey's own work, particularly his books *Colonialism, Neocolonialism, and the Transition to Capitalism* (1971) and *Class Alliances* (1973), only the second is available in English.

The underlying premise of those focusing on the articulation of modes of production is that the development of capitalism in the Third World is shaped by the precapitalist modes of production associated with it. According to Bradby, this is part of a more general phenomenon in capitalist development:

> The necessities of the expanded reproduction of capitalism result in the articulation of the capitalist mode of production with "pre-capitalist" modes. The nature of this articulation and its consequences for the "pre-capitalist" mode of production is a function first and predominantly, of the needs of the capitalist mode and second, of the internal structure of the "pre-capitalist" mode.[22]

In fact, Rey begins with an analysis of the transition from feudalism to capitalism in the original European centers of capitalist development. He then extends the analysis to those areas where capitalism was introduced from abroad. Rey's purpose is to develop an analytical model which can explain both the European experience as well as the experience of the "underdeveloped" countries.

The development of capitalism is seen as a process of extending capitalist relations of production and increasing the labor force from which surplus value can be extracted. This dynamic, once set in motion, pits capitalism against feudalism and other modes or production. To understand this transition, Rey finds it useful to begin with Marx's theory of capitalist ground rent. In a critique of Marx's theory Rey concludes that ground rent is the fundamental relation of production under feudalism, not capitalism.[23] This is a crucial link to understanding Rey's explanation of the transition from feudalism to capitalism, and the nature of the alliance between the aristocracy and bourgeoisie. As Bradby explains it:

> The growth of Flemish cloth manufacture was what permitted landlords to increase their rents by expelling peasants from the land and going over to leasing for wool production. At the same time this process served the interests of the nascent capitalist class by providing them with a labor-force. The rate of exploitation of both modes could increase simultaneously. The faster peasants were expelled from the land, the lower could industrial wages be kept and the higher would be the capitalist rate of exploitation; while the faster the agricultural population declined relative to the industrial one, and the larger the number of agricultural products required on the market, the faster could the feudal rate of exploitation grow.[24]

In short, the articulation here between feudalism and capitalism is not an antagonistic one but rather one of mutual concern and benefit.

The articulation between capitalism and feudalism is necessary, because capitalism cannot immediately eliminate preceding modes of production and the forms of exploitation that characterize them. In fact, feudal relations of production are reinforced. The feudal mode provides the agricultural provisions and labor power necessary to the capitalist mode of production.

Rey establishes three stages of articulation. In the first stage, the initial linkage is through the sphere of exchange. The feudal mode of production remains dominant, and the exchange relations reinforce the pre-existing mode rather than extending capitalist relations. Indeed, there is a dual necessity:

> For the landed proprietors there is the necessity to develop capitalism, because it is this development that assures them of their rents. For the capitalists, there is the necessity of maintaining landed property under a new form specific to the transition, because this form alone assures an adequate supply of both labor power and agricultural commodities.[25]

In the second stage, capitalism has "taken root" and becomes the dominant mode of production. Capitalism still needs feudalism in this stage; however, feudalism exists on the basis of capitalism and is subject to modification: "The development of large-scale industrial capital . . . destroys the artisan class entirely. Its penetration into certain branches of agriculture does away with the need for small peasants."[26]

The final stage of articulation takes place when peasant agriculture is destroyed by capital engaged in farming. At this point capitalism is capable of reproducing itself without the need for landed proprietors for its supply of labor power or raw materials.[27] The actual achievement of this stage of articulation has been reached only in the United States. Other advanced capitalist nations, such as England and West Germany, are still in the second stage.[28]

The transition to capitalism in the "neocolonies" follows in broad outline the experience of capitalism in Europe. It is different because capitalism is introduced from the outside and is articulated not with feudalism but with other precapitalist modes of production. Because capitalism appears as an import, already well armed and developed, it is tempting, Rey argues, "to analyze the necessity of its development exclusively in terms of the functioning of capitalism's laws."[29] This would be wrong, in Rey's view, because

> the transitional phase can only be understood through contemplation of
> internal features of the mode dominant prior to the intrusion of capital.
> The social formation must give birth in its own way to the transition of
> capitalism. The social formation in transition thus is subject to a double
> history whence erupts a contradiction between two orders of necessity. On
> the one side is the history of capital itself, a history whose essentials are
> outside the social formation in transition. On the other side is the history
> of the transition that is specific to the mode of production with which
> capital articulates.[30]

In other words, Rey assumes that capitalism has its own inherent laws
of development, but that the transition to capitalism will be different in
those cases where capitalism is imported from abroad and articulated
with precapitalist modes that differ from feudalism.

More specifically, Rey argues that whereas in the case of feudalism
the articulation is initially a peaceful one, the articulation between
capitalism and other precapitalist modes of production is characterized
by fierce, even violent resistance to the spread of capitalist relations.
Transitional modes of production are implanted by force in the colonial
period; they eventually give way once the conditions for capitalist
reproduction have been established.[31]

In sum, Rey argues that only in the transition from feudalism to
capitalism are the relations of production, based on ground rent, consistent with the needs of capital for agricultural goods and labor power.
The feudal aristocracy was better able than other precapitalist ruling
classes to meet these needs. According to Bradby,

> The interests of the feudal and bourgeois ruling classes coincided over a
> long period. No other social formation has seen a comparable growth.
> Only in the transition from feudalism does the working class grow out of
> the productive base rather than being developed through the superstruc-
> ture [e.g., as with colonialism].[32]

The only way that capitalism can eliminate antagonistic relations of
production is by implanting transitional modes of production within the
social formation. This means that the birth of capitalism in the Third
World will be more violent than the "original birth of capitalism from
feudalism."[33]

The second stage in the colonies, which takes place much later than in Europe, has the same effect. However, because the articulation is somewhat different it takes a different form.

> Traditional modes are not rooted out so thoroughly because they have never undergone such a radical experience as the expulsion of the peasants from their ancestral lands. While the destruction wrought by the landed proprietors is only reversible through emigration, there are many instances within the "neocolonial" societies in which the workers move to and fro between the traditional and the capitalist mode. . . . The traditional modes are not so solidly dominated because for a long period capitalism only occupied space within the "economic superstructure." It only sought to supply itself with means of production from agriculture, so these latter sectors were only rudimentarily affected by its presence, and the fact that these sectors were constrained to sell to the market did not provide a very solid base for integration of agriculture into the universe of the capitalist commodity.[34]

This stage of articulation represents the now current neocolonial stage of development in the Third World; in Rey's view it has not yet reached the third and final stage of articulation.

Imperialism, in the Leninist sense, comes into the picture during the second stage of articulation, after the capitalist mode of production becomes dominant. Here, particularly with the centralization and concentration of capital, capitalism requires greater quantities of raw materials and new sources of labor power. This drives capitalism into association (articulation) with other precapitalist modes of production. In this fashion, Rey integrates his articulation of modes of production with previous Marxist theory of imperialism.[35]

We have, then, a theory that explains the original development of capitalism out of feudalism, the spread of capitalism to other precapitalist modes of production in different parts of the world, and the differences (uneven development) between the original development and the development of capitalism in the Third World. This analysis challenges the earlier dependency view that capitalism has fully developed everywhere into a world system that contains developed and underdeveloped versions of capitalism. The articulation of modes of production shows that capitalism in the "neocolonies" is articulated with precapitalist modes of production and that the transition to capitalism is incomplete rather than underdeveloped.

The articulation of modes of production approach makes an important contribution to the Marxist theory of imperialism. However, there remain problems to be solved and issues to be worked out. One of the most serious is the problem of the degree to which capitalism in the Third World is influenced by external as opposed to internal forces. Another is the assumption of the parallelism of capitalist development. Although the transitions are seen to be necessarily different, it is still assumed that the end product will look the same: like capitalism in the original centers of development. Is it possible for different forms of capitalism to evolve in the Third World, for example the peripheral or disarticulated form suggested (though inadequately specified) by Amin? Another example is the suggestion that there exists a "colonial mode of production," which is neither precapitalist nor capitalist though it is the result of international capitalist forces, i.e., imperialism. The colonial mode of production is the result of the disarticulation of precapitalist modes.[36]

Another problem here concerns the necessity of capitalism to expand its relations of production in order to obtain raw materials and new sources of labor power. Are these equally important, or is their importance determined by particular historical circumstances? If the latter, then does this not call into question the theoretical validity of Rey's generalized stages of articulation? Might such stages differ according to historical circumstances? Furthermore, is violence inevitable in articulations with nonfeudal modes, or might it not depend upon specific circumstances?[37]

Finally, it is not clear whether capitalist development is blocked in the Third World, or merely taking a different transitional route to full capitalist development, something that has not been achieved to date. Reference to the process of development in the Third World as transitional rather than as underdevelopment implies a forward-moving social process, albeit one that may be slower and more complex than the original development of capitalism. One can only surmise in this view that capitalist development is not blocked, either by dependency or by precapitalist modes of production.

Historical materialism and the theory of imperialism

Another current trend in contemporary Marxist thought has been the attempt to evolve a theory of imperialism and backwardness consistent with materialist theory. Such works have sought to show that dependency theory is not consistent with Marx's materialist theory and is faulty on both empirical and theoretical grounds. In place of dependency theory, a materialist theory is advanced which is thought to be more empirically verifiable and theoretically correct. Although several works could be discussed under this heading, only the work of Elizabeth Dore and John Weeks will be discussed.[38] Their work is explicitly designated as materialist and is more extensive than that of some others.[39] Although they are in essential agreement with Robert Brenner on many points, Dore and Weeks concentrate much more on a theory of imperialism and backwardness, and less on the nature and origins of capitalism.

Weeks argues that a theory of the world economy must contain a theory of capitalist reproduction and make a distinction between domestic and international reproduction. Reproduction is defined as the specific ways a particular mode of production evolves and reproduces its social relations on an expanding scale. In the case of capitalism, capital accumulation is the crucial factor along with a conceptualization of the division of the world for purposes of explaining international accumulation.[40]

According to Weeks, a theory of accumulation must explain both the origins or initial establishment of capitalism and also its reproduction and expansion once established. If the central purpose of analyzing the world economy is to explain uneven development, then clearly the origins of capitalism are important. Weeks argues that dependency theory does not deal with these initial questions satisfactorily. Dependency theorists explain the "epoch-making transition from feudalism to capitalism in Europe" by reference to the advanced countries' appropriation of the surplus product of the now underdeveloped countries. Those countries that lose surplus experience stagnation and those that gain surplus experience rapid capital accumulation.[41]

Although dependency theorists imply division of the world into countries, according to Weeks the international dimension of their theory of accumulation rests upon a division of the world into developed and underdeveloped areas or regions. Therefore dependency theory cannot explain the existence of political boundaries, which Weeks considers an important factor in a theory of international accumulation and uneven development.[42]

One of the fundamental hypotheses that emerges from dependency theory is that the export of capital (both productive and financial) should be from developed capitalist countries to underdeveloped countries. Of course, this hypothesis cannot be empirically verified, as most capital flows into other developed capitalist countries, not underdeveloped countries. In Week's view, this calls into question the validity of dependency theory.

Counterposing a materialist theory to dependency theory, Weeks argues that all class societies are based on exploitation, but that the specific character of each class society is determined by the way in which the surplus product is appropriated. The existence of a surplus product does not necessarily imply capital accumulation as evidenced by precapitalist modes of production. The expanded accumulation of capital results from the progressive development of the forces of production, not the redistribution of surplus product among societies as in dependency theory. Weeks argues that to explain uneven development on a world scale, you must answer how, and under what circumstances, societies come to be characterized by progressive development of the forces of production.[43]

Drawing on Marx's analysis, Weeks argues that the process of primitive accumulation is a prior condition for the progressive development of the forces of production. Specifically, the "forcible separation of labor from rights in land" creates a "free" wage labor force. With the "freeing" of labor the means of production become commodities, and it is possible to bring labor and the means of production together by the medium of money. The social mechanism for organizing production is capital and its expansion results in capitalist society. In such a society, products circulate as commodities and the surplus product assumes a monetary form, surplus value. Surplus value, created by the exploitation of wage labor, is the basis for accumulation.

Accumulation is forced upon capitalists by the conflict among capitals. This conflict arises out of the necessity that the products of capitalist production be sold in order for capitalists to begin another round of production. The conflict among capitalists takes the form of an economic struggle that is fought out by cheapening commodities through technological change. Technological change in turn leads to production on an ever-expanding scale. According to Weeks, "this in itself is sufficient to explain why capitalism should reach out to under-developed areas." Materialist theory predicts "that capital will expand into all areas, and once there is more than one capitalist area, the movement of capital between developed capitalist areas is as much to be expected as between developed capitalist areas and underdeveloped areas.''[44]

It will be useful at this point to digress for a moment and examine more closely Week's argument that competition is an inherent part of capitalism. This is a crucial aspect of a materialist theory of imperialism, for the conceptions of competition held by contemporary Marxists have led to many of the theoretical problems noted in previous chapters. Weeks challenges the monopoly capital school's notion that monopoly negates materialist theory.[45]

Weeks notes that the neoclassical theory of competition based on free entry and the number of sellers in a specific market describes a real phenomenon and that the act of exchange plays an important role in the overall process of competition. This theory of competition has been adopted by many Marxists. However, Weeks argues that Marx's theory of competition is not so much an alternative to the neoclassical approach as it is a more general theory of competition, one that embraces the outward manifestation of competition in the sphere of circulation, but is rooted in the sphere of production.

Quoting from the *Grundrisse*, Weeks puts forth Marx's definition of competition: ''conceptually, *competition* is nothing other than the inner *nature of capital*, its essential character, appearing in and realized as the reciprocal interaction of many capitals.'' In more explicit terms:

> The essential difference between feudalism and capitalism is that in the latter capital is free to exploit labor under differing circumstances. The purchase of labor power is *prior to* circulation and realization. It is that purchase by capital of labor power which creates the conditions of competition. The necessary conditions or bourgeois production, free wage labor and a market for the means of production, mean that the possibility of capital marshalling the forces of production for an invasion of branches of industry where the rate of profit is above average is always present. Thus competition under capitalism is *not* determined by conditions in . . . the ''product market,'' but determined by the existence of a market for labor power . . . [even though] it may take its outward form as the struggle for sales in a single market. . . .[46]

In other words, the root of competition lies in the ability of capital, in its finance capital form, to buy labor power and means of production and to deploy them in the form of productive capital wherever they will yield the highest rate of profit. It is an objective necessity in capitalism that different individual capitals compete with one another. Competition results from the free movement of capital, which can only reproduce itself by continually throwing itself back into production. One outward manifestation of this competition is the struggle between different capitals, in their commodity form, for sales in a single branch of production. However, competition between different capitals is not restricted to this outward form. Capital in its financial capital form competes across all branches of production. This is the direct result of the availability of free wage labor and marketable means of production. Thus competition stems from the inner nature of capital and is inherent in the capitalist mode of production.

Weeks argues that it is important to note that this theory of competition in no way depends on numbers. Restriction of the number of sellers in a particular branch of production cannot eliminate or reduce competition among capitals, because it "does not touch the source of competition, which is the existence of free wage labor."[47]

Contrary to conventional wisdom, Weeks argues that it is an idealistic myth that there was a "golden age" of free competition in the early development of capitalism. According to Weeks, during the early development of capitalism competition was not well developed, because there were precapitalist fetters on capitalist expansion. Also, the lack of developed financial institutions made it difficult for capitalists to borrow sufficient funds to operate in branches of production other than their own.[48] It is only with the full development of capitalism and the complete development of financial institutions that capitalist competition reaches its higher stage. In other words, capitalism does not begin with "free competition of individuals," but rather with limited competition, which intensifies with the development of capitalism.[49]

Monopoly in this view becomes not the negation of competition but the intensification of competition on a new level. Weeks quotes from Marx on this point:

> We all know that competition was engendered by feudal monopoly. Thus competition was originally the opposite of monopoly and not monopoly the opposite of competition. So that modern monopoly is not a simple antithesis, it is on the contrary the true synthesis.

Thesis: Feudal monopoly, before competition.
Antithesis: Competition.
Synthesis: Modern monopoly, which is the negation of feudal monopoly as it implies the system of competition, and the negation of competition insofar as it is monopoly.[50]

In the synthesis, Marx argued that with the rise of monopoly, brought about by the tendency toward centralization and concentration, competition is no less vital to capital, because this is the only way that it can maintain itself; and as was shown above in Chapter I, Marx thought that the competition between monopolies would become more "desperate," particularly on a world scale.

It is at this point that Weeks restates Lenin's position that with the rise of monopoly, competition reaches its highest level in the form of imperialism. In the age of imperialism, "competition has burst through the confines of one country, and rages on an international scale." Imperialism is, in short, "capitalist competition raging on a world scale."[51]

Competition and uneven development are important to an understanding of imperialism for Weeks. Competition leads to the continued necessity of "revolutionizing the forces of production"; however, this process does not take place evenly, because of the tendency of uneven development "between capitals in the same branch of industry, between branches of industry, between regions and countries."[52]

With the rise of monopoly, uneven development becomes accentuated. The monopolization of certain branches of production by associated or individual capitals gives rise to super-profits, which attract other large capitals. The invasion of these branches of super-profitability, under monopoly conditions, takes place very erratically and sometimes with considerable delay. Because innovations tend to require an increasingly larger scale of production, smaller-sized capitals cannot "creep up" on the monopolists; this restricts the competitive struggles to the "powerful giants." However, because of the impossibility of eliminating competition without eliminating capitalism itself, the competitive contradiction must assert itself, though monopolies may be successful for a time at preventing technical advances (i.e., retarding the development of the productive forces and "nipping incipient competitors in the bud." These periods give capitalism in its imperialist age a "parasitic" character.[53]

However, according to Weeks, these periods can at best only be temporary phenomena, and at some point a competitor gains an edge and

> leaps ahead of the old monopolist, shattering the monopoly position, introducing the competitive contradiction suddenly and dramatically. This is the source of imperialist rivalry and conflict, accelerated when the competitors are from different national capitalist classes, and each turns to its state for aid in the struggle. It is the levelling of development between capitals that generates conflict, for levelling of power creates more-or-less matched contestants, and the possibility that the challenger will replace the old champion.[54]

Therefore, monopoly can only suspend temporarily the competitive contradiction, which must reassert itself at some point and, while destroying super-profits, pushes forward the development of the forces of production.

Materialist theory is thus not suspended because of the concentration and centralization of capital (monopoly). Competition becomes more intense with the rise of monopoly and provides the driving force behind capital accumulation and foreign expansion.

The main body of the materialist theory of world economy can be defined as the theory of the accumulation of capital located in the context of countries. Countries are defined as territories controlled by distinct ruling classes. The vehicle for rule is the state. Weeks draws three derivatives from this theory:

> (1) the analysis of the conflicts and cooperation between the ruling classes of advanced capitalist countries (which lead to interimperialist wars);
> (2) the conflicts and cooperation between advanced capitalist ruling classes and ruling classes of underdeveloped countries ("articulation of modes of production"); and
> (3) conflicts between ruling classes and oppressed peoples ("the national question").[55]

Materialist theory conceptualizes the accumulation process explicitly in terms of the social relations of produciton through which the surplus product is produced and appropriated. Capital accumulation takes place through the progressive development of the forces of production by the exploitation of wage labor, rather than the redistribution of the surplus, as argued by dependency theory. Materialist theory explains why capitalism did not occur anywhere before the capitalist era; moreover, it predicts capital flows to developed and underdeveloped countries as part of the general movement of capital. This conforms to the actual patterns of capital flows in the world economy.

In extending materialist theory to an analysis of backwardness, Dore and Weeks focus on the barriers to the accumulation of capital in the underdeveloped countries imposed by precapitalist relations of production. Like Brenner, they focus on the necessity of expanded labor productivity as the source of capital accumulation.

We have seen that the source of capitalist profit is surplus value and that in mature capitalism competition constantly drives the capitalist to increase his profits by increasing the productivity of labor, i.e., by increasing the production of what Marx called relative surplus value. However, for increases in the productivity of labor to permanently increase the rate of profit (ignoring the organic composition of capital), these increases must lower the value of labor power; this can be accomplished only if the increases in productivity take place in those branches of production that directly supply the workers' subsistence or supply the means of production used in such branches. [56]

When the increases in labor productivity take place in branches of production that are unrelated to the production of workers' subsistence, e.g., luxury goods, then there will be a temporary super-profit for the firm first introducing the innovation. As other firms duplicate that innovation, prices will be driven down so that the price just equals the new lowered value of that commodity. The rate of profit will fall back to, or might even fall below the previous level, unless there is a corresponding drop in the amount of constant capital necessary per unit of commodity. Therefore, increases in productivity that are isolated in one branch of production lower the total value of the commodity while leaving the rate of surplus value the same.

Dore and Weeks note that one of the central facts of capitalist development is that "the advance of the forces of production continually results in the reduction of necessary time since the means of subsistence are produced capitalistically." There is a "progressive cheapening of commodities and a rising rate of exploitation."[57]

Such is not the case in those backward countries where a significant portion of the subsistence goods are produced in precapitalist relations of production. Because of this, necessary labor time, which determines the value of labor power, is determined outside the capitalist sector of the underdeveloped country. This means that

> capital accumulation in backward countries will continually tend to be checked by the inability of capital to raise the rate of surplus value through the cheapening of commodities produced with capitalist social relations. Put another way, the problem of capitalist accumulation in backward countries is that the rate of surplus value does not rise as rapidly as the forces of production advance in the capitalist sector. The immediate barrier to capitalist accumulation is not external, but internal—the persistence of pre-capitalist formations.[58]

This conclusion is based on the following analysis by Dore and Weeks: Foreign capital enters the backward country because it can obtain a higher rate of profit there than it can at home. This capital brings with it a production process that is more advanced than that of local capital, and while it might have been associated with a falling rate of profit at home, it will be able to yield a super-profit in the backward country because it will be able to utilize labor more productively than local capital. Foreign capital is thus able to produce commodities at a lower value. Dore and Weeks emphasize that the higher rate of profit obtained by foreign capital is not the result of lower wages in the backward country; it is rather the outcome of foreign capital's ability to produce commodities at a lower value, due to a more advanced technology. They argue that low wages are an advantage to local and foreign capital alike and cannot, therefore, be a source of competitive advantage. In their view this ability to produce commodities more cheaply by foreign capital accounts for the movement of capital from the advanced to backward countries.[59]

Once the international capitalist establishes production in the backward country, he sells the commodity above its value, but below the value of the same commodity produced by local capitalists in the same branch of production. Foreign capital will thus be able to capture the market for this commodity and local competitors will be driven out of business unless they adopt the more efficient labor process. Dore and Weeks argue that if this does not occur, other international capitalists will be drawn to the high rate of profit in this branch of industry, and that despite the "considerable barriers" to competition in these countries there will still be "a tendency for the price of the commodity to be driven towards its new (lower) average social value."[60]

As prices fall toward the new lower value, super-profits will be squeezed out. The new rate of profit will be higher, lower, or the same as the previous rate of profit before foreign capital entered this branch, depending upon the rate of surplus value and the organic composition of capital. Dore and Weeks argue that because a substantial proportion of the workers' subsistence goods are not produced capitalistically, "there will be a dominant tendency . . . for necessary labor time to decline *slower* than the total value of commodities (per unit) declines." Furthermore, foreign capital brings in labor processes that have a higher organic composition of capital than domestic labor processes in the backward countries, and this, together with the slow decline in necessary labor time, produces a "tendency for the rate of surplus value to rise slower than the organic composition of capital."[61]

It follows from this that the rate of profit will fall in those branches of production that are invaded by foreign capital. The result will be that foreign capital will then move on to other branches of production where it can again realize temporarily higher profits. According to Dore and Weeks, this "same cycle is repeated—temporary high profits by selling above specific value and below average value, competitive elimination of local, less efficient producers, the re-emergence of competition by approximately equally efficient (usually international) capitals, and a fall in the rate of profit."[62]

Dore and Weeks conclude that

> international capital progressively destroys profitability in branch after branch, eliminating the local bourgeoisie as an independent capitalist class as it does so. It is this process that leads to the frequently observed denationalization of the ownership of the means of production in backward countries.[63]

The barrier to accumulation is the precapitalist relations of production, which prevent necessary labor time from falling fast enough; therefore the rate of surplus value does not rise fast enough to compensate for the increasing organic composition of capital. In short, precapitalist relations present an obstacle to profitable accumulation in those backward countries where a substantial proportion of the means of subsistence are produced under precapitalist relations.

The outflow of capital (surplus value) from the backward countries is not the cause of persistent backwardness but rather the symptom, argue Dore and Weeks. In their criticism of surplus extraction theories of underdevelopment (Baran and Frank), they note that capital must continually throw itself back into production in order to reproduce itself, produce surplus value, and realize a profit, not run from it.[64] In the backward countries it would appear that capital is fleeing because the conditions for maintaining profitability are absent.

Dore and Weeks do not pretend to have taken more than a first step toward an analysis of the barriers to capital accumulation in the backward countries, based on an approach that begins from the sphere of production, rather than beginning and ending in the sphere of circulation as did earlier theories of underdevelopment. They admit that there are a number of problems that require further theoretical work. One major problem they see is the issue of the impact of the expansion of capital upon precapitalist relations of production. They tentatively see expansion in the imperialist epoch reinforcing and rigidifying precapitalist economic formations; but more analysis is needed to specify exactly how and why this takes place.[65]

Class, state, and capital accumulation

Another current in recent Marxist thought on imperialism is represented by the work of James Petras.[66] The major thrust of his work has been to analyze the role of the state in class relations and capital accumulation. Petras provides a critique of previous Marxist thought on imperialism, namely dependency/world-systems theory, and offers an alternative conceptualization with which to analyze imperialism.

According to Petras, the analytical categories associated with dependency theory, although they capture some of the essence of imperialism in the Third World, are too vague and abstract. The key theoretical categories in dependency theory—such as metropolitan centers, satellites, core, and periphery—all abstract from "the most decisive processes of class formation and social relations." Petras argues that:

> It is not the world system that begets change in social relations, but rather social forces that emerge and extend their activities that produce the world market. The transformations wrought within societies by their insertion in the world market must be seen as an ongoing reciprocal relationship: between the forces of production and relations of production within a social formation and those that operate through the world market. From the perspective of international political economy, a comprehensive analytical framework must focus on the structural variations and transformations with the capitalist mode of production and the state capacities for exercising hegemony, both with a social formation and on a global basis.[67]

In other words, dependency theory focuses on exchange relations and leaves out of the picture the crucial, system-defining mode of production and relations of production. This problem was noted earlier in Chapter 4. Petras's uniqueness is his call for a focus on state and class relations within the mode of production.

Petras's conceptual framework centers on the mode of production, capital accumulation, class relations, and the state. Although critical of dependency theory, Petras defines the capitalist mode of production in such a way that it includes the peripheral social formations. Crucial to his conception is the determination of social relations of production by the mode of production. Petras argues that "the process of bringing together labor, capital, and machinery to produce surplus value defines the capitalist mode of production."[68] The particular way in which labor is brought into the production process, the specific relations of production are, according to Petras, variable. In cases where there was a large enough pool of labor available and no alternative forms of economic activity, free wage labor became the predominant social relation of capital. In the periphery, on the other hand, "coercive forms of labor recruitment" were necessary, along with coercive bonding to the production process.[69]

Petras does not, therefore, see Third World countries in terms of the articulation of capitalist and precapitalist modes of production. In his view these countries are capitalist; however, the basis for this claim is essentially different from that of dependency/world systems theory. It rests on an analysis of the mode of production and relations of production rather than market relations and a profit-maximizing psychology.

In examining class formation and capital accumulation in the periphery, Petras focuses on the way class structures "cross each other" and the "various combinations of class symbiosis and interlock." The state is the "pivotal institution shaping both the class structure and serving as its instrument in the developing process." However, the capitalist mode of production "possesses certain imperatives (dynamic) to which state activity is directed," namely, "facilitating the accumulation of capital." The policy decisions of the state "reflect the efforts by different social interests within the class structure to shape specific allocations of state resources to improve their relative position."[70] In other words, the dominance of the mode of production determines the alternatives facing the ruling class and the role of the state: "Modes of production and their laws of motion are, in the final analysis, class relations and are thus determined by the capacity of each class to impose its terms of control over production, including the disposition of the surplus."[71]

For Petras imperialism is the international expression of "capitalism's mission" to advance the forces of production. This advance is the result of the "logic of capital accumulation, a process that is, by its nature, uneven, exploitative, and contradictory."[72] In the periphery the process of accumulation, stimulated from the outside, led to the growth of internal classes. These classes grew in concert with their capacity to extend and develop their external linkages with foreign capital. The peripheral class structure is composed of "interlocking classes, which integrate and organize production and structure political activity toward facilitating the free flow of capital and goods between areas."[73]

In the colonial period, according to Petras, the exploitation of colonies was carried out through political and social forms of domination that were extensions of metropolitan institutions. Precapialist social formations and traditional political authorities served as "surrogates of imperial authority." The process of surplus extraction was directly creating an essential contradiction "between imperial capitalism extracting surplus value from colonized classes; the national struggle was, in large part, unmediated by internal class and political conflicts."[74]

With national independence and the formation of the nation state, new social strata arise, situated between imperial capitalism and the neocolonial labor force. Members of these intermediary strata are drawn from "political movements, the university, the army, and the civil service." They are a propertyless group rooted in the state bureaucracy. Through the levers of government policy they are able to associate themselves with foreign and state enterprises, and thereby to acquire property in a process of bourgeoisification.

Imperial exploitation in this stage is mediated then by internal class forces: "Imperial policy is oriented toward manipulating national 'intermediaries' as a protective covering, whereas the dominant national strata struggle to increase their social preponderance, vis-à-vis their own labor force."[75] Control over the government apparatus led to economic opportunities for the national elite.

Historically there are three strategies or "types of class alliances for capital accumulation" in the periphery, according to Petras. The first is the "neocolonial model," where the national regime joins with imperial capital to intensify surplus extraction from the labor force. Government policy is characterized by "coercion, and a demobilized population, open access to raw materials, tax and other incentives to foreign investors."[76] The imperial state and imperial capital are dominant in internal as well as external relations.

The second model is the "developmental" strategy. In this case, the national bourgeoisie dominates foreign capital as well as the national labor force. Under this strategy, the national elite acts to extend peripheral capital accumulation and national capitalization at the expense of the labor force. The result is the reconstitution of capital in its own hands. National capitalization is promoted through increased tax revenues, extending ownership to majority shares, limited foreign capital activities, and selected nationalization. This approach, then, squeezes the foreign sector while maintaining the exploitation of the domestic labor force. The success of this strategy is precarious, according to Petras, because it "depends on the avoidance of confrontations with foreign sectors and the labor force. Threats from either side may cause the national bourgeoisie to seek alliances: with populists if threatened by foreign interests, or with imperial groups if threatened by the left."[77] There is thus a tendency for this alternative to degenerate into dependent neocolonialism or to transform itself into a populist regime.

The third, and final strategy, is the national-popular alliance, which is composed of the bourgeoisie, petite bourgeoisie, workers, and/or peasants. The methods of capitalization of the economy are based on nationalization of foreign firms and state financing. The success of such policies is limited, in Petras' view, because initially they amount to little more than redistribution. The regime has difficulty finding substitutes for foreign exploitation, and it is forced to resort to state financing, which must come at the expense of the working classes. The problem is that the working classes are brought into the alliance on the promise of increased consumption rather than basic changes in the mode of production. Thus the foreign contradiction is replaced with a domestic contradiction. This limits the usefulness of this strategy for promoting national capital accumulation and the interests of the national bourgeoisie.[78]

From its own point of view, the imperial state's role is domination of the periphery. The imperial state must ensure the initial entry of capital, its expansion and its survival. According to Petras, this entails creation of the formal economic machinery of the government, elimination or restriction of internal dissidents, minimization of external competition, and creation of the necessary financial infrastructure through loans and aid. Petras argues, that without the intervention of the imperial state to pave the way, foreign capital would not have been able to establish itself.[79]

Beyond the initial stage, the expanded accumulation of capital required the "elaboration of worldwide financial networks to finance a great diversity of activities in a variety of locales." A world monetary system had to be fashioned via financial agreements, the development banks, credit agreements, etc. This promoted the development of multinational corporations and provided them with "mobile capital to facilitate and accelerate the accumulation of capital and intensify the extraction of surplus" in the periphery.[80] The imperial state must also resort to direct and indirect military and economic pressure to ensure the survival of capital whenever it is threatened by nationalist, populist, or socialist movements.[81]

The imperialist state thus has a dual role, according to Petras: that of state-builder and that of state "disaggregator." The purpose of state-building is to "provide a variety of access points to shape policy priorities and agendas in order to avoid the use of 'external pressures,' to avoid having to act from the outside. Within the periphery, the alienated state articulates the interests of imperial capital by promoting growth on the basis of the exploitation of national classes."[82]

In contrast, the role of the imperial state in "disaggregating" the peripheral state is to destabilize governments that become unfriendly to imperial capital:

> The emergence of national movements, and eventually governments, sets the stage for redefining relations with the imperial power. Yet, in most instances, controlling the government is not identical with controlling the state; the critical means of production, as well as important fractions of the army/police/state bureaucracy, remain, at least initially, still tied to the metropolis and serve to countermand the order of the national government. In this context, the imperial power may seek to renegotiate terms of dependency or disarticulate the national regime's development project through a variety of measures, and through agencies located outside or inside the national state.[83]

In summary, the capitalist mode of production unleashes the inherently expansionary process of capital accumulation, which gives rise to foreign expansion and imperialism. Imperial capital, with the aid of the imperial state, reshapes the class structure in the periphery to suit imperial needs for the exploitation of labor in the periphery. The resulting class relations, conflict, and contradiction determine class interests, policy, and capital accumulation. The imperial and the peripheral state play key roles in class domination and in advancing the accumulation of international and peripheral capital.

What then are the limits to the development of industrial capitalism and the accumulation of national capital in the periphery? According to Petras, there is no hope for such advances when imperial domination is present. In such cases, national development is distorted to meet the needs of foreign capital and, at best, national capital. The imperial state in conjunction with the peripheral state skews resource allocation and distributes income away from laboring or marginal groups. The familiar lopsided development patterns are the result then of imperial domination.

Perhaps the only hope other than socialism in the periphery is state capitalism. Petras cites South Korea, Libya, Algeria, Ethiopia, Peru, and Venezuela as examples of state capitalism, where the state has taken over the major initiatives for capital accumulation in the absence of a strong national bourgeoisie. However, these countries risk the reintegration into the imperial network, because they are dependent on foreign finance capital and imperial technology. Even if they manage to resist reintegration, Petras argues that explosive internal contradictions lead to struggle between the working class and the state, and create the conditions for revolutionary socialism. [84]

Petras has applied his conceptual approach to the study of several different Third World countries and to much of the history of imperialism in the periphery. Although his work yields many insights, particularly into state/class relationships and imperialism, there are shortcomings in his conceptual approach. Petras's emphasis on class forces at the level of the state is surely overdue, but this is accomplished at the expense of any real analysis of the process of capital accumulation and relations of production. The connections between the mode of production, capital accumulation, and class forces are vague and mechanistic. This leads Petras to the same questionable conclusion of dependency/world systems theory: that Third World social formations are capitalist. The real strength of Petras's analysis is his conceptualization and analysis of the role of the state as a class-based entity. This represents an advance over previous Marxist works on imperialism.

Imperialism and the law of value

The recent work of Anwar Shaikh is an attempt to explain the phenomena of imperialism on the basis of Marx's law of value, extended to the ''free and unrestricted commerce between nations.''[85] He tries to show, by extending Marx's law of value and theory of money to the formation of international prices, that the causes of uneven development and the increasing inequality between developed and underdeveloped countries can be explained. He argues that Ricardo's theory of comparative costs has always been implicitly, if not explicitly, assumed correct by previous Marxists, who have sought the causes of imperialism in monopoly and the export of capital rather than the free and unhampered trade between countries.

Shaikh begins by showing Ricardo's theory of comparative costs to be false because the quantity theory of money, upon which it depends, is incorrect. The crucial factor is the operation of the quantity theory of money, so that prices fall or rise directly as the quantity of money rises or falls. According to Shaikh, however, the quantity theory of money is untenable. His argument is based on Marx's critique of the quantity theory and Marx's own theory of money. In Shaikh's view, Marx argues that a pure increase in the supply of gold divorced from any change in the value of gold will not generally result in an increase in prices.

> An increased supply of gold can lead to an increase in effective demand, either directly insofar as it is spent by its original owners, or indirectly because it will expand bank reserves and the supply of loanable money-capital, which will tend to drive down interest rates, which may in turn increase capitalist borrowing for investment. However, even though this increase in effective demand may temporarily increase prices of some commodities, and hence raise the profits in some sectors, it must eventually lead to an expansion of production to meet the new demand. And as production expands prices will fall until (all other things being equal) they regain their original levels.[86]

Of course the assumption of full employment "is a vulgar fantasy."[87]

Applying this to the case of international exchange, Shaikh argues that the capitalists in Portugal are able to undersell their English competitors in the wine and cloth markets, which results in an outflow of gold from England and an inflow of gold into Portugal. This means that the supply of gold increases in Portugal and decreases in England. Instead of these pure changes in the supply of gold leading to changes in price levels, "the primary effect of an outflow of gold from England will be to diminish the supply of loanable money capital." And as cloth and wine production in England fall, it will also create a fall in the demand for money capital. The continuing drain of gold will raise interest rates, and thus diminish investments in other commodities, causing a general decline in English output.[88]

On the other hand, gold flowing into Portugal will have the opposite effects. Part of the inflow of gold will be absorbed in circulation as the production of wine and cloth expands, and part will be absorbed in the form of bank reserves. This will increase the supply of loanable money, lower interest rates, and expand investment and general production.[89]

Foreign trade in this instance will lead to a chronic trade surplus in Portugal and a chronic trade deficit in England, balanced by a continued outflow of gold. On the basis of commodity flows alone this situation will end in a collapse of the English currency and the collapse of trade, according to Shaikh. However, at some point Portuguese capitalists will find it advantageous to lend their increasing money capital abroad to take advantage of the rising interest rates in England due to the shrinking English reserves. The short-term financial capital flow will cause the rate of interest to reverse itself, to fall in England and rise in Portugal, until the two rates equalize.[90]

While this allows England to finance its chronic trade deficit by short-term international borrowing, it eventually has to pay back the loans plus interest, so that in the end England, "beset by chronic trade deficits and mounting debts, . . . must eventually succumb."[91]

According to Shaikh's analysis, trade between countries with approximately the same level of development will have a different trade pattern; and assuming, as in the neoclassical model, that both countries possess the same technology and level of productivity, trade will be determined by such factors as climate, location, availability of resources, experience, inventions, and most importantly, according to Shaikh, the competitive struggle among capitalists. In this case, it is expected that a more or less balanced trade pattern will emerge, and advantages (in particular commodities) in the short run will be constantly shifting back and forth.[92]

Shaikh concludes his analysis of commodity flows in international trade by saying that:

> these results represent automatic tendencies of "free" and *unhampered* trade among capitalist nations at different levels of development. It is not monopoly or conspiracy upon which uneven development rests, but free competition itself; "free" trade is as much a mechanism for the concentration and centralization of international capital as "free" exchange within a capitalist nation is for the concentration and centralization of domestic capital.[93]

In other words, the forces of uneven development operate internationally as well as nationally, and are predicated on free competition of capital.

According to Shaikh, the superiority of the developed capitalist country over the underdeveloped capitalist country lies in its more developed forces of production, i.e., its superior technology and a more conditioned work force. It is argued that even in the case where identical technologies are used in both countries, the productivity of the workers in the developed country will be higher. Further, the means of production will not be traded between the two countries, as each uses means of production appropriate to its own general level of development. While the capitalists of the backward countries can and do adopt the superior technologies of the developed ones, in general, Shaikh argues, "the vastly greater cost and scale of advanced techniques, the complex interdependence required among different techniques for any one to be viable, and the greater socialization required of the work force," work against the adoption of such techniques.[94]

Therefore, "modernization" as the result of trade alone seems to be negated. The factors that work against "modernization," however, work favorably concerning foreign direct investment by the capitalists in the developed counries who "have much larger capitals available for investment, are familiar with modern techniques, [and] have access to all the necessary skilled workers."[95]

Perhaps the most important factor favoring foreign direct investment in the underdeveloped countries is low wages. If transportation costs are ignored, Shaikh argues, the same price must rule everywhere and the cost of building and supplying a plant will be the same everywhere in the world. Therefore, the only difference can be in the cost of labor power, resulting from labor productivity and wage rates. While Shaikh considers other factors important to such investment decisions, cheap wage labor is the only general characteristic of all underdeveloped countries that affects investment decisions in all branches of production.[96]

Export industries are initially the target of foreign investors who, because of superior technology, can make exceptional profits in these sectors. Foreign investment will also take place in sectors that produce for domestic consumption only if the superior technology and the lower net cost of labor power enable the foreign capitalist to make a higher profit than he would at home. The profitability of existing domestic investment in the backward countries is not necessarily a guide to the profitability of foreign investment in these branches of production.[97]

Shaikh argues that competition among foreign capitals over superprofits will result in an increase in supply and a fall in price that will reduce excess profits. The process will stop when in these branches of industry the rate of profit on foreign capital is the same as it is in the developed capitalist countries. As the prices of production are driven down below previously existing prices, domestic capitalists in these branches will be driven out of business and will be forced into areas that are not affected by foreign domination.[98]

In answer to the question of whether foreign direct investment helps to overcome or to worsen the problems created by competition from foreign imports, Shaikh argues that domestic capital is absolutely worse off, inasmuch as "first their industries are ruined by cheap imports, and then those that survive are taken over by foreign capital!"[99] Shaikh goes on to argue that foreign capitalists are not limited to invading existing industries in the backward country, but will set up plants abroad in opposition to their competitors at home, i.e., establish what has come to be called an "export platform," and export the cheaper commodities (due to cheap labor in the backward countries) back home.[100]

Foreign direct investment on the one hand worsens the trade position of the backward "nation as a whole" by lowering the prices of exports, thus causing a deterioration in the terms of trade. On the other hand, the transplanting industries from the developed to the underdeveloped capitalist countries improves the export capability of the underdeveloped country, which "will tend to improve the underdeveloped nation's balance of trade, and create new avenues of employment for its labor."[101] However, while foreign capital can provide an offset to the chronic balance of trade deficits,

> it does so only at the expense of an eventual capital outflow (surplus-value transferred out in the form of repatriated profits), declining terms of trade, and increased foreign domination. Instead of negating international inequality therefore, foreign investment tightens the grip of the strong over the weak—not merely through monopoly and state power, but through "free" competition itself.[102]

In summary, Shaikh's analysis shows that the law of uneven development and the concentration and centralization of capital on a world scale manifest themselves in a continuous widening of the gap between the developed and underdeveloped capitalist countries on account of the "necessary form of development" of capitalism and free trade. This analysis is congruent with Marx's derivation of the laws of motion of capitalism based on free competition and free and equal exchange between capitalist nations.

Shaikh's analysis and conclusions concerning imperialism call into question all previous Marxist theories of imperialism that identify imperialism with the rise of monopoly and the export of capital. This is not to say that their analysis of the relationship between monopoly and the export of capital is wrong, but that this is not the source of imperialism. In Shaikh's view, imperialism is inherent in the capitalist mode of production from the very beginning when trade takes place between capitalist countries and when foreign expansion is limited to commodity exports. Nonetheless, with the rise of monopoly and the export of capital there does occur that qualitative change in the character of the system which manifests itself in intense interimperialist rivalries brought on by heightened competition between the monopoly establishments in different nations.

However, it seems confusing to call *this* stage imperialism, and previous stages something else, when Shaikh's analysis shows imperialism to be present from the very beginning. Presumably Shaikh would not disagree that imperialism takes on different forms or intensifies as capitalism develops. What he is arguing is that the generic roots of imperialism lie within the capitalist mode of production itself, and therefore must have been present from the very beginning.

In assessing Shaikh's theory of international exchange and imperialism, it should be noted that he does not pretend to have provided a complete analysis but only a beginning. He cites two major problems that must be resolved before this analysis can be considered complete. The first is a fuller development of Marx's theory of money, to include different forms of money and credit and the "confrontation" of more modern theories of money. The second problem is the question of whether the rise of monopoly is the antithesis of competition and if so, whether "it signals the end of the law of value and the beginning of the era of monopoly capital."[103] This issue is addressed in part by Weeks earlier in this chapter, and will be discussed more fully in Appendix I.

There are a number of other problems as well: the problem of the imperialism of free trade being rooted in merchant capital, which predates industrial capital, and the problem of applying the law of value to underdeveloped countries where a large number of commodities originate in noncapitalist sectors. Another related problem is the theoretical validity of international applications of the transformation of values into prices.

The usefulness of Shaikh's work is that it extends the law of value, which is crucial to Marx's understanding of capitalism, to an analysis of capitalist foreign expansion, i.e., imperialism. In so doing, he shows that the forces of foreign capitalist expansion and imperialism are rooted in free competition, free trade, and commodity exchange. His theoretical analysis extends the understanding of imperialism from a Marxist perspective.

The internationalization of capital

The origins of this current of recent Marxist thought can be traced to the work of Christian Palloix,[104] which has been extended and applied by several others, including James Cypher, Pat Clawson, and David Barkin.[105] One of the fundamental tenets of this theory is that capitalism has an inherent tendency to internationalize itself and thereby to expand the reproduction of the means of production and the relations of production on a world scale. In this view, capitalism breaks down all precapitalist modes of production and capital is compelled to accumulate as rapidly as possible the world over. This directly challenges the conclusions of previous Marxist thought.[106]

The dynamics of the internationalization of capital as derived by Christian Palloix are based on Marx's analysis of the circuits of capital in Volume II of *Capital*. Capital is conceptualized as a self-expanding value that represents not only an expansion of relations of production but also a movement of capital through stages or circuits. There are three essential stages that make up the circuits of capital: money, commodity, and production. These circuits represent the self-expansion of social capital and are represented by the following formula[107]:

The Circuits of Capital

$$
\overbrace{M\text{-}C \left\{ \begin{array}{l} M\text{-}L \\ M\text{-}Mp \end{array} \right. \overbrace{\ldots P \ldots C'\text{-}M'\text{-}C'}^{\text{II}} \left\{ \begin{array}{l} M\text{-}L \\ M\text{-}Mp \end{array} \right. \ldots P' \ldots C'}^{\text{I}}
$$
$$
\underbrace{\phantom{M\text{-}C \left\{ \begin{array}{l} M\text{-}L \\ M\text{-}Mp \end{array} \right. \ldots P \ldots C'\text{-}M'\text{-}C' \left\{ \begin{array}{l} M\text{-}L \\ M\text{-}Mp \end{array} \right. \ldots P' \ldots C'}}_{\text{III}}
$$

Circuit I represents the circuit of money capital (M . . . M'), Circuit II represents the circuit of productive capital (P . . . P'), and Circuit III is the circuit of commodity capital (C . . . C').[108]

Industrial capital, i.e., that capital engaged in capitalist production, is the only form that integrates all three circuits of forms of capital. The self-expansion of capital calls attention to the way in which capital is divided up into industrial and financial branches and into departments. The capital relation is not only reproduced but extended in the process of self-expansion. Capital exists and is reproduced with the unity of production and of circulation.[109]

The internationalization of this self-expanding process of social capital is necessitated by the fact that, beyond some point, the unity of the three circuits can no longer be fully realized within a single capitalist formation; more specifically, the commodity form is no longer produced within one country. According to Palloix, the "commodity or rather the commodity-group, can only be conceptualized, produced, and realized at the level of the world markets."[110] The internationalization of capital is part of a process that results from the "world-wide universality of the capitalist mode of production."[111] Competition is thought to be one of the underlying forces behind this movement.[112]

This creates both a tendency toward the equalization of the conditions of production and exchange worldwide, and a tendency toward the differentiation of production and exchange worldwide. According to Palloix, internationalization manifests itself as the expression of national divisions, universality of the capitalist mode of production, and the law of uneven development.[113] The international and the national mirror each other as well as amplify each other. They are both shaped by and molded by capital:

> Internationalization has its roots in the law of uneven development; it assures the reproduction of world-wide inequalities, not as a final goal of capital, but as a condition of increasing the rate of surplus value through M–L, through M–MP, and through their fusion within the process of production.[114]

Marx argues in Volume II of *Capital* that industrial capital draws diverse modes of social production into the process of circulation and thus into the circuit of industrial capital. The capitalist mode of production is conditional on modes of production "lying outside its own stage of development." Marx goes on to write:

> But it is the tendency of the capitalist mode of production to transform all production as much as possible into commodity production. The mainspring by which this is accomplished is precisely the involvement of all production into the capitalist circulation process. And developed commodity production itself is capitalist commodity production. The intervention of industrial capital promotes transformation everywhere, but with it also the transformation of all direct producers into wage-laborers.[115]

This forms the basis for the transformation of precapitalist modes of production and for the internationalization of capital, although Marx did not take it this far.

Historically the internationalization of capital has taken place in three stages, which correspond to the three circuits of capital: the early importance of commodity capital in expanding foreign trade, the later importance of money capital in the form of the export of capital noted by Lenin, and the more recent importance of the expansion of productive capital worldwide, giving rise to the multinational corporation. Let us elaborate on each of these three stages and their relationship to the circuits of capital.

In the first stage, the circuit of commodity capital is internationalized. This gives rise to the world market; it presupposes only commodity production on a world scale. The dynamic characteristic of the internationalization of the commodity capital circuit is continuous trade expansion. During this stage, capitalism did not transform the relations of production it found in the peripheral societies; it does, however, contribute "to pressures forcing a transition to capitalist relations of production," according to Clawson. Clawson goes on to argue that industrialization is against the interests of the imperialists, who are interested only in cheap raw materials and markets. It is also against the interests of the local ruling classes, who want to remain in the "good graces" of the imperialists and are content to exploit their own labor force through the "traditional mechanisms of land-leasing, commerce, and money-lending."[116] In other words, when precapitalist social formations are linked to the capitalist mode of production internationally through the commodity-capital circuit, "this link may fail to dissolve and may in fact perpetuate and strengthen the [noncapitalist mode of production]."[117]

The transition to capitalist relations of production takes place in the second stage, when the circuit of money capital is internationalized. This stage coincides with Lenin's conception of imperialism. The ultimate force behind the internationalization of money capital is capitalism's inner tendency to transform all production into developed commodity production. According to Marx, the "intervention of industrial capital promotes this transformation everywhere, but with it also the transformation of all direct producers into wage-laborers."[118] This stage is characterized by primitive accumulation and is facilitated by the internationalization of the circuit of money capital. The latter promotes both the accumulation of money capital on a scale necessary for capitalist production, and capitalist relations of production. These represent the "twin elements of the internationalization of the circuit of money-capital."[119]

The final stage, the internalization of productive capital, has only just recently begun to take place. The dominance of the capitalist mode of production in the Third World has created a new industrial bourgeoisie that is determined to increase its role in the world economy. According to Clawson, this class is trying to "cement the connections between their local economies and the world economy," and is "pushing for the internationalization of production."[120] The internationalization of production reinforces the internationalization of the other circuits and spreads capitalist relations of production more widely. This extends the international division of labor and accelerates the tendency toward industrialization in the Third World. At the same time it ties the Third World more closely into the process of international capital accumulation. The predominant features of this stage are the new international division of labor and the rapid industrialization of several Third World countries.[121]

The basic argument here is that the spread of capitalism throughout the world is the result of the laws of motion of capitalism or, more specifically, the laws of capital accumulation. In this view, the transformation of the Third World is understood as the result of the dynamics of the particular period in the internationalization of capital and the particular response of the precapitalist social formation. Although on one level it appears that the internationalization of capital equalizes capitalist development everywhere, in fact it "reinforces uneven development by allowing imperialist countries to develop more rapidly."[122]

The internationalization of capital view has not been completely worked out. Perhaps the biggest shortcoming is the awkwardness with which the move is made from abstract circuits of capital to the actual concrete historical specification of the internationalization of capital. Of particular importance here is the problem of articulation of modes of production, discussed earlier in this chapter. The main focus of the internationalization of capital view has been on the internationalization of the capital accumulation process via the three circuits of capital, rather than on the specifics of articulation. In terms of the latter, positive reference is made to the work of Pierre-Phillipe Rey by Clawson and Cypher.[123] These two views can thus be seen as complementary, with the internationalization of capital school providing a more rigorous theoretical underpinning for the international expansion of capitalism as well as for the rise of capitalism in the Third World.

Although the internationalization of capital approach has proven useful in several case studies, similar problems emerge in them.[124] There appears to be a great deal of surface plausibility, yet there is a lack of in-depth understanding. Perhaps the greatest merit of this approach is that the analysis is based on the integration of the three moments of production (production, circulation, and distribution) through the circuit of capital. It thus avoids the bias and shortcomings of previous Marxist analyses based on the sphere of exchange only.

Conclusion

The diversity and complexity of recent Marxist thought on imperialism is striking. Many of the shortcomings of previous Marxist theory have been corrected and there is a more thorough understanding of the rise of capitalism, its inner nature and dynamic, the causes of foreign expansion, and the impact of capitalism on noncapitalist societies. The magnitude of such an undertaking is certainly gigantic and its scope far-reaching, especially when compared to the narrow disciplinary and subdisciplinary focus of the work of most non-Marxist social scientists.

The recent currents of Marxist thought on imperialism mark off a new stage in the development of a Marxist theory of imperialism. This stage represents a fundamental break with earlier postwar Marxist theory.

The intellectual history of the Marxist theory of imperialism has had four fairly distinct stages, beginning with the work of Marx and Engels in the first half of the nineteenth century. The early Marxists at the turn of the century mark a second stage. The third stage, which begins after World War II and extends to the early 1970s, includes the work of those associated with monopoly capital/dependency–world systems/unequal exchange theories, and culminates in the grand synthesis by Samir Amin. The mid-seventies mark the beginning of the now current fourth stage in the development of the Marxist theory of imperialism.

Each stage represents efforts to develop and extend the theory of imperialism by drawing on past theory and extending it to take account of new phases in the development of capitalism. There have been many twists and turns, and much overlap, so it is hard to trace a logical evolution of thought. As Robert Heilbroner has noted "the work of Marx's followers has been characterized by bitter divisions and conflicting interpretations of Marx's work," so that it is "difficult to find the elements that unify the whole."[125] However, there does seem to be a sort of rough correspondence between the stages of thought and the stages of the internationalization of capital. It might be more than coincidence that the current emphasis on production and relations of production coincides with the current period of the internationalization of productive capital.

In any event, the strands of thought discussed in this chapter add considerable theoretical depth to the theory of imperialism, despite a lack of theoretical integration or synthesis among the various currents and between current theorizing and previous Marxist theory. One of the most significant contributions has been to show the specifically capitalist nature of imperialism in terms of a mode of production with specific productive relations and in terms of the logic of capital accumulation. Second, the inclusion of class analysis at the point of production as well as at the level of the state provide a dimension missing in previous theory. Third, the recognition of transitional historical stages between successive modes of production casts the "blockage of economic development" in an entirely different light. Fourth, the enriched understanding of capitalist competition has produced a greater understanding of the nature of capital and capitalist tendencies hitherto misunderstood. Finally, imperialism is seen as an extension of the central dynamic of capitalism on a world scale, extending both capitalism and uneven development. The process of capitalist development in the Third World is subject to the laws of international capital accumulation and the dynamic set in motion by the articulation of foreign with domestic modes of production.

These current analyses take us a long way from previous Marxist theory. Although there are many differences between these new currents and past theory, the most fundamental is the recent emphasis on the sphere of production and relations of production. The basic revisions of Marx's methodological and conceptual approach undertaken in the past have been shown to be misinformed and the source of serious theoretical problems. The newest group of Marxists applies Marx's method, conceptualization, and theoretical apparatus skillfully and flexibly, but not dogmatically or mechanistically. Fresh new interpretations and extensions of Marx's analysis have brought new life to the Marxist intellectual tradition rather than a new orthodoxy.

Although these recent currents of Marxist thought on imperialism correct many of the deficiencies of previous theory, add considerable depth, and extend the Marxist theory of imperialism, they are still incomplete and represent in most cases only initial forays into new areas. Furthermore, the current literature is fragmented and lacks integration, despite the strongly held belief by Marxists in the organic nature of society. Foster-Carter has noted the disciplinary biases of some of the current literature. In his evocative description, recent Marxist analysis is "like a tide going out, [creating] little rock pools increasingly unconnected to one another." He chastises Marxists for conducting narrow and circumscribed discussions that deal with issues separately, "without thought of their mutual implications," and he recommends a long-overdue theoretical synthesis.[126]

Foster-Carter's call for a theoretical synthesis was made in 1978. In retrospect, his recommendation seems premature. In the years since 1978 additional currents of thought have emerged, yet more "rock pools" seemingly unconnected to each other. Yet this should not be seen as a failure of synthesis, but as further progress along the path to an integrated theory of imperialism, for significant gains have been made in important aspects of the theory of imperialism. Moreover, some fragmentation is necessary, indeed is desirable, if Marxists are to construct a theory of imperialism that can explain the economic, social, political, historical, and ideological aspects of imperialism.

In Marxist theory, as compared with mainstream social science, there already exists a high level of integration. As is evident in this chapter, Marxist economists, sociologists, political scientists, and historians, in spite of their disciplinary focus, have a great deal in common, certainly more than their non-Marxist counterparts. And although synthesis and integration of contemporary Marxist theory is still necessary, so is the continuation of research along narrow fronts, for it is important to avoid a premature, ill-founded synthesis.[127] The aim is to produce a well-founded, well-integrated theory of imperialism. This calls for work on all fronts.

There is no reason not to suppose that such an outcome is far off. The rapid growth of literature on imperialism in the postwar period has been the result of a large increase in the number of Marxist "intellectuals," particularly in the United States (where there were very few before the 1960s) but also in Europe and in Third World countries. The 1960s and early 1970s brought a radicalization of students as well as of some established scholars who were able to go on to carry out study and research. This group accounts for much of the recent literature on imperialism.

The development of the Marxist theory of imperialism can be seen in terms of its historical development and in terms of the sociology of knowledge. In the Kuhnian jargon of "scientific revolutions," the development of Marxist theory of imperialism, and of Marxism in general, represents an unfinished revolution. The objective, although not the ultimate objective, is to build an integrated theory of imperialism as part of a more general Marxist theory. The work of Marxists has been that of "problem solving" and "paradigm building" in a not always smooth or continuous process of Marxist intellectual historical development. Nonetheless, in the postwar period an enormous advance has been made in the development of a theory of imperialism. This forward movement shows no signs of abating; indeed it should accelerate given the forces already set in motion.

A Critique of Baran and Sweezy

Paul Baran and Paul Sweezy's theory of monopoly capitalism, notwithstanding its large following, has been subjected to far-reaching criticism from all sides.[1] For many Marxists the most serious issue is their break with Marx's approach on what will be shown here to be highly questionable grounds.

Baran and Sweezy derive the law of the tendency for the surplus to rise relatively from an incomplete analysis (even when restricted to the sphere of circulation) of the generation of surplus. In monopoly enterprises costs tend to decline while prices remain constant or increase. This causes the surplus to rise. But what happens, under conditions of monopoly, to the surplus that is "generated" in the competitive branches of production? The interaction between competitive and monopoly branches of production is completely ignored by Baran and Sweezy. Yet, while monopoly enterprises dominate the most important branches of production, competitive branches are by no means insignificant. And no one would dispute that the surplus, or surplus value for that matter, rises absolutely in competitive as well as monopoly capitalism. No general tendency for the surplus can be derived without a complete analysis of the interaction between different branches of production.

Moreover, no tendency for the surplus to rise relatively has been convincingly established. There is no empirical evidence of continuously widening profit margins for monopoly enterprises. The empirical evidence offered by Baran and Sweezy shows only a very slight increase and is highly dependent on classification of all government spending as surplus. This identification has been seriously questioned by several critics, who conclude that the tendency for the surplus to rise is not proven.[2]

A third issue of major importance is Baran and Sweezy's contention that stagnation is the natural state of capitalism, interrupted by periods of expansion caused by external stimuli. This is the exact opposite of Marx's emphasis on the dynamic aspects of capital accumulation, periodically interrupted by crises. Underlying Baran and Sweezy's contention is an underconsumptionist theory of crisis, developed in an earlier work by Sweezy.[3]

Sweezy had abandoned Marx's theory of crisis, based on the tendency for the rate of profit to fall, in favor of a theory of realization crisis, according to which capitalists are forced to sell below value and thus must accept a decline in the rate of profit. According to Sweezy, the ultimate cause of a realization crisis is an imbalance between the rates of growth in departments I and II. In capitalism there is a tendency to use more and more machines and materials per worker, which means that the ratio of the rate of growth of consumption to the rate of growth of means of production declines. Therefore

> it follows that there is an inherent tendency for the growth in consumption to fall behind the growth in the output of consumption goods. As has already been pointed out, this tendency may express itself either in crises or in stagnation, or in both.[4]

Here Sweezy argues that a realization crisis may manifest itself in either crisis or stagnation, but later he argues that the normal tendency of capitalism is toward stagnation. Crises disappear altogether from his analysis.[5]

Further, Sweezy argues that it is

> equally logical to speak of a tendency for the provision of means of production to exceed the requirements for means of production. Properly understood, then, "underconsumption" and "overproduction" are opposite sides of the same coin.... The label used is a matter of taste, the point of origin a relatively unimportant detail dependent upon a multitude of particular circumstances.[6]

In other words, underconsumption and overproduction are merely different manifestations of one and the same thing, underconsumption.

The major problem with Sweezy's analysis is that it is restricted to the sphere of circulation and divorced from the labor theory of value.

For Sweezy, the sphere of circulation determines the sphere of production. In other words, production gears itself to the dictates of the market, i.e., the level of effective demand. For Marx, production and the contradiction between capital and labor are primary, not the circulation of commodities and distribution. It seems highly unlikely that Marx, had he developed a complete theory of economic crises, would have analyzed and explained them in a way that negated his entire previous analysis of the laws of motion of capitalism.[7]

Exactly what role underconsumption plays in economic crises has been a source of considerable debate among Marxists, but that question lies outside the scope of this book.[8] Several other difficulties with Baran and Sweezy's analysis call for commentary here.

First, Sweezy is wrong when he asserts that there can be no expanded reproduction with a proportional growth in consumption goods and means of production and with a rising ratio of means of production to workers. The error lies in Sweezy's assumption that increasing the output of producers' goods can only increase the production of consumption goods. This ignores the fact that producers' goods can be used in the production of more producers' goods. Taking this into consideration, one can show *theoretically*, and contrary to Sweezy's analysis, that the expanded reproduction of capital can take place.[9]

Second, it has been shown that underconsumption, rather than causing crises, is the *result* of crises originating in the sphere of production. Overproduction, or overaccumulation of *capital*, eventually removes the conditions of profitability. The realization crisis is the result of the falling rate of profit, which falls because less variable capital is advanced relative to total capital. This in turn results in a distribution of income that leads to underconsumption.[10]

A third problem with underconsumptionism is that stagnation is *not* a permanent state of capitalism. Marx sees stagnation as a way the system temporarily reestablishes the conditions of profitability, through a "withdrawal" and "partial destruction" of capital, part of which is accomplished in the sphere of circulation when commodities are sold below their value. Capitalists do not realize all the surplus value contained in these commodities and part of their capital is destroyed. Thus, the "realization crisis is not the cause of crisis, and it is not even simply a result of crisis, it is a result of crisis which helps to secure the condition of expansion."[11] Crises and expansion are both part of the "elementary logic," as Baran and Sweezy call it, of capitalism, and no external factors need be brought in. Crisis and expansion are both part of a dialectical process that is largely ignored by Baran and Sweezy.[12]

This analysis calls into question the whole notion of stagnation and surplus absorption in monopoly capitalism. Periods of expansion do not result from external stimuli; stagnation itself reproduces the conditions of a new expansion. In this view, the expansion that followed the Great Depression was not altogether due to military spending and the aftermath of the war. The destruction of capital in the 1930s and the physical destruction and reorganization of capital caused by World War II restored profitability, and this paved the way for war spending and deficit spending to exert a stimulating effect on the economy. More importantly, it is argued that this paved the way for U.S. imperialism, which enabled U.S. capitalists to counteract the tendency toward the overproduction of capital and the falling rate of profit at least up until the late 1960s. The ensuing crisis of profitability perhaps accounts for the current downward spiral.[13]

The fourth theoretical issue concerns the usefulness of replacing surplus value with the concept of economic surplus. As was noted in Chapter 3, there is no generic relationship between the concepts of surplus and of surplus value. It has been contended that the concept of surplus "has different uses and illuminates different aspects of reality."[14] It will be useful to discuss the differences between these two concepts and to evaluate Baran and Sweezy's contention that surplus value is no longer a useful concept in the analysis of contemporary capitalism.

The crucial difference between the two concepts is the "historical generality of economic surplus and the historical specificity of surplus value." This means that the concept of economic surplus can be used to analyze any mode of production, whereas surplus value can be applied only to those societies where commodities are produced by free wage labor, i.e., capitalism. According to Barclay and Stengel,

> The reason for this limitation is that, like all of Marx's concepts, surplus value is relational...that is to say that it describes a particular social relation, a dialectic of class conflict between producers and non-producers in a particular historical period.[15]

On the other hand,

> the concept of the economic surplus is not built upon the social relations of production. It is defined in the aggregate, for society as a whole, and cannot be represented as the sum of the surpluses deriving from the relations between individual laborer and capitalist. Thus, it ignores the dialectics of production, exploitation, and class conflict which are contained in the labor process [sphere of production].[16]

This difference goes far toward explaining the confusion in *Monopoly Capital* over the generation and absorption of economic surplus. Economic surplus is a macro concept with an incomplete micro foundation; more importantly, it is not explicitly related to exploitation. It is essentially a static concept, despite Baran and Sweezy's attempt to force it into a dynamic analysis of the laws of motion of monopoly capitalism. What they achieve is not a dynamic analysis but one comparing alternative static states that has obvious shortcomings in explaining the dynamic process of capitalist accumulation.[17] This is a major flaw in Baran and Sweezy's theory of monopoly capitalism.

It has been argued that the usefulness of the concept of economic surplus lies in its ability to show more clearly the contradiction between what a society is and what it could be. More specifically, it allows one to focus on the ways a particular society or mode of production disposes of its economic surplus and to compare this with some as yet nonexisting "more rational order." Barclay and Stengel note that, as "a result, while surplus value goes behind the appearances of the market to a deeper level of social relations, economic surplus transcends these appearances by going to the plain of pure reason." In other words, it provides a kind of "benchmark by which capitalist society...is found wanting."[18]

This concept, however, reveals neither the laws of motion of capitalist society nor exactly what must be changed to achieve a more rational society. On the other hand, the concept of surplus value does reveal this:

> Surplus value, by definition, is at the disposal of the capitalist class, for accumulation, luxury consumption, or waste. The capitalist class by virtue of its exclusive ownership of the means of production, has the power and position to decide how labor is employed, how the resources of

the society are used, and, consequently, what is produced. In order to move in the direction of a more rationally ordered society, it follows that this power over the disposal of surplus value must be wrested from the capitalist class by its dialectical opposite, the proletariat.[19]

Barclay and Stengel argue that when analyzing irrationality, waste, and the form of growth under monopoly capitalism, the concept of economic surplus comes into its own.[20] However, Baran and Sweezy's analysis of these aspects of monopoly capitalism, though couched in terms of surplus, is not dependent upon that concept. The claim that the sales effort and arms production are wasteful and not socially useful could be made just as easily and convincingly without the concept of surplus, as some liberal economists have done. However, such a claim would certainly be more meaningful if it were explained in terms of the concept of surplus value, which reveals the laws of capitalist motion and the irrationality and waste inherent in the process of capital accumulation.

The final issue to be dealt with here is whether the law of value is applicable to monopoly capitalism. Shinzaburo Koshimura has shown that an extension of Marx's analysis based on the labor theory of value to the monopoly stage of capitalism is perfectly legitimate and produces conclusions consistent with Marx's conclusions on monopoly in Volume III of *Capital*.[21] For whatever reason, Baran and Sweezy completely ignore the latter. It will be useful to reproduce here Marx's insight into the effect monopoly would have on the law of value:

> if equalization of surplus-value into average profit meets with obstacles in the various spheres of production in the form of artificial or natural monopolies, and particularly monopoly in landed property, so that a monopoly price becomes possible, which rises above the price of production and above the value of the commodities affected by such a monopoly, then the limits imposed by the value of the commodities would not thereby be removed. The monopoly price of certain commodities would merely transfer a portion of the profit of the other commodity-producers to the commodities having the monopoly price. A local disturbance in the distribution of the surplus-value among the various spheres of production would indirectly take place, but it would leave the limit of this surplus-value itself unaltered....The limits within which the monopoly price would affect the normal regulation of the prices of commodities would be firmly fixed and accurately calculable.[22]

Koshimura extends Marx's analysis and argues that the "logic of monopoly prices and monopoly profit is nothing but an extension of the theory of value," and that this whole question must be answered in terms of the "process of production and circulation."[23]

Koshimura then proceeds to show how monopoly affects the production cycle, the interconnections between branches, and the creation and distribution of surplus value. He establishes the limits within which monopoly price would affect the normal regulation of the prices of commodities. Koshimura concludes that monopoly capitalism is another stage in the unfolding of the law of value, and that the usefulness of the labor theory of value does not stop when capitalism reaches its monopoly stage, but goes on to explain how the laws of motion of capitalism are modified, not replaced by new laws, under conditions of monopoly.

Clearly Marx's "analytical model" could not have depended upon the "assumption of competition," at least not the kind of competition that Baran and Sweezy have in mind. What they mean by competition— a large number of sellers in a particular branch of production—is what the neoclassical economists mean. However, Marx, certainly aware of the effect of numbers on price in the sphere of circulation, saw that the limitation of the number of sellers in any particular branch in no way reduced the competition between capitals in the sphere of production. In fact, as Baran and Sweezy note, the form that competition takes in monopoly capitalism is in many ways more intense; however, because their analysis is limited to the sphere of circulation, the real essence of competition in capitalism is lost.

According to Marx, the essence of competition is the free movement of capital, which depends upon the existence of free wage labor. As competition gives rise to monopoly, competition is intensified, not negated, as capital is able to escape the confines of one branch of production and the confines of one country.[24] It was this latter aspect of monopoly capitalism that the early Marxists, except Luxemburg, argued was the essence of imperialism, the extension of capital, and the intensification of the worldwide competition between capitals. Only Lenin argued that competition was not negated at the national level.

Monopoly certainly has an impact in the sphere of circulation. However, it does not negate the fundamental laws of motion of capitalism, nor does it make Marx's approach and method obsolete. Marxist analysis, with its focus on the sphere of production, reveals the real nature of capitalism and its inner workings. It is not accidental that Baran and Sweezy, who use a different approach and method, fail to show how the relations of production, exploitation, and capital accumulation combine to determine the laws of motion of monopoly capitalism. These crucial factors are totally absent from their work. In short, there is no convincing evidence that monopoly negates the basic essence of the capitalist mode of production as identified by Marx over a century ago. This remains, however, an unsettled area of concern among contemporary Marxists.

APPENDIX II

A Critique of Emmanuel's
Theory of Unequal Exchange

Arghiri Emmanuel's work has been the subject of much debate and criticism.[1] Among the theoretical problems with Emmanuel's theory of imperialism, perhaps the most central from a Marxist perspective is his treatment of wages as an independent or predetermined variable. This issue is discussed below, followed by a discussion of the problems of the rate of surplus value and the value of labor power, and the tendency for the rate of profit to equalize. Finally an alternative formulation of unequal exchange will be presented.

Emmanuel's treatment of wages affects his entire analysis of unequal exchange and his subsequent theory of imperialism; it is central in his argument. A discussion of this issue will bring into relief the fundamental differences between Emmanuel's methodological approach and that utilized by Marx.

Wages, or the value of labor power (Emmanuel uses these interchangeably), are a subject taken up very early in Emmanuel's work. In the first chapter of *Unequal Exchange*, Emmanuel notes that while "at the moment of equilibrium the prices of commodities and the respective rates of reward of the two factors correspond, we must admit that there does not, at first glance, seem to be any purely rational proof as to which of the two is the determinant and which the determined."[2] In short, a problem arises at the level of the prices of production: How to determine cause and effect? Do wages determine prices or do prices determine wages? This problem is important for Emmanuel, because if he cannot establish the determinant as wages, then the neoclassical economists will win the debate with their subjective theory of prices.

To illustrate this problem, Emmanuel increases the general rate of wages in Marx's transformation schema to show that there is no change

196

in value, yet the prices of production do change. But how, asks Emmanuel, is one to determine which way the causality runs? "How then can we say whether it is the alteration in wages that has determined the alteration in equilibrium prices or whether it is the latter, due to supply and demand, that has determined the alteration in wages?"[3]

After a lengthy discussion of this problem, Emmanuel concludes that the "correspondences shown in Marx's diagram of prices of production are not reversible. Wages and profits are indeed the independent variables in the system, and prices the dependent variables."[4] Emmanuel's discussion of this "problem" is not important, except insofar as it is carried out entirely within the realm of exchange. The question arises: Why should there be a problem in the first place, when for Marx prices of production are not, in any event, determined by costs of production but by socially necessary labor time? Unless one sees a break between the law of value and prices of production, there should be no problem. However, this is exactly what Emmanuel does see, as is implicit in his treatment of the "wage-price problem." He later makes this point explicitly in a response to his critics:

> The reason is that what we have here is a false problem [the transformation problem], in the sense that what is involved is a change not of form but of content. Therefore, we either seek to keep the content, which will be translated into mathematical language by the equations already mentioned—but then the elements discovered in this way are not correct—or we calculate the prices of production correctly, but then we alter not only the form but the whole content as well, and this cannot be done without that "break" that my critics talk about.[5]

Thus Emmnanuel breaks away from the sphere of production and can maintain that wages are independent, and prices of production are dependent, variables. However, what starts out as a break turns into a determination of the sphere of production by the sphere of circulation, i.e., reverse causality. Emmanuel argues that under simple commodity production, where prices are proportional to value, there is no problem establishing the independence of wages, because they are determined by physiological subsistence levels. However, under the expanded reproduction of capital, with capitalist relations of production, the conditions are created that allow wages to rise above this biological subsistence level. A historical and moral element comes into play.[6]

The basis for Emmanuel's claim is as follows:

> As there has been no change in the natural features of human life and no change in man himself apart from what resulted from his economic and social evolution, it had to be deduced that wages had ceased to be the primary fact assumed by the classical economists. This does not of course mean that wages had ceased to be the independent variable of the system. But it was henceforth still the independent variable only as regards the dependence of prices upon wages, and no longer the independent variable in the total socioeconomic function throughout all time.[7]

However, if the value of labor power is determined in the sphere of production, according to the law of value, allowing for a historical and moral element, it certainly follows logically that the prices of production are also determined in accordance with the law of value. For Emmanuel, even the value of labor power is not directly determined by "economic causes" but is "in the immediate sense, *ethical*: it is *economic* only in an indirect way, through the mediation of the moral and historical element, which is itself determined, in the last analysis, by economic causes."[8]

The separation allows Emmanuel to move further away from the sphere of production and to argue that the only way wages can rise above the value of labor power is by the intervention of an "extraeconomic factor" that works outside the law of value and ensures the perpetuation of a super-wage above the value of labor power. According to Emmanuel, these factors can only be political or the result of trade unions. Thus, the differentiation of wages between countries can only be explained by these "institutional" factors that enter into the determination of the value of labor power.[9]

In what sense then can Emmanuel claim that wages are an independent variable, when he admits that in the last analysis they are determined by economic causes? If he were to go no further than this, his theory of imperialism would crumble, and he could not argue that wages are independent and determine unequal exchange and the course of capitalist development. He does not stop here, but goes on to make a clean break from the sphere of production. It will be useful to quote Emmanuel at length here to establish the break:

I do not dream of denying [that] . . . *in the final instance* the value of labor power, however ethical and institutional it may be, is based, like all other institutions, upon the economic foundations of society. But this is why I also say that it is not a question of interdependence in the neo-classical sense, but of dialectical interaction . . . .[10]

Emmanuel goes on a few lines later to say that

The real problems, so far as this study is concerned, are different [from the real dynamic of the process]. It is above all the question whether, *here and now*, and all other things being equal, it is economic conditions that directly determine national equilibrium wages, or whether it is the inequality between these wages that influence prices and economic development. I believe the second proposition to be the correct one, and I think that I have shown this to be so.[11]

Emmanuel has succeeded in cutting into the dialectical process of wage formation at the moment wages have in fact been determined, the "here and now." However, it is clear from his analysis of unequal exchange that he is more than just interested in the "here and now," because he proceeds to argue as if there were a chain of causality running from the sphere of appearances (exchange) backward to the sphere of production. Thus, low wages in the underdeveloped countries dictate the movement of capital, the international division of labor, and the organic composition of capital, not to mention Emmanuel's "organic composition of labor.".

For a Marxist this is the equivalent of the tail wagging the dog. However, if "in the final instance" the value of labor power is based upon the "economic foundations" of society, as Emmanuel says it is, then why, in the final instance, is not the blocking of development, for example, based upon the economic foundations of society, rather than low wages? The reason is that if Emmanuel granted this, unequal wages and unequal exchange would no longer be causes but rather symptoms. The real causes, therefore, lie not in unequal wages or exchange, but with the laws of motion of capitalism.

One cannot break into this series of moments anywhere one wishes, as Emmanuel does, because, as Marx went to great lengths to show, the sequence is all important. What is sequential for Marxists becomes for Emmanuel a circle of mutual cause and effect without any apparent starting point. Emmanuel chooses to start with the "here and now" (where, of course, not just wages but everything else is already determined) and proceeds as if dealing with a model that allows the manipulation of variables. Emmanuel has built a model that is severed from its theoretical base—and in fact works to destroy that base.[12]

Both Charles Bettelheim and Ernest Mandel in their critiques of Emmanuel have advanced a theory of wages that more correctly explains unequal wages between developed and underdevelopoed countries.[13] Wages are in no sense independent of the productive forces and relations of production, but are determined by the development of these forces and relations, i.e., by the laws of development of capitalism. More specifically, Mandel argues that wages are

> dependent on the long-term trend of the industrial reserve army and the long-term trend in the productivity of labor in the consumer goods sector and agriculture. These, in turn, are determined by two factors: the starting-point for the demand and supply of labor-power, and the secular tendency of the accumulation of capital.[14]

Both Mandel and Bettelheim argue (with some differences) that the growth of productive forces (accumulation of capital) in the underdeveloped countries has been hindered or blocked by the expansion (imperialism) of the industrialized capitalist countries. Thus wages in the underdeveloped countries are prevented from rising and the laws of capital accumulation on a world scale produce an international division of labor that guarantees the polarized development of the forces of production and expanded reproduction of economic inequalities.

Another theoretical issue raised by Emmanuel's work is his determination of unequal rates of surplus value.[15] The problem lies in Emmanuel's failure to distinguish between use value and exchange value in claiming that the rate of surplus value is higher or lower on the basis of difference in the standard of living (use values consumed). Just because workers in industrial capitalist countries consume more use values than do workers in underdeveloped countries does not mean that the rate of surplus value is lower in the industrial countries. The rate of surplus value depends upon the productivity of labor, which determines the value of commodities consumed by workers.

Elizabeth Dore and John Weeks argue that it is possible for the exchange value of labor power to be lower where the standard of living is higher because of the greater productivity of labor. They conclude, however, that it is not possible to establish theoretically that differences in the standard of living (appearances) mean differences in the exchange value of labor power (wages).[16] If this is true, then Emmanuel cannot assert that because workers in underdeveloped countries have a lower standard of living, the exchange value of labor power is also lower there. His assumption that the rate of surplus value is higher in the Third World is questionable.

Bettelheim argues that the rate of surplus value is higher in the industrial countries because they are more efficient. Emmanuel counters with the following argument. First, there is no reason why the necessary labor time in the underdeveloped countries "should not be even longer than the total labor time, since as we have seen, the latter is institutionally limited to eight hours a day."[17] Emmanuel offers no proof, merely an assertion, that the total labor time everywhere is limited to the eight-hour day; however, he does recognize exceptions. He argues that the necessary labor time is greater than the total time, and that therefore

the value of a kilo of flour would represent not less but more than eight hours, so that the worker in the export sector who receives a kilo of wheat for a working day of eight hours would not only not produce any surplus value for his employer, would not merely not be exploited, he would be exploiting his employer! An unexpected but inexorable consequence [of Bettelheim's argument] . . . .[18]

Just how this consequence follows is not at all clear. How does the fact that the rural worker's standard of living is lower than that of the export worker cause the value of a kilo of wheat to be more than eight hours, even if the rural worker is compelled to work more than eight hours a day? What counts is the efficiency with which wheat is produced. If it takes eight or more hours to reproduce a kilo of wheat, then the export worker will obviously not have a wage that allows him to consume a kilo of wheat; in other words, the exchange value of his labor power will be less than that of a kilo of wheat. Thus, Emmanuel has not here established that necessary time is greater than total time. Further, it is difficult if not impossible to make such comparisons between workers who are in sectors that manifest different relations of production.

Emmanuel argues next that, if Bettelheim is correct that the rate of surplus value is positive and lower in the underdeveloped country, then the equalization of rates of profit on a world scale would produce a transfer of value from the industrialized countries to the underdeveloped countries; the underdeveloped countries ''exploit'' the advanced countries. This conclusion, Emmanuel notes, ''would not be ill received by some neo-classical theoreticians.''[19] The very tenuous assumption of equalization of the rates of profit on a world scale will be dealt with later.

The third argument Emmanuel makes against Bettelheim is based on the assumption that most of the goods consumed in the developed enclaves of the underdeveloped countries are imported from the advanced countries. On this assumption, Emmanuel claims that Bettelheim's analysis can be extended to claim that a worker in the interior of an underdeveloped country who consumes local produce is less exploited, because it takes him more time to produce his subsistence than it takes a worker in a metropolitan center of the same country who consumes imported produce.[20]

Emmanuel argues that Bettelheim's ''mistake'' lies in his determination of worker's necessary labor time

> on the basis of the *individual* value instead of social value of the subsistence goods. The worker's necessary time is not determined by the individual value of the subsistence goods in a particular enterprise or a particular place, but by their *social* value *in the entire system under consideration.*
>
> In the context of world economy, the only value that counts in measuring necessary time is social (world) value, and not the individual (national) value of the goods represented by wages.[21]

Emmanuel is treating the international system as a world system wherein all commodities, regardless of the conditions under which they are produced, have one social world value. This value is presumably equal to the socially necessary labor time to produce these commodities for the world. Even if we grant this assumption, for Emmanuel's conclusion to follow, the *exchange value* of these commodities, which he does not take into account, must be everywhere equal. In this case, for example, if the workers in Country A have a standard of living equal to 10 kilos of wheat per day and Country B has a standard equal to 1 kilo, while the exchange value of wheat (not the actual value, which varies from place to place) is equal to .1 labor hour per kilo, then the necessary time in A will be one hour while the necessary time in B will be equal to .1 hour and the rate of surplus value (assuming the working day is the same everywhere) will be higher in the country with the lower standard of living.

If the exchange values are not equalized on a world scale, or if there is no "tendency towards such equalization, then Emmanuel's social world value becomes a lifeless abstraction. Emmanuel does not attempt to establish the basis for social world values. Had he, he would have had to establish under exactly what conditions the exchange values of the commodities that make up the workers' standard of living are equal the world over. This would be true only where commodities are exchanged on a world scale and where international prices of production are formed. However, as Marx makes clear, where markets are isolated from each other, trade may lead not to a set of international prices of production but rather to different exchange values. This gives rise to a merchant's profit, which is attained by exploiting the difference in the exchange value of commodities in different markets. In this case, it is nonsensical to speak of a world social value or to calculate necessary labor time on the basis of some hypothetical one, when in fact actual exchange values differ from country to country.

Furthermore, it is very doubtful that a majority of the commodities that make up the workers' standard of living in the underdeveloped countries enter into international exchange, even when we restrict our analysis to the consumption of those workers in the export sector. It is very likely that these commodities have an exchange value based on local conditions of production.

Even if we grant that these commodities enter into international exchange, how does the law of value affect this exchange when the commodities are produced under different conditions of production, and in many cases under different relations of production as well? The law of value tells us that a great deal of the labor expended in the underdeveloped countries, where producers are less efficient, would not be recognized in international exchange as having created any value. The prices of these commodities would be above the more efficient producers' elsewhere, but below the value of the less efficient producers' in the underdeveloped countries.

According to the laws of capitalist development, the inefficient producers will be forced to adopt the methods of the efficient producers in order to lower the value of their output, or else be driven out of business. Dore and Weeks argue, however, that these tendencies exist only when certain social relations of production give rise to competition. Such tendencies are absent when the competition is between capital and peasant producers from a different mode of production.[22] Thus, we are unable to establish any tendency toward a common exchange value for items of working-class consumption on an international level.

There is perhaps one case where unequal rates of surplus value can be established. This is a case provided by Amin.[23] He assumes that the organic composition of capital in the export sector, where modern methods are used, is the same as in the industrial countries. The workers in this sector, however, have lower real wages than their counterparts in the industrial countries; thus, the rate of surplus value is higher in the underdeveloped countries. Amin calculates the necessary labor time on the basis of international exchange values for the items of working-class consumption. However, the same criticisms used above concerning the existence of such values hold here. If the value of labor power is determined by local conditions, while the exchange value of the commodity that labor produces—but does not consume—is determined at the international level, can we still argue that the rate of surplus value is higher in the underdeveloped country? This is a theoretical problem, concerning the value of labor power when subsistence production is noncapitalist. Both Amin and Emmanuel fail to recognize the problem of establishing the value of labor power and the exchange value when there are two different modes of production involved.

Concerning the rate of exploitation, empirical evidence points to the use of obsolete technology and equipment in underdeveloped countries, suggesting a lower organic composition of capital[24]; but this does not necessarily prove that the rate of surplus value is lower in the underdeveloped countries. It is, however, unlikely that on average the commodities that the underdeveloped countries export have the same organic composition of capital as those exported by the developed countries. We are thus no closer to establishing the objective basis for unequal rates of surplus value on a world scale. Serious problems exist at both the theoretical and empirical levels.

A final criticism of Emmanuel's theory concerns his assertion that there is a tendency toward the equalization of rates of profit on a world scale. This assumption has been doubted by Mandel and criticized by Dore and Weeks. Mandel argues that there is no such empirical trend toward equalization and supplies data to confirm this.[25] However, Emmanuel's thesis does not require that the rate of profit actually ever be equalized. In fact, he argues that it never will be, because of the higher risk of foreign investment, which requires a certain premium to compensate foreign investors.[26] Since risk is a subjective factor, any and all differences in the rate of profit between home and host country can be attributed to it. This same argument is used by classical economists to explain the higher rates of profit in the Third World. But while the risk factor may be important, it is not a very satisfactory way of disposing of the empirical fact that rates of profit are still very much higher in the underdeveloped countries and do not seem to be narrowing.

Dore and Weeks criticize Emmanuel at the theoretical level.[27] They argue that the equalization of rates of profit is only a tendency, while Emmanuel treats it as an equilibrium point. If it is a tendency, then a majority of capital would flow to the underdeveloped countries prior to the point where equalization occurs. This would mean that the rate of capital accumulation would actually be faster in the underdeveloped countries until equalization occurs. If the tendency were to persist, then unequal exchange would never come into play, although there still might be a transfer of surplus value from the underdeveloped countries in the form of super-profits. Emmanuel does not deny the existence of super-profits. He simply thinks unequal exchange is predominant.

Emmanuel would argue here that there could be no massive inflow of capital into the underdeveloped countries because of the underconsumption caused by low wages. Therefore, the equalization of the rate of profit would take place long before there was any substantial movement of capital. Amin makes a similar argument; however, his analysis of the block to the capital inflow is much different and he attempts to root it in the laws of development of capitalism.[28]

These shortcomings concerning the tendency for the rate of profit to equalize are a major obstacle for the theory of unequal exchange. At most it can be said that unequal exchange is a tendency that may in fact never take place. Even assuming that it does, Dore and Weeks claim that "the worst that can happen is that the relative surplus will be the same in advanced and backward countries, i.e., at the worst, the surplus remaining in backward countries is sufficient to match the rate of accumulation of advanced countries."[29]

Emmanuel would counter here that this does not mean that the rate of development would be the same. In fact, Emmanuel argues that development is blocked in the underdeveloped countries because of unequal wages, not unequal exchange, which according to Emmanuel would create a backflow of capital to the developed countries rather than an equalization of the rate of accumulation. Nonetheless, the worst that can happen from *unequal exchange* is to match the surplus remaining in the underdeveloped country to that of the industrial country. While there might very well be a backflow of capital, Emmanuel's analysis is still faulty as was shown above concerning the treatment of wages as an independent variable.

An alternative approach
to unequal exchange

An alternative theory of unequal exchange, based on the laws of development of capitalism and the law of value, has been put forth by James Becker.[30] At the outset Becker chooses an approach radically different from Emmanuel's. While Emmanuel treats the transformation of values into prices as a logical problem to be solved in Marx's "model," Becker argues that

> the famous transformation of values into prices is not primarily a logical problem, as it is widely assumed to be, but a historical process whose developing interrelations of price to value are to be explained and their implications assessed. The transition from feudalism to capitalism features a transformation of values, a conversion of traditional ratios of exchange into new, monetary forms, and an establishing of ratios between these values and these prices, which are themselves subject to continuing evolution with the new market order.[31]

It is by treating unequal exchange within this historical transformation that Becker is able to come to an understanding of unequal exchange different from Emmanuel's.

Becker sees unequal exchange on a world scale as the result of the global extension of interdependence. Expansion produces certain irregularities and unevennesses which "are *everywhere* an integral part of one general organic interrelation. Any proper explanation at the global level must, in other words, encompass the local phenomena as well."[32] Becker first establishes the law of unequal exchange at the "local level," explaining just exactly how it produces the "unevenness" and "irregularity" of national capitalist development:

> The law . . . asserts a tendency of terms of exchange [within an economy] to move in favor of the more advanced productive forces—more precisely, in favor of those controlling the more developed forces of social labor—and to move against the technically retarded laborers and, to a lesser degree, against those controlling the more retarded forces. Within a system of capitalist relations of production, the law of unequal exchange yields a torsion effect upon terms of exchange that, on the one hand, accelerates accumulation of those whose terms are favorable or rising, while repressing accumulation of those whose terms are unfavorable or falling. One might say simply that the relations between these prices and values that the law predicts show a recurrent tendency to cut the pie in favor of those who have already had more than their share. The unbalanced growth that follows is one overall effect of the general exchange, given the relations of production to which we have referred. Another is the familiar irregularity, the expansion followed by collapse and contraction.[33]

Just how the terms of trade move against the technically backward workers will be shown later.

The twisting of the terms of trade to the advantage of the advanced branches from the very inception of industrial accumulation produces a "forced draft accumulation of constant capitals." The exchange mechanism, in conjunction with the competition between capitals, transfers surplus value from branches with below-average organic compositions to branches with above-average compositions. This is the basis, Becker argues, for the tendency toward overproduction in department I (means of production) and in all branches with a higher than average organic composition of capital. This overproduction is matched by underconsumption and retardation in the remaining branches. Becker concludes here by saying that "the law of unequal exchange in this way contributes to the evolution of periodic crises in exchange relations between these departments . . . ."[34]

Becker's main purpose is not to explain capitalist expansion and the uneven development of productive forces on a world scale; his discussion in this area, though incomplete, is instructive. He argues that, because of the operation of the law of unequal exchange, the extension of interdependence globally ensures that countries with more branches of production below the average organic composition will usually experience unfavorable terms of trade in their exchanges with countries where the majority of the branches of production have above-average composition. Becker notes that while the differential development of the forces of production (Becker takes this as given for his limited purposes) between developed and underdeveloped countries "yields inequalities in exchange, the continuing accumulation of capitals under these conditions may serve only to enlarge and extend the original unevenness."[35]

The operation of this law on a world scale produces crises just as in the domestic economy. Becker argues that the tendency to unequal exchange was especially powerful during the 1960s. This led to a situation where financial crises and debt crises periodically threatened international trade. Trade imbalances flooded some countries with deficit country currencies, threatening breakdowns of the international order.[36]

The law of unequal exchange also affects the production and exchange of labor power itself. The torsion effect works to distort the terms of exchange of all grades of labor. More highly skilled labor is paid above its exchange value and less-skilled labor is paid a wage lower than the exchange value of its labor power. This is so, Becker argues, because the more highly skilled labor requires more constant capital relative to variable capital in its production, so that the "composition of the productive capitals varies directly with the level of training and skill of the laborer being reproduced."[37]

This torsion effect, the paying of workers in the higher grades wages in excess of their exchange value, stimulates the overproduction of this type of labor, while paying workers in the lower grades wages below their exchange value represses the production of this type of labor. According to Becker, the surplus value is pulled out "of labor of less expensive grades and transferred . . . to advanced sectors for overpayment and, hence, overproduction of advanced grades."[38]

Becker distances himself from Emmanuel on the question of whether labor of the advanced countries exploits the labor of the underdeveloped countries:

> At the level of world economy, too, both the advanced and retarded branches of productive labor contribute to their common exploitation, and although the latter contribute relatively more than the former to the surplus shared out among the capitalists of all countries, the overpayment of the former and the underpayment of the latter are circumstances for which neither is responsible. These are merely the consequence of the extension of capitalist relations of production at the global level. Of course, this system of distorted and differential wage payments does, nationally and internationally, serve also a political purpose quite useful to capital. The fact that the better-skilled administratively more useful workers are everywhere overpaid, while the less skilled industrial and agricultural workers are everywhere underpaid, helps to keep labor everywhere divided and, hence, conquered. Overpayment distracts the more privileged from the fact that they, too, are exploited along with the less privileged through a mechanism that takes from both of them the surplus value that they mutually and cooperatively produce.[39]

Whereas Emmanuel speaks of nations exploiting each other and of the workers of the industrial countries exploiting the workers in the underdeveloped countries, Becker analyzes unequal exchange in a way that shows workers everywhere to be victims of the system; however much one group of workers appears to benefit at the expense of the other, it only does so because this is necessary to maintain capitalist hegemony and the progressive accumulation of capital. The divergent political implications of Emmanuel's and Becker's approaches are quite apparent.

For Becker, unequal exchange is a phenomenon produced by the laws of development of capitalism. It is the result, not of unequal wages, but of the competitive struggle of capitals. Unequal exchange develops in a logical and predictable fashion; indeed, Becker calls it the "law of unequal exchange." Unequal exchange, reflected in the terms of trade between different capitals and in the wages of workers in various grades, takes place because it is functional to the development of capitalism. At the same time it is a contradictory process that produces interruptions and crises in the process of capital accumulation. Becker distinguishes the strict and the broad senses of ''nonequivalence.'' As his analysis shows, there is no qualitative difference in unequal exchange at different levels; it always has the same generic root. Unlike Emmanuel, who argues that unequal wages are prior to unequal exchange and produce certain laws of motion of capitalism, Becker argues that the laws of motion of capitalism produce unequal exchange, one result of which is unequal wages.

While Becker's analysis is incomplete, particularly concerning the value of labor power and uneven development, it is a useful alternative to Emmanuel's theory of unequal exchange and imperialism. As Becker shows, a more fruitful analysis of unequal exchange can take place using Marx's basic method and approach, without throwing out the law of value. His analysis avoids many of the difficulties of Emmanuel's theory of unequal exchange.

Notes

CHAPTER 1

1. The following are readers on imperialism: Kenneth Boulding and Tapan Mukerjee, eds., *Economic Imperialism*; K. T. Fann and Donald C. Hodges, eds., *Readings in U.S. Imperialism*; Roger Owen and Bob Sutcliffe, eds., *Studies in the Theory of Imperialism*; Robert I. Rhodes, ed., *Imperialism and Underdevelopment: A Reader*; and Harrison M. Wright, ed., *The "New Imperialism."*

2. Between the time the present work was written and its publication there appeared an excellent book by Anthony Brewer, *Marxist Theories of Imperialism*, which covers much of the same ground but with a quite different emphasis.

3. For a recent and original interpretation see Melvin Rader, *Marx's Interpretation of History*.

4. See Ben Fine and Laurence Harris, *Rereading Capital*, and John Weeks, *Capital and Exploitation*, for the most recent interpretations of Marx.

5. Marx, *Capital*, Vol. III, p. 237.

6. Ibid., pp. 238-239.

7. Marx, *Capital*, Vol. I, pp. 450-451.

8. Ibid., p. 451.

9. Marx, *The Poverty of Philosophy*, as quoted by John Weeks, "Marx's Theory of Competition and the Theory of Imperialism," p. 17.

10. Marx, *Capital*, Vol. I, p. 451.

11. Shlomo Avineri, ed. *Karl Marx on Colonialism & Modernization*, pp. 132-133.

12. Ibid., p. 136.

13. Ibid., p. 137

14. Ibid., see introduction.

15. See Marx, *Grundrisse*, Introduction.

16. See Ben Fine and Laurence Harris, "Controversial Issues in Marxist Economic Thought," pp. 141-178.

17. Ibid.

18. Marxist revisionism can be traced all the way back to Engels, who as the chief interpreter and editor of Marx's work after his death, distorted Marx's ideas without so intending. See John Weeks, *Capital and Exploitation*, for substantiation of this point in reference to fundamental differences between Marx and Engels on the labor theory of value.

19. The key theoretical work here is Paul Baran and Paul Sweezy, *Monopoly Capital*.

20. Fine and Harris, "Controversial Issues...."

21. Even at the national level this fetish has been compelling, and many contemporary Marxists dealing with national issues have likewise fallen victim to it.

22. Some attribute this to the class background of contemporary Marxists. See Barbara and John Ehrenrich, "The Professional-Managerial Class," *Between Labor and Capital*, ed. Pat Walker (Boston: South End Press, 1979).

23. These conclusions are the same as those of Fine and Harris in their criticism of the neo-Ricardians. See "Controversial Issues...."

CHAPTER 2

1. On this point see Tom Kemp's review of the interwar literature in his *Theories of Imperialism*.
2. Vladimir Lenin, *Imperialism: The Highest Stage of Capitalism* (1916), pp. 81–82.
3. Nikolai Bukharin, *Imperialism and World Economy* (1915–1918), p. 112.
4. Ibid., pp. 112–114.
5. Rudolf Hilferding, *Finance Capital: A Study of the Latest Phase of Capitalist Development* (1910). Because the English translation of this work was not yet published at the time this chapter was written, most of the citations below are to pages in the original, *Das Finanzkapital*, as cited in secondary sources.
6. By far the most complete summary of Hilferding's analysis is that of Paul Sweezy in his *Theory of Capitalist Development*. What follows draws heavily on Sweezy's interpretation.
7. Hilferding, *Das Finanzkapital*, p. 239, as quoted in Lenin, *Imperialism*, p. 18.
8. Sweezy, *Theory of Capitalist Development*, p. 259.
9. Hilferding, *Das Finanzkapital*, p. 283, as quoted in Lenin, p. 47.
10. Hilferding, p. 132, as quoted in Sweezy, p. 261.
11. Hilferding, p. 218, as quoted in Sweezy, p. 266.
12. Hilferding, *Finance Capital* (ed. T. B. Bottomore), p. 234.
13. See Anwar Shaikh "An Introduction to the History of Crisis Theories," p. 228.
14. Hilferding, p. 427, as quoted in Sweezy, p. 376.
15. Hilferding, p. 426, as quoted in Sweezy, p. 375.
16. Hilferding, pp. 427–428, as quoted in Sweezy, p. 376.
17. Hilferding, p. 428, as quoted in Sweezy, p. 377.
18. Hilferding, p. 389, as quoted in Sweezy, p. 300.
19. Hilferding, p. 401, as quoted in Sweezy, p. 304.
20. Hilferding, p. 406, as quoted in Lenin, p. 121.
21. Hilferding, p. 406, as quoted in Sweezy, p. 305.
22. Michael Barratt Brown, "A Critique of Marxist Theories of Imperialism," p. 49.
23. Sweezy, pp. 268–269.
24. For a contemporary account and analysis of such financial groups see James Knowles, "The Rockefeller Financial Group," *Superconcentration/Supercorporation*, ed. Ralph L. Andreano (Andover, Mass.: Warner Modular Publications, 1973), M343.
25. Two contemporary studies are David Kotz, *Bank Control of Large Corporations in the United States* (Berkeley: University of Calif. Press, 1978); and Edward Herman, *Corporate Control, Corporate Power* (New York: Cambridge University Press, 1981).
26. Rosa Luxemburg, *The Accumulation of Capital* (1913), and *The Accumulation of Capital—An Anti-Critique* (1915/1921).
27. See especially Rosa Luxemburg, *The Mass Strike: The Political Party and the Trade Unions and the Junius Pamphlet*, and *What Is Economics?*
28. Luxemburg, *Accumulation of Capital*, p. 131, as quoted by Tom Kemp in *Theories of Imperialism*, p. 49.

29. Luxemburg, *Anti-Critique*, pp. 56–57.
30. Ibid., p. 59.
31. Ibid., p. 60.
32. Ibid., p. 59.
33. Ibid., p. 60.
34. *Accumulation of Capital*, p. 445, as quoted by Paul Sweezy in *Theory of Capitalist Development*, pp. 205–206.
35. George Lee, "Rosa Luxemburg and the Impact of Imperialism," *Economic Journal* (December 1971), pp. 847–863.
36. Ibid., pp. 848–849.
37. Ibid., p. 850.
38. Luxemburg, *Junius Pamphlet*, p. 213.
39. Lee, pp. 851 and 862.
40. Luxemburg, *Accumulation of Capital*, pp. 419–428.
41. Ibid., p. 421.
42. Ibid., p. 419.
43. Ibid., p. 417.
44. This point is made by Kenneth Tarbuck in his introduction to Luxemburg, *Anti-Critique*, p. 31.
45. For two different explanations of this process, see Samir Amin, *Unequal Development*, pp. 85–87, and Anwar Shaikh, "An Introduction to the History of Crises Theories," pp. 226–227.
46. Luxemburg, *Anti-Critique*, p. 57.
47. Tarbuck, Introduction to ibid., p. 30.
48. Sweezy, p. 205.
49. This point was made by Nikolai Bukharin in his critique of Luxemburg, *Imperialism and the Accumulation of Capital* (1925), pp. 243–247.
50. This point was made by Bukharin in ibid., pp. 252–253.
51. Tarbuck, introduction to Luxemburg, *Anti-Critique*, pp. 31–32.
52. Ibid., p. 32. It should be noted that by "unequal exchange of values" Tarbuck does not mean the unequal exchange of labor time.
53. This same conclusion is reached by Tarbuck, in his introduction to Luxemburg, *Anti-Critique*, pp. 23–24; see also Sweezy, p. 205, and Tom Kemp, pp. 52–53.
54. This point has recently been established by Robert Brenner and is discussed in depth in Chapter 7 of this study. See his article "The Origins of Capitalist Development: A Critique of Neo-Smithian Marxism," pp. 25–92.
55. See George Lee on this point in his "Luxemburg and Imperialism," pp. 859–861.
56. Bukharin's *Imperialism and World Economy* was published with an introduction written by Lenin.
57. Nikolai Bukharin, *Imperialism and the Accumulation of Capital* (1925).
58. Tarbuck, introduction to ibid., p. 246.
59. Bukharin, *Imperialism and World Economy*, p. 26.
60. Ibid.
61. Ibid., pp. 26–27.
62. Ibid., p. 21.
63. Ibid., p. 30.
64. Ibid., pp. 32–34.
65. Ibid., p. 36.

66. Ibid., p. 39. Bukharin does not integrate this movement of labor into his theory of imperialism, nor have other Marxists. Hannah Arendt has developed a theory of imperialism around the motive to create outlets for this excess and dissatisfied population and surplus capital. See her *The Origins of Totalitarianism*, 2nd ed. enl. (London: Allen and Unwin, 1958).

67. Bukharin, *Imperialism and World Economy*, pp. 41–42.

68. Ibid., pp. 41–42.

69. Ibid., pp. 45–46.

70. Bukharin, *Imperialism and Accumulation*, p. 256. Emphasis added.

71. Bukharin, *Imperialism and World Economy*, p. 119.

72. Ibid., p. 120.

73. Ibid., p. 58.

74. Ibid., p. 72.

75. Ibid., p. 104.

76. Ibid., pp. 81–82.

77. Ibid., pp. 82–84.

78. Ibid., p. 84.

79. Ibid., pp. 84–88.

80. Ibid., p. 93.

81. Ibid., p. 95.

82. Ibid., p. 96.

83. Ibid., p. 97.

84. Ibid., pp. 97–98.

85. Ibid., p. 103.

86. Ibid., p. 99.

87. Ibid., pp. 101–103.

88. Ibid., p. 120.

89. Ibid., p. 120.

90. Ibid., pp. 136–140.

91. Ibid., pp. 140–143.

92. Bukharin, "The Theory of 'Organized Economic Disorder'," pp. 331 ff.

93. *Imperialism: The Highest Stage of Capitalism* (1916).

94. Ibid., p. 14.

95. Ibid., p. 15.

96. Ibid., p. 89.

97. Ibid., p. 124.

98. Ibid., p. 88.

99. Ibid., p. 89.

100. Ibid., p. 31.

101. Ibid., pp. 35–36. Emphasis in original.

102. Sweezy, *Theory of Capitalist Development*, p. 269.

103. Lenin, *Imperialism*, p. 44.

104. Ibid., pp. 28–29.

105. Ibid., p. 62.

106. Ibid.

107. Ibid., p. 63.

108. Ibid.

109. Ibid., p. 64.

110. Lenin has been criticized on this point. It is argued that most capital flowed to the independent rather than dependent countries, therefore, the colonies could not

have been a major attraction for capital and were thus not necessary to finance capital. However, Lenin refutes this argument in his "Notebooks on Imperialism" where he argues that even though most capital flowed to independent countries, the colonies were of major importance as sources of superprofits which supplemented the normal profits on other operations. See V. I. Lenin, *Collected Works*, Vol. 39 (Moscow: Progress Publishers, 1968), pp. 195–196.

111. Lenin, *Imperialism*, p. 65.
112. Ibid., pp. 124–126.
113. Ibid., p. 67.
114. Ibid., p. 68.
115. Ibid., p. 70.
116. Ibid., p. 85.
117. Ibid., p. 77.
118. Ibid., p. 82.
119. Ibid., p. 84.
120. Ibid., p. 89.
121. See, for example, Tom Kemp, a contemporary follower of Lenin who makes this mistake in his *Theories of Imperialism*, Ch. V.
122. For a good cross-section of positions put forth by non-Marxists see Harrison Wright, ed., *The New Imperialism*, 2nd ed. rev. (Lexington: D. C. Heath and Co., 1976). Two very good works by Marxists who weigh most of the major points against Lenin and make counter-arguments are Michael Barratt Brown, *The Economics of Imperialism*, passim. Also see Kemp, *Theories of Imperialism*, Chs. V, VII–IX.
123. Brown, *Economics of Imperialism*, pp. 170–183.
124. D. K. Fieldhouse is one of the chief proponents of this view. See his "Imperialism: An Historiographical Revision," *Economic History Review*, 2nd Ser., 14, 2 (December 1961), and his later works. For a contemporary view see Benjamin Cohen, *The Question of Imperialism*.

CHAPTER 3

1. See "The Meaning of Economic Imperialism" in James O'Connor, *The Corporations and the State*.
2. See Harry Magdoff, *Age of Imperialism* (1969); *Imperialism from the Colonial Age to the Present* (1978); and "Imperialism Without Colonies," in *Studies in the Theory of Imperialism*, eds. Roger Owen and Bob Sutcliffe (1972). For Magdoff's other numerous writings see bibliography.
3. Paul Baran and Paul Sweezy, *Monopoly Capital*, p. 3.
4. Ibid., pp. 3–4.
5. Ibid., p. 4.
6. Ibid., pp. 5–6.
7. Ibid., p. 53. Emphasis added.
8. Paul Baran, *Political Economy of Growth*, pp. 22–23.
9. Baran and Sweezy, *Monopoly Capital*, p. 2 and 112.
10. Baran, *Political Economy of Growth*, fn. p. 22.
11. Ibid., pp. 23–24.
12. Ibid., p. 24. Emphasis added.

13. See William Barclay and Mitchell Stengel, "Surplus and Surplus Value," p. 58.

14. Baran and Sweezy, *Monopoly Capital*, pp., 57–64.

15. Ibid., p. 71.

16. The issue of competition and Baran and Sweezy's treatment of it are discussed in Appendix I.

17. Baran and Sweezy, *Monopoly Capital*, pp. 71–72.

18. The validity of this assumption will be discussed below.

19. Baran and Sweezy, *Monopoly Capital*, Ch. 4. This analysis will be expanded vis-à-vis imperialism in Chapter 5, below.

20. Ibid., p. 108.

21. This view is consistent with Sweezy's earlier position on the cause of economic crisis in *The Theory of Capitalist Development*, Part III. For substantiation on this point see M. F. Bleaney, *Under-Consumption Theories*.

22. Baran and Sweezy, *Monopoly Capital*, p. 108.

23. Ibid., p. 219.

24. Ibid., pp. 91–104.

25. Ibid., p. 222.

26. Ibid., p. 125.

27. Ibid., p. 126.

28. Ibid., pp. 126–127.

29. Ibid., pp. 147–148.

30. Anthony Brewer's recent book, *Marxist Theories of Imperialism*, focuses solely on this aspect of imperialism.

31. See Baran and Sweezy, *Monopoly Capital*, and their article "Notes on the Theory of Imperialism."

32. O'Connor, "Meaning of Economic Imperialism."

33. Ibid., p. 122.

34. Ibid., p. 125.

35. Baran and Sweezy, "Notes on the Theory of Imperialism," in *Economic Imperialism*, eds. Kenneth Boulding and Tapan Mukerjee, p. 157.

36. Ibid., p. 159.

37. Ibid., p. 163.

38. Baran and Sweezy, *Monopoly Capital*, pp. 105–108.

39. O'Connor, "Meaning of Economic Imperialism," p. 142.

40. Baran and Sweezy, *Monopoly Capital*, p. 179.

41. See Baran and Sweezy, *Monopoly Capital*, Ch. 7, and "Notes on the Theory of Imperialism."

42. *Monopoly Capital*, pp. 187 ff.

43. Ibid., p. 201. See also "Notes on Imperialism." For a much more current and complete analysis of the global operations of multinational corporations see Richard Barnet and Ronald Müller, *Global Reach* (New York: Simon and Schuster, 1974).

44. Baran and Sweezy, "Notes on the Theory of Imperialism," pp. 165–166.

45. Ibid., p. 166.

46. Ibid., p. 169.

47. O'Connor, "Meaning of Economic Imperialism," p. 121.

48. Harry Magdoff makes economic rivalry central to his theory of imperialism, which is discussed below in Chapter 6. This issue is discussed in Bob Rowthorn, "Imperialism in the Seventies—Unity or Rivalry?" *New Left Review*, No. 69 (September–October, 1971); Ernest Mandel, "Where is America Going?"

New Left Review, No. 54 (March–April, 1969); and James Petras and Robert Rhodes, "The Reconsolidation of U.S. Hegemony," *New Left Review*, No. 97 (May—June 1976).

49. O'Connor, "Meaning of Economic Imperialism," p. 125.

50. Ibid., pp. 127–129.

51. Ibid., p. 127.

52. Ibid., pp. 129–130.

53. Ibid., p. 131.

54. Ibid., pp. 133–134.

55. Ibid., pp. 134–136.

56. Ibid., pp. 136–138.

57. Ibid., p. 142.

58. Ibid.

59. Ibid., p. 138.

60. Ibid., pp. 139–140.

61. Ibid., p. 141.

62. Ibid.

63. Much of the text of *The Age of Imperialism* had appeared previously in articles published in 1966 and 1968.

64. See note 2.

65. Magdoff, *Age of Imperialism*, p. 166.

66. Ibid., p. 167.

67. Ibid., p. 35.

68. Ibid., pp. 35–36.

69. Ibid., pp. 36–38. Magdoff argues that through protective tariffs and other trade barriers, foreign investment is an effective method of invading the markets of competitors. It is also an effective method of capturing foreign sources of raw materials as well as taking advantage of lower costs and higher profits.

70. Ibid., pp. 38–39.

71. Ibid., p. 39.

72. Ibid., pp. 39–40.

73. Ibid., p. 39.

74. Magdoff, "Imperialism Without Colonies," pp. 152–155.

75. Ibid., p. 148.

76. Ibid., p. 147, fn. 3.

77. Ibid., p. 169.

78. Ibid., p. 155.

79. Ibid., pp. 155–156.

80. Ibid., p. 156.

81. Ibid., p. 160.

82. Ibid., p. 161.

83. Ibid., pp. 157–160. For a more sophisticated yet concise analysis of monopoly competition and foreign expansion see Arthur MacEwan, "Capitalist Expansion, Ideology, and Intervention," *The Review of Radical Political Economics*, Vol. 4, No. 1 (Winter 1972), pp. 36–58.

84. Magdoff, "Imperialism Without Colonies," p. 148.

85. Ibid., p. 165.

86. Magdoff, *Age of Imperialism*, p. 40.

87. Ibid.

88. Magdoff, "Imperialism Without Colonies," p. 168.

89. Ibid., pp. 168–169.

CHAPTER 4

1. In addition to Paul Baran and Andre Gunder Frank, discussed here, this group includes such well-known theorists as Fernando Cardosa, James Cockcroft, Theotonio Dos Santos, Celso Furtado, and Thomas Weisskopf. See the Bibliography for references to their works.

2. Paul Baran, *The Political Economy of Growth*, p. 137.

3. Ibid., p. 138.

4. Baran offers very little proof that these conditions were developing elsewhere; however, this is not a crucial point in his later explanation of backwardness.

5. Baran, *Political Economy of Growth*, p. 141.

6. Ibid., pp. 141-142.

7. Ibid., p. 143.

8. Ibid.

9. Ibid., p. 144.

10. Ibid.

11. Ibid., pp. 164-167.

12. Ibid., p. 167.

13. Ibid., pp. 167-170.

14. Ibid., pp. 170-173.

15. Ibid., pp. 173-176.

16. Ibid., pp. 178-184.

17. Ibid., p. 177.

18. Ibid., pp. 194-195.

19. Ibid., p. 215.

20. Ibid., p. 221.

21. Paul Baran, "On the Political Economy of Backwardness," p. 289.

22. Ibid., p. 300.

23. Frank's most important works on this theme are *Capitalism and Underdevelopment in Latin America* (1969); *Latin America: Underdevelopment or Revolution?* (1969); *Lumpenbourgeoisie, Lumpendevelopment* (1972); and *Dependent Accumulation and Underdevelopment* (1979).

24. Frank, *Capitalism and Underdevelopment in Latin America*, p. 3.

25. Ibid., p. 9.

26. Ibid., p. 147.

27. Ibid., pp. 14-15.

28. Frank, *Latin America: Underdevelopment or Revolution?* p. 225.

29. Frank, *Capitalism and Underdevelopment*, pp. 221-241.

30. Frank, *Lumpenbourgeoisie, Lumpendevelopment*, pp. 18-19.

31. Ibid., p. 13.

32. Ibid., pp. 17-18. Frank cites Adam Smith to substantiate his claim that the motives for European commercial expansion were individual profit motives.

33. Frank, "Economic Dependence, Class Structure, and Underdevelopment Policy," p. 22.

34. Frank, *Lumpenbourgeoisie, Lumpendevelopment*, p. 13.

35. Frank, *Capitalism and Underdevelopment*, pp. 148-150. See Frank's case studies of Brazil and Chile in the same book.

36. Ibid., pp. 44-45.

37. Frank, "Economic Dependence," p. 44.

38. Ibid., pp. 44-45.

39. Frank, *Lumpenbourgeoisie, Lumpendevelopment*, p. 101. Frank rests his case here on the analyses of Baran and Sweezy and Magdoff.

40. Ibid.

41. Ibid., p. 120.

42. Ibid., pp. 94–100. Frank here agrees with O'Connor's contention that control is exercised with minimal inflow of foreign capital. For further empirical proof see Ronald Müller, "The Multinational Corporation and the Underdevelopment of the Third World."

43. Frank, *Lumpenbourgeoisie, Lumpendevelopment*, pp. 104–121. The radical analysis of the profile and composition of demand has been extended further by Celso Furtado and Theotonio Dos Santos. See Furtado, "The Concept of External Dependence in the Study of Underdevelopment," and Dos Santos, "The Structure of Dependence," both in *The Political Economy of Development and Underdevelopment*, ed. Charles K. Wilber.

44. Frank, *Lumpenbourgeoisie, Lumpendevelopment*, pp. 110–111.

45. Frank, *Capitalism and Underdevelopment*, p. 211.

46. Some contend that the United States is an example which contradicts Frank's argument that it is impossible for a satellite to break away and achieve capitalist development. Frank would presumably argue that only in the southern colonies were the satellite conditions consistent with a colonial class structure based on ultraexploitation. In the northern colonies these conditions were not imposed, for reasons already cited. After 1876 the South became an internal satellite of the North. However, even granting that there might be a strong case made for such an interpretation, there still remains a problem for Frank. He would either have to admit that successful capitalist development is possible, albeit based on internal colonialism and imperialism, or else argue that the United States is underdeveloped.

47. See, for example, Frank's *Latin America: Underdevelopment or Revolution?*, which contains a substantial critique of mainstream views.

48. See, for example, the work of Raul Prebish and H. W. Singer, for what can be referred to as "liberal dependency theory" and has also been called "structuralist theory." See also the currently most popular development textbook, Michael Todaro's *Economic Development in the Third World* (New York: Longmans, 2nd ed., 1981).

49. For a good survey of the history and issues see Ronald H. Chilcote, "Dependency: A Critical Synthesis of the Literature," and his more recent survey "Issues of Theory in Dependency and Marxism."

50. This argument was first advanced by Ernest Laclau in "Feudalism and Capitalism in Latin America."

51. This thesis has been expanded by Immanuel Wallerstein to explain world history. See his "The Rise and Future Demise of the World Capitalist System: Concepts for Comparative Analysis"; and *The Modern World-System: Capitalist Agriculture and the Origins of the European World-Economy in the Sixteenth Century*.

52. Frank, *Capitalism and Underdevelopment*, p. 15.

53. Frank, *Lumpenbourgeoisie, Lumpendevelopment*, p. 27. Frank actually refers to these various productive relationships as different "modes of production" while still maintaining that these countries are fully capitalist. It is clear that Frank does not use these categories the way Marx did.

54. Laclau, "Feudalism and Capitalism," p. 25.

55. This point has been established by Robert Brenner in "The Origins of Capitalist Development: A Critique of Neo-Smithian Marxism."

56. Ibid.
57. The work of Laclau and Brenner has already been cited above. Other theorists include Raul Fernandez and Jose F. Ocampo, "The Latin American Revolution: A Theory of Imperialism, Not Dependence," and Elizabeth Dore and John Weeks, "International Exchange and the Causes of Backwardness."
58. See Dore and Weeks, cited above.
59. Ibid., p. 65.
60. Ibid.
61. This quote is from an earlier unpublished version of the article cited above.
62. William Barclay and Mitchel Stengel, "Surplus and Surplus-Value," p. 59.
63. Ibid.

CHAPTER 5

1. Emmanuel also challenges Ricardo's theory of comparative advantage and its neoclassical equivalent.
2. Arghiri Emmanuel, *Unequal Exchange: A Study in the Imperialism of Trade*, p. 61.
3. Ernest Mandel makes this same observation in *Late Capitalism*, p. 354.
4. Emmanuel, *Unequal Exchange*, p. 160.
5. Ibid., p. 163.
6. Ibid., p. 130.
7. Ibid., p. 89.
8. Ibid., p. 130.
9. Ibid., p. 131.
10. Ibid.
11. Ibid.
12. Ibid., pp. 371–372. Emphasis added.
13. Ibid., p. 372.
14. Ibid., pp. 373–374.
15. Ibid., p. 129.
16. Ibid., p. 376. Emphasis added.
17. Ibid., p. 267.
18. Ibid., pp. 269–270.
19. See Samir Amin, "The End of a Debate"; Michael Barratt Brown, *The Economics of Imperialism*, pp. 229–235 and pp. 240–245; Charles Bettelheim, Appendices I and III in *Unequal Exchange*; Geoffrey Pilling, "Imperialism, Trade and 'Unequal Exchange,'" pp. 164–185; Anwar Shaikh, "Foreign Trade and the Law of Value," Parts I and II; and Elizabeth Dore and John Weeks, "International Exchange and the Causes of Backwardness."
20. See Bettelheim in *Unequal Exchange*, Appendix I, and Mandel in *Late Capitalism*, pp. 362 ff.
21. For a discussion of the neo-Ricardians see Ben Fine and Laurence Harris, "Controversial Issues in Marxist Economic Theory."
22. Bettelheim, *Unequal Exchange*, Appendix I; and Dore and Weeks, "International Exchange," pp. 13–16.

CHAPTER 6

1. Samir Amin, *Unequal Development*, p. 75.
2. Samir Amin, *Accumulation on a World Scale*, Vol. II, p. 531.
3. Amin, *Unequal Development*, pp. 173–174.
4. Ibid., pp. 171–172.
5. Ibid., pp. 101, 173, 182.
6. Ibid., p. 287.
7. Ibid., p. 287.
8. Discussed in Chapter 2, above.
9. Amin, *Unequal Development*, p. 191.
10. Ibid., p. 76.
11. Ibid., p. 184.
12. Ibid., p. 185.
13. Ibid.
14. Ibid., p. 68.
15. Ibid., p. 170.
16. Ibid., p. 178.
17. Ibid., p. 175.
18. Ibid., p. 185.
19. Ibid., p. 77.
20. Ibid., p. 178.
21. In neoclassical terms this equalization should occur in the absence of capital movements due to factor price equalization.
22. Amin, *Unequal Development*, p. 145. It is interesting to note that Amin eschews the labor theory of value for the purposes of analyzing the national economy because monopoly prevents the equalization of rates of profit and thus prices have "no apparent rationality." Yet, under the same conditions internationally, i.e., monopoly, Amin finds the labor theory of value useful to explain international prices. See *Unequal Development*, p. 68.
23. It should be noted that in Amin's example the organic composition of capital is five times greater in the low wage country, the same as it is in Emmanuel's example. However, even if this was reversed "unequal exchange" will still take place. This assumption is clearly noncritical. See *Unequal Development*, p. 140.
24. Ibid., pp. 138–145.
25. See Amin's "End of the Debate." In Amin's view he had ended the debate over unequal exchange without abandoning the theory itself.
26. Oscar Braun, *Comercio internacional e imperialismo* (Buenos Aires, 1972).
27. Amin, *Unequal Exchange*, p. 151.
28. Ibid., p. 144.
29. Ibid.
30. Ibid., p. 187.
31. Ibid., p. 188.
32. Amin's analysis of economic crises is one that compresses into one explanation features of Marx's analysis and Harrod's "multiplier" and "accelerator" analysis of the cycle. It is very difficult to follow Amin because of his admixture of terms and concepts from different paradigms.
33. Ibid., p. 102.
34. Ibid., pp. 102–103.

35. Ibid., pp. 103-104, 188.
36. Ibid., p. 77.
37. Ibid.
38. Ibid., p. 179.
39. Ibid., pp. 179-180.
40. Ibid., p. 181.
41. Ibid., p. 189.
42. Ibid., p. 189.
43. See Elizabeth Dore and John Weeks, "International Exchange and the Causes of Backwardness."
44. For a discussion of this controversy see Anwar Shaikh, "An Introduction to the History of Crisis Theories," and MFZ, "Against Sweezy's Political Economy," *The Communist* (Fall-Winter 1977).
45. Amin, *Unequal Development*, p. 287.
46. Ibid., p. 288.
47. Ibid., p. 203.
48. Ibid., p. 204.
49. Ibid.
50. Ibid., p. 205.
51. Ibid., p. 206.
52. Ibid., pp. 193 and 210.
53. Ibid., p. 193.
54. Ibid., p. 209.
55. Ibid., p. 212.
56. Ibid.
57. Ibid.
58. Ibid., pp. 213-214.
59. Ibid., p. 214.
60. Ibid., pp. 200-201.
61. Ibid., p. 201.
62. Ibid., p. 236.
63. Ibid., p. 238.
64. Ibid., pp. 238-239.
65. Ibid., p. 288.
66. See the Bibliography for references to these authors' works.
67. For a case study that shows just such a rearticulation despite dependency see Charles Barone, "Dependency, Marxist Theory, and Salvaging the Idea of Capitalism in South Korea," *Review of Radical Political Economics* (Spring 1983).
68. See Ben Fine and Laurence Harris, "Controversial Issues in Marxist Economic Theory," *The Socialist Register* (1976).

CHAPTER 7

1. Bill Warren, "Imperialism and Capitalist Industrialization."
2. For a good critique see James Petras, Philip McMichael, and Robert Rhodes, "Industrialization in the Third World," *New Left Review* (May-June 1974).
3. Bill Warren, *Imperialism: Pioneer of Capitalism*, pp. 5-6.

4. See Immanuel Wallerstein, *The Capitalist World-Economy*; *The Modern World-System*; "Dependence in an Interdependent World"; and "The Rise and Future Demise of the World Capitalist System."

5. See Andre Gunder Frank, *Dependent Accumulation and Underdevelopment*; *Crisis: In The World Economy* and *Crisis: In The Third World*.

6. For critical literature see Ira Gerstein, "Theories of the World Economy and Imperialism"; James Petras, *Critical Perspectives on Imperialism and Social Class in the Third World*, pp. 32 ff.; Aidan Foster-Carter, "The Modes of Production Controversy," pp. 73 ff.; and Ronaldo Munck, "Imperialism and Dependency: Recent Debates and Old Dead-Ends."

7. For an interesting account of such orthodox responses see Ronaldo Munck, "Imperialism and Dependency."

8. See, for example, John Weeks, *Capital and Exploitation*.

9. See Ernesto Laclau, "Feudalism and Capitalism in Latin America"; Raul Fernandez and Jose Ocampo, "The Latin American Revolution: A Theory of Imperialism, Not Dependence"; Elizabeth Dore and John Weeks, "International Exchange and The Causes of Backwardness"; Ben Fine, "On the Origins of Capitalist Development"; and Robert Brenner, "The Origins of Capitalist Development: A Critique of Neo-Smithian Marxism."

10. Brenner, "Origins of Capitalist Development," p. 32.

11. Ibid., p. 34.

12. Ibid., pp. 34–36.

13. Brenner is referring to Paul Sweezy and his exchange with Maurice Dobb in Dobb *et al.*, *The Transition From Feudalism to Capitalism*, and to Immanuel Wallerstein.

14. Brenner neglects to point out that in the early development of capitalism and in mature capitalism the production of absolute surplus value plays a continued role alongside the production of relative surplus value. See Ben Fine, "On the Origins of Capitalist Development," on this point.

15. Brenner, "Origins of Capitalist Development," pp. 67–77.

16. Ibid., p. 78.

17. Ibid., p. 85.

18. Ibid., p. 85.

19. Ibid., pp. 89–90.

20. Ibid., p. 91.

21. Barbara Bradby, "The Destruction of National Economy"; Aidan Foster-Carter, "The Modes of Production Controversy." See also the work of Haruza Alavi, "India and the Colonial Mode of Production"; D. McEachern, "The Mode of Production in India"; Martin Murray, "Recent Views on the Transition From Feudalism to Capitalism."

22. Bradby, "Destruction of National Economy," p. 127.

23. Pierre-Philippe Rey, *Class Alliances*, pp. 12 ff.

24. Bradby, "Destruction of National Economy," pp. 143–144.

25. Rey, *Class Alliances*, p. 43.

26. Ibid., p. 44.

27. Ibid., p. 45.

28. Ibid., p. 52.

29. Ibid., p. 40.

30. Ibid.

31. Ibid., pp. 114–116.

32. Bradby, "Destruction of National Economy," p, 147.
33. Ibid.
34. Rey, *Class Alliances*, pp. 116–117.
35. Ibid., pp. 82 ff.
36. These issues are more fully discussed in Foster-Carter, "The Modes of Production Controversy," pp. 64 ff.
37. For a more thorough discussion see ibid., p. 68, and Brady, "Destruction of National Economy," pp. 148 ff.
38. See Dore and Weeks, "International Exchange"; also "The Intensification of the Assault Against the Working Class in 'Revolutionary' Peru." John Weeks, "Marx's Theory of Competition and The Theory of Imperialism"; "The Differences Between Materialist Theories and Why They Matter"; *Capital and Exploitation*.
39. For others see Raul Fernandez and Jose Ocampa, "The Latin American Revolution: A Theory of Imperialism, Not Dependence"; and Raul Fernandez, "Imperialist Capitalism in the Third World: Theory and Evidence from Colombia."
40. Weeks, "Materialist Theory," p. 118.
41. Ibid., p. 119. See Dore and Weeks, "International Exchange," for an extended critique of Baran, Frank, Emmanuel, and Amin.
42. Weeks, "Materialist Theory," p. 120.
43. Ibid., pp. 120–121.
44. Ibid., p. 121.
45. Weeks, "Marx's Theory of Competition," and *Capital and Exploitation*, chapter 6.
46. Weeks, "Marx's Theory of Competition," pp. 11–12.
47. Ibid., p. 12.
48. Ibid., pp. 13–15.
49. Ibid., p. 16.
50. Marx, *The Poverty of Philosophy*, in *Marx and Engels Collected Works*, Vol. 6, 1845–1848, p. 195 (as cited by Weeks in ibid).
51. Weeks, "Marx's Theory of Competition," p. 17.
52. Ibid., pp. 17–18.
53. Ibid., p. 21.
54. Ibid., p. 20.
55. Weeks, "Materialist Theory," p. 122.
56. Dore and Weeks, "Relative Surplus Value and the Barriers to Accumulation in Backward Countries."
57. Ibid.
58. Ibid.
59. Ibid.
60. Ibid.
61. Ibid.
62. Ibid.
63. Ibid.
64. Dore and Weeks, "International Exchange," pp. 84 ff.
65. Dore and Weeks, "Relative Surplus Value . . . ." These problems have been solved in part by Brenner and by the articulation of modes of production school.
66. Petras's articles appear regularly in *Monthly Review, New Left Review, Latin American Perspectives*, and many other journals.

67. James Petras, *Critical Perspectives on Imperialism and Social Class in the Third World*, pp. 33-34.
68. Ibid., p. 67.
69. Ibid., pp. 66-67.
70. Ibid., pp. 63 ff.
71. Ibid., p. 70.
72. Ibid., p. 40.
73. Ibid., p. 70.
74. Ibid., p. 41.
75. Ibid., p. 41.
76. Ibid., p. 44.
77. Ibid., pp. 45-46.
78. Ibid., pp. 46-47.
79. Ibid., p. 49.
80. Ibid., p. 49.
81. Ibid., p. 50.
82. Ibid., p. 52.
83. Ibid., p. 53.
84. Ibid., pp. 84 ff.
85. Anwar Shaikh, "Foreign Trade and the Law of Value," Parts I and II.
86. Ibid., Part II, p. 32.
87. Ibid., p. 33.
88. Ibid., p. 38.
89. Ibid., p. 38.
90. Ibid., pp. 38-39.
91. Ibid., p. 39.
92. Ibid., p. 41.
93. Ibid., pp. 40-41.
94. Ibid., p. 42.
95. Ibid., pp. 42-43.
96. Ibid., pp. 43-44.
97. Ibid., pp. 44-45.
98. Ibid., p. 45.
99. Ibid., p. 45.
100. Ibid., pp. 45-46.
101. Ibid., p. 46.
102. This quote does not appear in the published version, but appears in manuscript, p. 75.
103. See manuscript, p. 76.
104. See Christian Palloix, "The Self Expansion of Capital on a World Scale," a partial translation of his *L'internationalisation du capital* (1975). See also "The Internationalization of Capital and the Circuit of Social Capital."
105. James Cypher, "The Internationalization of Capital and the Transformation of Social Formations: A Critique of the Monthly Review School"; Pat Clawson, "The Internationalization of Capital and Capital Accumulation in Iran and Iraq"; David Barkin, "The Internationalization of Capital: An Alternative Approach."
106. Although on the surface this view may seem similar to the thesis of Bill Warren in "Imperialism and Capitalist Industrialization," there is a substantial difference. Warren asserts that successful capitalist industrialization is rapidly taking place in the Third World. His analysis, however, never goes beyond surface appear-

ances. The "internationalization of capital" approach is profoundly different in methodology and although it identifies a tendency to reproduction of capitalism worldwide, such a tendency is tempered by uneven development and articulation of modes of production.

107. Palloix, "Self-Expansion of Capital on a World Scale," p. 19.
108. Ibid., p. 19.
109. Ibid., p. 19.
110. Ibid., p. 20.
111. Ibid., p. 23.
112. Cypher, "Internationalization of Capital," p. 35.
113. Palloix, "Self-Expansion of Capital on a World Scale," p. 23.
114. Ibid., p. 23.
115. *Capital*, Vol. II (New York: International Publishers, 1967), p. 110.
116. Clawson, "Internationalization of Capital and Capital Accumulation," pp. 65–66.
117. Cypher, "Internationalization of Capital," p. 34.
118. See Clawson, "Internationalization of Capital and Capital Accumulation," p. 67.
119. Ibid.
120. Ibid., p. 70.
121. Ibid., p. 71.
122. Ibid., p. 71.
123. Ibid., pp. 64–65; and Cypher, "Internationalization of Capital," p. 42.
124. See Clawson on Iran and Iraq; see also Barkin's brief but suggestive application of this approach to Mexican agriculture in "Internationalization of Capital: An Alternative Approach."
125. Robert Heilbroner, *Marxism: For and Against* (New York: Norton, 1980), p. 19.
126. Foster-Carter, "Modes of Production Controversy."
127. See the discussion of Samir Amin in Chapter 6.

Appendix I

1. For an extensive bibliography of those who have critiqued Baran and Sweezy see William Barclay and Mitchell Stengel, "Surplus and Surplus-Value," pp. 63–64.
2. See James O'Connor, *The Corporations and the State*, pp. 50–51; Michael Barrett Brown, *The Economics of Imperialism*, pp. 215–217; and M. F. Bleaney, *Underconsumption Theories*, pp. 230–233.
3. See Paul Sweezy, *Theory of Capitalist Development*, Part III, particularly Ch. X.
4. Ibid., pp. 182–183.
5. Ibid., p. 180 and p. 217. Though it is not always recognized as such by underconsumptionists, stagnation as the normal state of capitalism is the logical conclusion of all underconsumption theories. See M. F. Z., "Against Sweezy's Political Economy," p. 99; Bleaney, *Underconsumption Theories*, pp. 50–51; and Anwar Shaikh, "An Introduction to the History of Crises Theories," p. 224.
6. Sweezy, *Theory of Capitalist Development*, p. 183.
7. Ibid.

8. For an excellent critical analysis of underconsumption theories see Bleaney, *Underconsumption Theories.*

9. On this point see Shaikh, "Crises Theories," pp. 229-230.

10. On this point see M. F. Z., "Against Sweezy," pp. 96-100.

11. Ibid., p. 103.

12. On this point see ibid., pp. 96-100.

13. This interpretation is based on ibid., pp. 104-106.

14. Barclay and Stengel, "Surplus and Surplus-Value," p. 56.

15. Ibid., p. 57.

16. Ibid., p. 58.

17. Barclay and Stengel have reached a similar conclusion. See ibid., p. 58.

18. Ibid.

19. Ibid., pp. 58-59.

20. Ibid., pp. 59-60.

21. See Shinzaburo Koshimura, *Theory of Capital Reproduction and Accumulation*, pp. 128-158.

22. Karl Marx, *Capital*, Vol. III, p. 861.

23. Koshimura, *Theory of Capital Reproduction*, p. 129.

24. This interpretation relies heavily on John Weeks, "Marx's Theory of Competition and the Theory of Imperialism."

APPENDIX II

1. See Samir Amin, "The End of a Debate"; Michael Barratt Brown, *The Economics of Imperialism*, pp. 229-235 and pp. 240-245; Charles Bettelheim, Appendices I and II in *Unequal Exchange*; Geoffrey Pilling, "Imperialism, Trade and 'Unequal Exchange,'" pp. 164-185; Anwar Shaikh, "Foreign Trade and the Law of Value," Parts I and II; and Elizabeth Dore and John Weeks, "International Exchange and the Causes of Backwardness."

2. Arghiri Emmanuel, *Unequal Exchange*, p. 22.

3. Ibid., p. 23.

4. Ibid., p. 28.

5. Ibid., Appendix V, p. 395.

6. Ibid., pp. 109-110.

7. Ibid., p. 116.

8. Ibid., p. 120.

9. Ibid., pp. 115-116.

10. Ibid., p. 127.

11. Ibid., pp. 127-128.

12. Both Bettelheim and Geoffrey Pilling come to the same conclusions.

13. See Bettelheim in *Unequal Exchange*, Appendix I, and Ernest Mandel, *Late Capitalism*, pp. 362-365.

14. Mandel, *Late Capitalism*, p. 362.

15. This issue is taken up by both Bettelheim, *Unequal Exchange*, Appendix I; and Dore and Weeks, "International Exchange," pp. 13-15.

16. Dore and Weeks, "International Exchange," p. 16.

17. Emmanuel, *Unequal Exchange*, p. 381.

18. Ibid., p. 381.

19. Ibid., pp. 381-382.
20. Ibid., p. 382.
21. Ibid., pp. 382-383.
22. Dore and Weeks, "International Exchange," p. 21.
23. Amin, "End of the Debate."
24. See Mandel, *Late Capitalism*, Chapter 11.
25. Ibid.
26. Emmanuel, *Unequal Exchange*, p. 71.
27. Dore and Weeks, "International Exchange," pp. 13-15.
28. Amin, "End of the Debate," pp. 31-51.
29. Dore and Weeks, "International Exchange," p. 15.
30. James F. Becker, *Marxian Political Economy*, Chapter 7.
31. Ibid., p. 110.
32. Ibid., p. 162.
33. Ibid.
34. Ibid., p. 169. Becker establishes this tendency in a rather unique way using Marx's reproduction schemes; see pp. 164-168.
35. Ibid., p. 160.
36. Ibid., pp. 170-171.
37. Ibid., pp. 173-174.
38. Ibid., p. 176.
39. Ibid., pp. 178-179.

Bibliography

Alavi, Hamza. "India and the Colonial Mode of Production," *The Socialist Register*. London, 1975.

Amin, Samir. *Accumulation on a World Scale*. 2 vols. New York: Monthly Review Press, 1974.

————. "Comment on Gerstein," *The Insurgent Sociologist*. Vol. VII, No. 2 (Spring 1977), 99–103.

————. *Neo-Colonialism In West Africa*. New York: Monthly Review Press, 1973.

————. "Self-Reliance and the New International Economic Order," *Monthly Review* (July–August, 1977).

————. *The End of a Debate*. Dakar: United Nations African Institute for Economic Development and Planning. I DFP/ET/R/2558. 1973.

————. *Unequal Development*. New York: Monthly Review Press, 1976.

Avineri, Shlomo, ed. *Karl Marx on Colonialism and Modernization*. Garden City: Anchor Books, 1969.

Baran, Paul A. "On the Political Economy of Backwardness," *The Manchester School of Economics and Social Studies* (January 1952). Reprinted in *Imperialism and Underdevelopment*, ed. Robert Rhodes.

————. *The Political Economy of Growth*. New York: Monthly Review, Inc. 1957.

————, and Paul M. Sweezy. *Monopoly Capital*. New York: Monthly Review Press, 1966.

————. "Notes on the Theory of Imperialism," *Monthly Review*, Vol. 17, No. 10 (March 1966). Reprinted in *Economic Imperialism*, eds. Kenneth Boudling and Tapan Mukerjee.

Barclay, William and Mitchell Stengel. "Surplus and Surplus Value," *Review of Radical Political Economics*, Vol. 17, No. 4 (Winter 1975).

Barkin, David. "The Internationalization of Capital: An Alternative Approach," *Latin American Perspectives*. Vol. VIII, Nos. 3, 4 (Summer and Fall 1981).

Becker, James F. *Marxian Political Economy*. Cambridge: Cambridge University Press, 1977.

Bettelheim, Charles. Appendices to Arghiri Emmanuel, *Unequal Exchange*.

Bleaney, M. F. *Under-Consumption Theories*. New York: International Publishers, 1976.

Boulding, Kenneth, and Tapan Mukerjee, eds. *Economic Imperialism*. Ann Arbor: University of Michigan Press, 1972.

Bradby, Barbara. "The Destruction of National Economy," *Economy and Society*, Vol. IV, No. 2 (May 1975).

Brenner, Robert. "The Origins of Capitalist Development: A Critique of Neo-Smithian Marxism," *New Left Review*, No. 104 (July-August 1977).

Brewer, Anthony. *Marxist Theories of Imperialism*. London: Routledge and Kegan Paul, 1980.

Brown, Michael Barratt. "A Critique of Marxist Theories of Imperialism." In *Studies in the Theory of Imperialism*, eds. Roger Owen and Bob Sutcliffe.

————. *After Imperialism*. London: Heinemann, 1970.

————. *Essays on Imperialism*. Montreal: Black Rose Books, 1972.

————. *The Economics of Imperialism*. Baltimore: Penguin Books, 1974.

Bukharin, Nikolai. *Imperialism and the Accumulation of Capital*. New York: Monthly Review Press, 1972.

————. *Imperialism and World Economy*. New York: Howard Fertig, 1966.

————. "The Theory of 'Organized Economic Disorder'" and "Toward a Theory of the Imperialist State." In N. I. Bukharin, *Selected Writings on the State and the Transition to Socialism*, ed. Richard B. Day. Armonk, N. Y.: M. E. Sharpe, 1982.

Cardoso, Fernando Henrique. "Dependency and Development in Latin America," *New Left Review*, No. 74 (July-August 1972).

————, and Enso Faletto. *Dependency and Development in Latin America.* Berkeley: University of Calif. Press, 1979.

Chilcote, Ronald H. "Dependency: A Critical Synthesis of the Literature," *Latin American Perspectives* (Spring 1974).

————. "Issues of Theory in Dependency and Marxism," *Latin American Perspectives* (Summer/Fall, 1981).

Clawson, Patrick. "The Internationalization of Capital and Capital Accumulation in Iran and Iraq," *The Insurgent Sociologist.* Vol. VII. No. 2 (Spring 1977).

Cockcroft, James D., Andre Gunder Frank, and Dale L. Johnson. *Dependence and Underdevelopment.* New York: Anchor Books, 1972.

Cohen, Benjamin. *The Question of Imperialism.* New York: Basic Books, 1973.

Cypher, James, "The Internationalization of Capital and the Transformation of Social Formations: A Critique of the Monthly Review School," *Review of Radical Political Economics.* Vol. 11, No. 4 (Winter 1979).

Disney, Nigel. "Accumulation on a World Scale," *The Insurgent Sociologist.* Vol. III, No. 2 (Spring 1977).

Dobb, Maurice, et al. *The Transition from Feudalism to Capitalism.* London: New Left Books, expanded edition, 1976.

Dore, Elizabeth and John Weeks, "International Exchange and the Causes of Backwardness," *Latin American Perspectives.* (Spring 1979).

————. "The Causes of Backwardness and the Uneven Development of Capitalism." Mimeographed. Washington, D.C.: The American University, 1977.

————. "The Intensification of the Assault Against the Working Class in 'Revolutionary' Peru," *Latin American Perspectives*, Vol. III, No. 2 (Spring 1976).

Dos Santos, Theotonio. "The Structure of Dependence." In *The Political Economy of Development and Underdevelopment*, ed. Charles K. Wilber.

Emmanuel, Arghiri. "Myths of Development Versus Myths of Underdevelopment," *New Left Review*, No. 85 (June 1974).

————. *Unequal Exchange: A Study of the Imperialism of Trade.* Trans. Brian Pearce. New York: Monthly Review Press, 1972.

Erlich, Alexander. "A Hamlet Without the Prince of Denmark," *Politics and Society* (Fall 1973), 35–53.

Fann, K. T., and Donald G. Hodges, eds. *Readings in U.S. Imperialism.* Boston: Porter Sargent, 1971.

Fernandez, Raul A. "Imperialist Capitalism in the Third World: Theory and Evidence from Columbia," *Latin American Perspectives*, Vol. 6, No. 1 (Winter 1979).

————, and Jose F. Ocampo. "The Latin American Revolution: A Theory of Imperialism, Not Dependence," *Latin American Perspectives*, Vol. 1, No. 1 (Spring 1974).

Fieldhouse, D. K. "Imperialism: An Historiographical Revision," *Economic History Review*, 2nd Ser., 14, 2 (December 1961).

Fine, Ben. "On the Origins of Capitalist Development," *New Left Review*, No. 109. (May/June, 1978).

————, and Laurence Harris, "Controversial Issues in Marxist Economic Theory," *The Socialist Register* (1976).

————. "Surveying the Foundations," *The Socialist Register*, 1977, pp. 106–120.

Foster-Carter, Aidan. "The Modes of Production Controversy," *New Left Review*, No. 107 (January–February 1978).

Frank, Andre Gunder. *Capitalism and Underdevelopment in Latin America.* New York: Monthly Review Press, 1967; revised and enlarged ed. 1969.

————. *Crisis: In the Third World.* New York: Holmes and Meier, 1981.

————. *Crisis: In the World Economy.* New York: Holmes and Meier, 1980.

————. *Dependent Accumulation and Underdevelopment.* New York: Monthly Review Press, 1979.

————. *Latin America: Underdevelopment or Revolution?* New York: Monthly Review Press, 1969.

————. *Lumpenbourgeoisie, Lumpendevelopment: Dependency, Class and Politics in Latin America*. New York: Monthly Review Press, 1972.

Furtado, Celso. "The Concept of External Dependence in the Study of Underdevelopment." In *The Political Economy of Development and Underdevelopment*, ed. Charles K. Wilber.

————. "The Brazilian 'Model' of Development." In *The Political Economy of Development and Underdevelopment*, ed. Charles K. Wilber.

Gerstein, Ira. "Theories of the World Economy and Imperialism," *The Insurgent Sociologist*, Vol. VII, No. 2 (Spring 1977).

Hilferding, Rudolf. *Finance Capital: A Study of the Latest Phase of Capitalist Development*, trans. Tom Bottomore. London: Routledge and Kegan Paul, 1981.

Jalee, Pierre. *The Pillage of the Third World*. New York: Monthly Review Press, 1970.

————. *The Third World in World Economy*. New York: Monthly Review Press, 1971.

Kemp, Tom. *Theories of Imperialism*. London: Dobson Books, 1967.

Kidron, Michael. *Capitalism and Theory*. London: Pluto Press, 1974.

Kiernan, V. G. *Marxism and Imperialism*. London: Edward Arnold, 1974.

Koshimura, Shinzaburo. *Theory of Capital Reproduction and Accumulation*, ed. Jesse G. Schwartz. Kitchener, Ont.: DPG, 1975.

Laclau, Ernesto. "Feudalism and Capitalism in Latin American," *New Left Review*, No. 67 (May/June 1971).

Lee, George. "Rosa Luxemburg and the Impact of Imperialism," *The Economic Journal* (December 1971).

Lenin, V. I. *Imperialism*. New York: International Publishers, 1929.

————. "Notebooks on Imperialism," *Collected Works*, Vol. 39. Moscow: Progress Publishers, 1968.

Lichtheim, George. *Imperialism*. New York: Praeger Publishers, 1971.

Luxemburg, Rosa. *The Accumulation of Capital*. Trans. Agnes Schwarzschild. London: Routledge, 1951.

————. *The Accumulation of Capital—An Anti-Critique*. New York: Monthly Review Press, 1972.

————. *The Mass Strike: The Political Party and the Trade Unions* and *The Junius Pamphlet*. New York: Harper Torchbooks, 1971.

MacEwan, Arthur. "Capitalist Expansion, Ideology and Intervention," *Review of Radical Political Economics*, Vol. 4, No. 1 (Winter 1972).

Magdoff, Harry. "Economic Aspects of U.S. Imperialism," *Monthly Review*, Vol. 21, No. 9 (February 1970).

———— "How to Make a Molehill out of a Mountain: Reply to Szymanski," *The Insurgent Sociologist*, Vol. VII, No. 2 (Spring 1977).

————. "Imperialism—A Historical Survey," *Monthly Review*, Vol. 24 (May 1972).

————. *Imperialism: From the Colonial Age to the Present*. New York: Monthly Review Press, 1979.

————. "Imperialism Without Colonies." In *Studies in the Theory of Imperialism*, eds. Roger Owen and Bob Sutcliffe.

————. "Imperialist Expansion: Accident and Design," *Monthly Review*, Vol. 25, No. 8 (January 1974).

————. "Is Imperialism Really Necessary?" *Monthly Review*, Vol. 21, Nos. 5 and 6 (October and November 1970).

————. "Militarism and Imperialism." Paper delivered at the annual meeting of the American Economic Association, December 30, 1969. Reprinted in Paul M. Sweezy and Harry Magdoff, *The Dynamics of U.S. Capitalism*.

————. *The Age of Imperialism*. New York: Monthly Review Press, 1969.

————. "U.S. Foreign Policy and Underdevelopment," *Monthly Review*, Vol. 22, No. 10 (March 1971).

Mandel, Ernest. "After Imperialism?" *New Left Review*, No. 25 (May–June 1964).

————. *Late Capitalism*. London: New Left Books, 1975.

————. "The Laws of Uneven Development," *New Left Review*, No. 59 (January–February 1970).

————. "Where is America Going?" *New Left Review*, No. 54 (March–April 1969).

Marx, Karl. *Capital*. Vols. I–III. New York: International Publishers, 1967.

————. *Grundrisse*. London: Penguin Books, 1973.

————. *Karl Marx on Colonialism and Modernization*, ed. with an Introduction by Shlomo Avineri. Garden City: Anchor Books, 1959.

————. *The German Ideology*. New York: International Publishers, 1970.

————, and Frederick Engels. *The Communist Manifesto*. New York: International Publishers, 1948.

McEachern, D. "The Mode of Production in India," *Journal of Contemporary Asia*, 1976.

McMichael, Philip, James Petras, and Robert Rhodes. "Imperialism and the Contradictions of Development," *New Left Review*, No. 85 (May–June, 1974).

Müller, Ronald. "The Multinational Corporation and the Underdevelopment of the Third World." In *The Political Economy of Development and Underdevelopment*, ed. Charles K. Wilber.

Munck, Ronaldo. "Imperialism and Dependency: Recent Debates and Old Dead-Ends," *Latin American Perspectives*, Vol. VIII, Nos. 3, 4 (Summer/Fall 1981).

Murray, R. "Underdevelopment, International Firms, and the International Division of Labour." In *Towards a New World Economy*. Rotterdam: Rotterdam University Press, 1972.

Novak, George. "The Law of Uneven and Combined Development and Latin America," *Latin American Perspectives*, Vol. III, No. 2 (Spring 1976).

O'Connor, James. *The Corporations and the State*. New York: Harper & Row, 1974.

Owen, Roger, Bob Sutcliffe, eds. *Studies in the Theory of Imperialism*. London: Longmans, 1972.

Palloix, Christian. *L'internationalisation du capital*. Paris: Maspero, 1975.

————. "The Internationalization of Capital and the Circuit of Social Capital." In *International Firms and Modern Imperialism*, ed. Hugo Radice. London: Penguin, 1975.

————. "The Self-Expansion of Capital on a World Scale," *Review of Radical Political Economics*. Vol. 9, No. 2 (Summer 1977).

Petras, James. *Critical Perspectives on Imperialism and Social Class in the Third World*. New York: Monthly Review Press, 1978.

————, and Robert Rhodes. "The Reconsolidation of U.S. Hegemony," *New Left Review*, No. 97 (May–June 1976).

Pilling, Geoffrey. "Imperialism, Trade and 'Unequal Exchange': The Work of Aghiri Emmanuel," *Economy and Society* (May 1973).

Radice, Hugo, ed. *International Firms and Modern Imperialism*. Baltimore: Penguin Books, 1975.

Rey, Pierre-Philippe. *Class Alliances*. Translated with an introduction by James F. Becker. In *International Journal of Sociology*, Vol. XII, No. 2 (Summer 1982).

————. *Colonialisme, Neo-Colonialisme, et Transition au Capitalisme*. Paris: Maspero, 1971.

Rhodes, Robert I., ed. *Imperialism and Underdevelopment: A Reader*. New York: Monthly Review Press, 1970.

Rowthorn, Bob. "Imperialism in the Seventies—Unity or Rivalry?" *New Left Review*, No. 69 (September–October 1971).

Shaikh, Anwar. "An Introduction to the History of Crisis Theories." In *U.S. Capitalism in Crisis*, ed. Crisis Reader Editorial Collective. New York: Union for Radical Political Economics, 1978.

————. "Foreign Trade and The Law of Value," Parts I and II, *Science and Society* (Fall and Spring 1980).

Sweezy, Paul M. "Monopoly Capital and the Theory of Value," *Monthly Review*, Vol. 25, No. 8 (January 1974).

————. "On the Theory of Monopoly Capitalism," *Monthly Review*, Vol. 23, No. 11 (April 1972).

————. *The Theory of Capitalist Development*. New York: Monthly Review Press, 1942.

————, and Harry Magdoff. *The Dynamics of U.S. Capitalism*. New York: Monthly Review Press, 1972.

————, Harry Magdoff and Leo Huberman, eds. "Imperialism in the Seventies: Problems and Perspectives," *Monthly Review*, Vol. 23, No. 10 (March 1972).
Taylor, John. *From Modernization to Modes of Production: A Critique of the Sociologies of Development and Underdevelopment*. London: Macmillan, 1979.
The Review of Radical Political Economics, Vol. 5, No. I (Spring 1973). Special Issue: "Capitalism and World Economic Integration: Perspectives on Modern Imperialism."
The Review of Radical Political Economics, Vol. 3, No. I (Spring 1971). Special Issue: "Case Studies in Imperialism and Underdevelopment."
Thomas, Clive Y. *Dependence and Transformation*. New York: Monthly Review Press, 1974.
Wallerstein, Immanuel. "Dependence in an Interdependent World," *African Studies Review*. (April 1974).
————. *The Capitalist World-Economy*. London: Cambridge University Press, 1979.
————. *The Modern World-System: Capitalist Agriculture and the Origins of the European World Economy in the Sixteenth Century*. New York: Academic Press, 1974.
————. "The Rise and Future Demise of the World Capitalist System," *Comparative Studies in Society and History*. Vol. 16, No. 4 (1974).
Warren, Bill. "Imperialism and Capitalist Industrialization," *New Left Review*, No. 81 (September–October 1973).
————. *Imperialism: Pioneer of Capitalism*. London: New Left Books, 1980.
Weeks, John. "Accumulation in the Manufacturing Sector of Peru, 1954–1975." Mimeographed. Washington, D.C.: The American University, 1976.
————. *Capital and Exploitation*. Princeton: Princeton University Press, 1981.
————. "Marx's Theory of Competition and the Theory of Imperialism." Mimeographed. Washington, D.C.: The American University, 1977.
Weisskopf, Thomas. "Capitalism, Underdevelopment and the Future of the Poor Countries," *Review of Radical Political Economics*, Vol. 4, No. 1 (Winter 1972).
————. "Theories of American Imperialism: A Critical Evaluation," *Review of Radical Political Economics*, Vol. 6, No. 3 (Fall 1974).
Wildstrand, Carl, ed. *Multi-National Firms in Africa*. New York: Africana Publishing Company, 1975.
Wilber, Charles K., ed. *The Political Economy of Development and Underdevelopment*. New York: Random House, 1973.
Wolpe, H. (ed). *The Articulation of Modes of Production*. London: Routledge and Kegan Paul, 1980.
Wright, Harrison M., ed. *The "New Imperialism"*. Lexington: D. C. Heath and Company, 2nd ed., 1976.
M.F.Z. "Against Sweezy's Political Economy," *The Communist*, Vol. 2, No. 1 (Fall–Winter, 1977).